The Vegetarian Feast

The Vegetarian Feast

*Revised and Updated
Plus 50 New Recipes*

Martha Rose Shulman

HarperPerennial
A Division of HarperCollins Publishers

HarperCollins books may be purchased for educational, business, or sales promotional use. For information please write: Special Markets Department, HarperCollins Publishers, Inc., 10 East 53rd Street, New York, N.Y. 10022.

FIRST EDITION

Designed by Nancy Singer

Library of Congress Cataloging-in-Publication Data

Shulman, Martha Rose.
    The vegetarian feast/Martha Rose Shulman—Rev. and updated plus 50 new recipes
        p. cm.
    Includes index.
    ISBN 0-06-095001-3
    1. Vegetarian cookery. I. Title.
TX837.S468 1995
641.5'636—dc20   94-18744

95 96 97 98 99 ❖/RRD 10 9 8 7 6 5 4 3 2 1

For Mary and for Max
with love and gratitude

Contents

Foreword to the
New Edition

Not too long ago when I was teaching a Mediterranean cooking class in New York, one of the students asked me if I was planning to do an updated version of *The Vegetarian Feast*. She had bought the book in 1979, and still cooked black bean enchiladas, one of its signature recipes, every time her son came home from college. But many of the recipes in the book contained more fat than she likes to use now. I too had become a lower-fat cook, dedicated to reducing fats in recipes without sacrificing flavor. Although I hadn't exactly relished fats back in the seventies, when I looked at my recipes in *The Vegetarian Feast*, I could see that they needed an overhaul.

And so I began this revision. It has been one of the most interesting undertakings of my career, enabling me to look at myself learning to cook. I feel fortunate to have had the opportunity; a novelist, after all, does not get to revise his or her first novel fifteen years down the line, even though he has matured and his style and outlook have probably changed.

When I wrote this book in the mid-seventies, I was already committed to applying healthy principles to good cuisine. I did not become a vegetarian out of principle, but because it seemed the easiest way to combine healthy habits with delicious foods. I wanted, passionately, to create a tasty cuisine that did not include much in the way of processed or "adulterated" foods. *Nutrition* was a key word, and a relatively new idea back then.

But our knowledge of nutrition was quite different at the time. The role that fats play in the diet was not as well understood as it is now. I knew that fat calories were the hardest calories to burn, but I still used more fat than I now know was necessary. Many tablespoons of butter and oil and cups of cheese, most of the nuts, and almost all of the cream (there wasn't much of that ingredient to begin with) have been discarded in this edition of *The Vegetarian Feast*.

In the seventies Americans were much more protein-fixated than we are now, so we vegetarians tended to compensate for the absence of meat by incorporating lots of high-fat cheese or nuts into our diet. I was very keen on proving that complete protein could be had at every meal, by combining grains, beans, and dairy products in the right proportions. Now nutritionists tell us that protein combining can be done as efficiently over the course of a day, so we have been able to simplify our menus. I also thought that by incorporating as much texture as I could into a dish I would compensate for the absence of meat; so my dishes tended to be busy, with nuts thrown in often, sometimes where they had no place to be.

A self-taught cook, I took as my early mentors not so much other vegetarians as classical cooks. Julia Child was my main inspiration. As I reread the recipes in the original *Vegetarian Feast* I could see myself learning her techniques, then applying them to my dishes. For example, the soups I learned from Julia and other classical cooks were thickened with roux, the way sauces are, so many of mine were, too. Now I would never thicken a soup with a roux; I use potatoes in the new soups chapter, a much simpler and more efficient way to thicken a puréed soup.

Over the last fifteen years my gastronomic horizons have widened enormously. How could they not? I lived and cooked in Paris for twelve years, and traveled widely in the Mediterranean and studied its cuisines. Living in France lightened my touch and refined my palate. My dishes became simpler, more to the point, and my tastes, as those of so many Americans, became decidedly Mediterranean (with an enduring love of Mexican food). You will find, in this new edition, that olive oil is the oil of choice. Fifteen years ago we had not really discovered it, and had certainly not created a demand for the fine imported virgin oils that are so readily available today.

When I wrote *The Vegetarian Feast* I was exploring each and every cuisine. Any appealing dish that was vegetarian, or could be successfully converted, was a candidate for the book; consequently the book is quite eclectic. That aspect remains. But because my palate has matured, the flavors in the dishes themselves are more focused.

I was struck, as I took a close look at the recipes, by what I didn't know at the time I wrote them. For example, as I retested and revised the recipe for picante zucchini gratin (originally called picante zucchini), I saw that at the time I hadn't realized I was making a gratin. I've changed the names of certain recipes to reflect this.

I've also made some additions. There is a pasta chapter in this new edition. It's hard to believe that pasta was not such a big thing at the time I wrote this book. It would have been much easier to convince people that vegetarian eating could be easy and full of familiar flavors and ingredients if we had been as in love with this food then as we are now. Today I could write a whole book of vegetarian pasta recipes.

As I brought this book from the past to the present, I discarded a few recipes from the original. These dishes appealed to me then, but I wouldn't cook them now (rose hips soup, for example). I've also added a few recipes to the side dishes chapter—gratins and a few more grain dishes— and some dressings to the salad dressing repertoire. Mainly what I've done is reduce the fat content of just about every recipe in the book. (I did leave in some deep-fried items, like the egg rolls, although there I give you a spring roll alternative that isn't fried.) Sometimes this involved changing the cooking technique completely; for example, I transformed the deep-fried won tons in the original book to marvelous simmered won tons served in a fragrant ginger broth. Sometimes reducing the fats required nothing more than eliminating a tablespoon of butter here, oil there, or exchanging butter or safflower oil for olive oil, and in far smaller quantities. I've simplified recipes wherever it was called for, paring down long lists of ingredients and taking out many handfuls of the sprouts and sunflower seeds of the seventies. However, the delicious flavors (and an occasional irresistible high-fat dish) remain.

I am grateful to Susan Friedland, at HarperCollins, who was enthusiastic from the beginning about giving a new life to this book. Thanks for getting this off the ground and for being so supportive throughout the project.

Martha Rose Shulman
Berkeley, January 1995

Introduction

When I wrote the original version of this book I felt that I had to explain my vegetarian eating habits, to convince people that I was really not weird or ascetic or *against* eating meat. But today the word *vegetarian* no longer conjures up images of hair shirts and hippies. Many people—76 percent of American shoppers, according to one market research study—have cut way down on their meat consumption, and although they would not describe themselves as strict vegetarians, they hardly ever eat red meat.

The reason for this goes beyond our growing concern with health. Today's vegetarian food is much more appealing than it used to be. The cuisine has grown up: It's gone from heavy to light, from gray to bright; and its moral overtones have vanished. Restaurants easily accommodate both carnivores and vegetarians with one menu. Like American cuisine in general, vegetarian food now expresses a love of ethnic flavors and a merging of cuisines.

Exotic flavors were always present in my vegetarian cooking. I turned to other cuisines when I began to explore the possibilities of meatless eating, and didn't have to look very far to put together a repertoire of delicious dishes. That's why this book is so eclectic. From Mexico, for example, there is garlic soup—Sopa de Ajo (page 64), Tortilla Soup (page 60), Guacamole (page 221), Black Bean Enchiladas (page 97), and Chalupas (page 100). From the Middle East come tantalizing dishes like Hummus (page 21), Tabouli (page 220), Baba Ghanoush (page 24), and

Turkish Cucumber Soup (page 92). Italy, of course, offers its exquisite, fragrant tomato sauces and pastas, full-bodied, comforting Minestrone (page 74), hearty pizzas, Eggplant Parmesan (page 132), and delicate Stracciatella (page 54). India—with its millions of vegetarians—has delightful curries, spicy dals, and cooling raitas. Chinese delicacies—egg rolls, won tons, subtle vegetable combinations—are well known and loved here in the United States. Japanese cooking makes extensive use of tofu, or bean curd, a versatile food that's light and high in protein; it's a staple in my own diet, and I use it in my stir-fries. And the cuisine of France, my greatest source of inspiration, offers sublime sauces, a wide range of salads and vegetable dishes, and eminently useful culinary basics—the soufflé, the quiche, the omelet, the gratin, and the crêpe—which give any cook a seemingly limitless framework.

In the last twenty years, the big questions about vegetarianism—how do we get enough protein? how can we prepare this kind of food quickly? is it a high-calorie cuisine?—have been cleared up for many people. Still, for others the questions linger. The answers are simpler than they were twenty years ago, because we know more about diet now.

• Protein. Many nutritionists now feel that a healthy diet, one that includes an abundance of whole grains, beans, and vegetables, will provide enough protein. Others recommend paying close attention to "protein complementarity." This refers to combining different types of foods to obtain "complete protein." Proteins are made up of amino acids. There are eight "essential amino acids" that we must obtain from food in order to get enough protein. Every protein-rich food contains these amino acids, but in lesser or greater amounts. Meat, fish, fowl, dairy products, eggs, and soy products are high in all of them. Other foods—grains and flours, nuts and seeds, legumes (beans), fruits, and vegetables are low in some amino acids and high in others. To obtain balanced, complete protein, one simply combines foods from these groups over the course of a day. We usually do this naturally—we eat tortillas with beans, bread with cheese, cereal with milk.

• Time. The notion of the time-consuming aspect of the vegetarian diet comes from the fact that it takes beans so long to cook, bread so long to rise, and grains a certain amount of time to cook. But all of this cooking is *unsupervised*, and can be done in advance. Also, beans can come from a can if necessary, certain grains like couscous and bulgur can be reconstituted in no time in hot water, and good bread is now easily obtained from local bakeries. Any kind of cooking demands organization, and in the case of beans, you do have to be organized enough to remember to soak your beans before you cook them and cook them before you need them. But this is not just bean cuisine. Actually, vegetable preparation, not grain or bean cooking, is the most time-consuming element of this food—or any food, for that matter—but the dishes themselves—especially the pastas and the omelets, go very quickly indeed.

• Calories. The reason so many Americans are eating less meat is that this is one of the easiest ways to keep saturated fat consumption at a minimum, provided that high-fat dairy products—cheese, butter, whole milk—and nuts and oils are eaten in moderation. The calories in a vegetarian diet are mostly from complex carbohydrates, the type of calories we burn up most quickly. It's fat calories that put people at risk from life-threatening diseases.

INGREDIENTS

Much of the mystery of vegetarianism revolves around ingredients you may have never heard of. These are, for the most part, grains, legumes, soy products, nuts and seeds, and some seasonings (see the next chapter for more detail). The natural foods industry in this country has grown tremendously in the past twenty years; you should have no trouble obtaining most of the foods called for in this book, even in supermarkets.

If you live in a small town, check to see if there is a natural foods store nearby; if you live in a city, you will have no problem finding them. Natural foods stores are often as large and user-friendly as supermarkets. In some areas there are still food co-ops, which were common, especially in college towns, in the sixties and seventies. They operate on varying principles, some asking membership fees and labor hours from their members, others just membership fees, and some are open to the public. These stores are usually oriented toward natural foods and have wide selections, including dairy products, eggs, produce, and often unadulterated meat. The prices are usually lower than regular retail stores, and most of the products, including spices, are sold in bulk. But these days the supermarkets and large whole foods stores also sell their whole foods products in bulk. You can also order products by mail.

Produce, eggs, and dairy products: Since the basis of a good dish is its ingredients, it's worth finding the best, which means fresh produce in season and fresh dairy products. Local farmers do still exist, and farmers' markets are increasingly present in large cities. Neighborhood stores and fruit stands are more likely to carry local produce than the supermarket chains. Farmers' and local markets often stock fresh eggs; even fresh "cage" eggs (from caged chickens, as opposed to chickens that run loose in a yard) are more suitable than the mass-produced eggs that sit on supermarket shelves. I can't overemphasize the superior quality of fresh eggs. Crack a noncommercial egg into a bowl next to a commercial one. It will be shades yellower—the commercial egg will look almost white in comparison—and it will hold its shape. It's heartbreaking to have your omelet refuse to hold its shape simply because the eggs are old. You'll also notice that fresh eggs taste richer. And they are safer than mass-produced eggs.

Shop around for dairy products, too. Look for cheese that has not been "ultrapasteurized"; raw milk cheeses have the best flavor. Cottage cheese varies from brand to brand, as does yogurt; look at the carton and buy the brand with the least amount of additives (and the latest date). It may not last as long as the more processed brands, but what's the sense of eating week-old food that had little food value in it to begin with? Also, buy low-fat or nonfat yogurt, milk, and cottage cheese.

Fresh herbs: Many of the recipes in this collection call for fresh herbs. Herbs are now widely available in supermarkets, farmers' markets, and specialty food stores. They're also easy to grow, either in small pots in a sunny window or on a sunny balcony, or outside in a garden or in pots. They require well-drained soil, and most herbs like lots of sunlight. Dried herbs can often be substituted, but there is nothing like the taste and aroma of herbs freshly picked. Try growing basil, dill, mint, rosemary, sage, tarragon, and thyme. It's nice to have parsley around, too, but that's one herb you can always find in the grocery store.

Ingredients Used in This Book

I have listed on the next few pages the grains, flours, legumes, nuts and seeds, oils, and miscellaneous items that you will find in my recipes. You'll see many more products in natural foods stores, but I've narrowed it down to what will be called for in the pages that follow.

• **Grains:** Store in tightly covered containers on shelves or in a pantry. They look nice in glass jars. Grains are susceptible to weevils if kept too long. Your store of grains should include:

> Brown rice
> Millet
> Wheat berries
> Bulgur (partially cooked cracked wheat)
> Buckwheat groats
> Rolled or flaked oats

Other grains to consider are rye and quinoa.

• **Flours:** Store in tightly sealed containers on shelves or in the refrigerator. Wheat germ must be refrigerated, as it gets rancid very quickly. Other flours should be refrigerated if you live in a very warm climate, or if you don't use them up quickly, as they are vulnerable to weevils. Flours include:

Whole wheat
Whole-wheat pastry
Unbleached white
Wheat germ
Rye
Yellow stone-ground cornmeal

• **Legumes:** Store in tightly sealed containers on shelves or in a pantry. Again, glass jars are fine. Beans will keep for a long time.

Adzuki, or azuki, beans (small red Japanese beans)
Black beans
Black-eyed peas
Chick-peas (also called garbanzo beans)
Kidney beans
Lentils
Mung beans (for sprouts)
Navy beans and small white beans (can be used inter-changeably)
Giant white beans (favas)
Pinto beans
Soybeans
Soy flakes (split, partially cooked, and dehydrated soy-beans; they cook faster than whole soybeans and can be substituted for soybeans)
Soy grits (cracked, partially cooked soybeans; a good sup-plement with grains, cooked along with the grains)

• **Pasta:** Keep pasta in large jars, or in the bags or boxes they come in. Try to have a few shapes on hand, such as:

Fettuccine (flat noodles, about ¼ inch wide)
Linguine (flat thin noodles)
Fusilli (spiral-shaped noodles)
Rotelle (wheel-shaped noodles)
Penne (ridged hollow macaronilike noodles)
Spaghetti

Couscous (looks like a grain, but it is actually a grainlike semolina pasta)
Whole-wheat noodles (fettuccine or spaghetti)

• **Nuts and seeds:** I refrigerate my nuts and seeds to ensure freshness; they can also be kept in the freezer. Basic nuts and seeds include:

Almonds
Brazil nuts
Cashews
Peanuts (these are really a legume, but are used as nuts in cooking)
Pecans
Pine nuts
Sesame seeds
Sunflower seeds
Walnuts

• **Oils:** Cold-pressed oils, which can be found in natural foods stores, contain no preservatives and must be refrigerated upon opening. They get rancid quickly, which is something you can't always taste. Unless the label on an oil says it is cold-pressed, there is no need to refrigerate; I keep my imported olive oil in the cupboard. Oils to have around are:

Canola oil: Recommended as an all-purpose oil, this has virtually no flavor.
Olive oil: A rich, tasty oil used in salad dressings and in Mediterranean cooking.
Peanut oil: A moderately strong-tasting oil, good for Asian and Indian dishes.
Safflower oil: An all-purpose oil with a slightly strong flavor.
Dark Chinese sesame oil: A rich, nutty oil that gives a nice Asian flavor to dishes. Used sparingly, sesame oil is more of a condiment than a cooking oil.
Soy oil: A strong-tasting, cheap oil, used for stir-fries and tempuras.
Sunflower seed oil: This oil is quite mild and can be used interchangeably with canola oil.

Walnut oil: A rich, nutty oil, this makes a tasty salad dressing.

Below is a list of other ingredients called for in the book, each followed by a short explanation:

• **Alfalfa seeds:** Very small seeds that make excellent sprouts. Found in natural foods stores; will keep indefinitely in a covered jar.

• **Arrowroot powder:** A white powder, like cornstarch, used to thicken sauces. Proportions of arrowroot to liquid for a glaze or thickened sauce are 1½ tablespoons arrowroot to 1 cup liquid. To prevent lumping, dissolve the arrowroot in some liquid before adding it. It is found in supermarkets and natural foods stores along with the spices, and can be used interchangeably with cornstarch. Keeps indefinitely in a covered container.

• **Buckwheat noodles** (or **soba**): Nutty-flavored noodles made from buckwheat. Found in Asian import stores and natural foods stores.

• **Carob powder:** Also known as "St. John's bread," this product consists of finely ground pods from a leguminous evergreen. Very low in fat compared to chocolate, for which it is used as a substitute. Found in natural foods stores; will keep indefinitely in a covered container.

• **Chia seeds:** Small seeds that are very high in protein. Add to breads to enrich. Found in natural foods stores; will keep for a long time in covered containers.

• **Dried mushrooms:** Dehydrated mushrooms, which, when simmered in water or stock, provide an aromatic broth. Asian varieties like shiitakes are found in some supermarkets and wherever Asian ingredients are sold. European mushrooms, like porcini or morels, can be found in imported food stores and gourmet markets. Store in tightly covered containers.

• **Filo dough:** a thin strudel dough found in import stores, some supermarkets, and Greek markets. Comes in long packages of two sizes, both consisting of paper-thin sheets of dough that are dusted with cornstarch, stacked, and folded up. The two-ounce packages contain four to eight sheets per package; these are larger than the sheets in the one-pound packages and are more heavily dusted. Keep refrigerated; can also be frozen.

• **Gingerroot**: A spicy root used mostly in Asian and Indian dishes, either freshly grated or dried and powdered. Fresh ginger can be found in supermarket produce departments and Asian and Spanish markets; the dried powder is readily available in supermarkets. Store fresh gingerroot, once cut, covered with sherry in a jar in the refrigerator; it will keep indefinitely this way.

• **Honey**: Always use mild honey, such as clover or acacia.

• **Marmite**: A yeast extract imported in small jars from England and Canada. A very viscous spread, high in protein and B vitamins, used in this book as a flavoring for stocks and soya pâté. Can be found in import stores, natural foods stores, and gourmet markets. Keeps indefinitely in a sealed jar; no need to refrigerate.

• **Miso paste**: A fermented paste made from soybeans and grains. High in protein; very salty. Used in soups, spreads, dressings, and sauces. Sealed in plastic or in a jar, it will keep indefinitely; I keep mine refrigerated. Found in natural foods stores.

• **Molasses**: I use blackstrap molasses. It has a strong flavor and is used in certain desserts and breads.

• **Postum**: A powdered coffee substitute, somewhat sweet, made from grains and molasses. Found in supermarkets on the coffee shelves and in natural foods stores; will keep indefinitely in a covered jar.

• **Rose hips**: The fruit of the rose plant, which, when dried, makes a good tea; rose hips can also be used to flavor fruit soups and compotes. High in vitamin C. Found in natural foods stores; will keep indefinitely in a covered jar.

• **Savorex:** A yeast extract like Marmite, produced in this country by Loma Linda Products. Available in many natural foods stores. Because it isn't imported, it doesn't cost as much as Marmite.

• **Sea salt:** Salt from evaporated sea water; higher in trace minerals and tastier than regular table salt. Found in natural foods stores and gourmet groceries. Have both fine and coarse sea salt on hand.

• **Sesame tahini:** Raw sesame butter, used in many Middle Eastern dishes, in sauces, dressings, and spreads. Delicious by itself on bread, like peanut butter. Can be found in natural foods stores and imported foods stores. Keep refrigerated once opened. Tahini (especially the canned variety) sometimes separates. The ground sesame seeds will be on the bottom, very hard and dry, with about an inch of oil floating on top. If this happens, just blend the contents of your can in a blender or food processor and put the unused tahini back into the can. It shouldn't separate so drastically again.

• **Spray-dried milk:** A highly concentrated powdered milk, about twice as concentrated as commercial brands. Comes whole or skim; can be found in natural foods stores. Good for enriching milk; I use it instead of cream in quiches and soups. Keeps indefinitely in a covered container.

• **Sprouts:** Tender young shoots of seeds, beans, and some grains. Very high in simple proteins, sugars, vitamins, and minerals. Crisp and tasty; a wonderful, nutritious addition to salads, main dishes, and soups; also a beautiful garnish. My favorites are alfalfa, lentil, and sunflower seed; each has a distinctive taste. For sprouting directions, see page xxxviii. Sprouts can be stored in sealed plastic bags or jars in the refrigerator for up to a week.

• **Sugar:** I use very little refined sugar, but it does appear in some recipes. More often I use unrefined brown sugar, sometimes called "turbinado" sugar. This is easy to find in whole foods stores and many supermarkets.

- **Tamari:** A very strong soy sauce with a distinctively rich flavor. You will quickly note the difference between it and commercial brands. Found in natural foods stores; will keep indefinitely in a covered jar or bottle. Kikkoman soy sauce is my second choice after tamari.

- **Tofu:** Bean curd, a kind of "cottage cheese" made from soybeans and molded in solid cakes. Comes packaged in water and must always be kept in water in the refrigerator. Very high in complete protein. By itself it is very bland, but it absorbs flavors beautifully because it is very porous, and it's fun to cook with. Found in natural foods stores and most supermarkets in the produce section, and Asian import stores. If your city has an Asian population, you can probably get it fresh, and fresh tofu is unbelievably light and delicate.

- **Vegetable bouillon cubes:** These are bouillon cubes that dissolve in boiling water to make a simple vegetable broth. Can be found in some supermarkets and most natural foods stores and co-ops. There are several brands, and they vary in price and also in the number of preservatives they contain, so shop around. When pressed for time, use for tamari-bouillon broth instead of vegetable stock.

- **Vegetable salt:** Seasoned salt made from salt and dehydrated herbs and vegetables. Found in natural foods stores and some supermarkets. The two brands I am familiar with are Herbamare and Vegesal, but there are more. Use along with or in place of salt or sea salt as a seasoning.

EQUIPMENT

If you're an experienced cook, you may want to skip this section, as you probably know what you need. The novice should remember that it takes—or should take—a while to acquire a *batterie de cuisine*. A friend of mine who is also a professional cook was once fired from her job teaching cooking at a gourmet cookware store. The reason she was asked to leave was that she wasn't selling their expensive gadgets—Cuisinarts, crêpe pans, fancy utensils. Instead she urged her students to invest their money in a good set of knives and learn to use them, and to figure out what they should have in their kitchen as they went along.

You can begin to cook with a minimum of equipment: a couple of mixing bowls, one set of measuring cups and spoons, one or two good knives, one or two pots and pans, a skillet or wok, and a baking dish. I was cooking professionally for three years before I invested in an expensive set of pots and pans; it took me that long to know what kind of cookware would best suit my cooking.

When I began, I was cooking on a very low budget and bought many of my first items at secondhand stores, garage sales, and auctions. These are excellent sources for beautiful old utensils at very low prices. The blenders I've bought for five dollars at garage sales have outlived the fancy multi-speed blender I bought new last year.

If you've never been to a restaurant supply house, I urge that you go. You'll be amazed at all the different kinds and sizes of equipment—not only cookware and cooking utensils, but also glasses, plates, flatware, serving utensils, pitchers, and salt shakers—all at unbeatable prices.

As my cooking became more refined, I began to know what I wanted and needed, and what to choose in restaurant supply houses and gourmet cookware stores. Good equipment does make a difference, but it's silly to buy it before you know what you need, and you can discover that only through cooking.

Here's what I have in my kitchen:

Cutting and Chopping Equipment

• **Knives:** A paring knife, an all-purpose 8-inch, and a 10-inch. I rarely use the 10-inch except when I'm cutting several things at once; if I were to have only one knife, I'd choose the 8-inch. I use both stainless and carbon steel. Good brands include Sabatier, Zanger-Icel, J. A. Henckels-

Solingen, Trident, and Forschner. Carbon steel keeps a sharp blade for a long time and is easy to sharpen on a stone or steel. But carbon steel knives rust, so choose stainless if you tend to forget to dry things.

Also, a stainless-steel all-purpose knife (for fruits and acidic vegetables and potatoes); a serrated bread knife.

Utensils

• **Wooden spoons:** Have at least three.

• **Whisks:** A medium-sized can serve as an all-purpose whisk. There's a nice flat whisk that is good for sauces; the shape allows you to scrape sauces up from the sides and bottom of the pan while whisking.

• **Balloon whisk** or **egg beater**

• **Spatulas:** A flat wooden or metal one and a rubber or plastic one.

• **Pastry brush**

• **Graters:** A four-sided hand grater and a Mouli grater; a nutmeg grater.

• **Food mill:** Good for puréeing soups.

• **Garlic press**

• **Mortar and pestle**

• **Pepper mill**

• **Citrus juicer**

• **Pastry cutter**

• **Pastry board**

• **Pastry board scraper**

• **Rolling pin:** A large, heavy one. If you make many pie crusts, it's worth the investment.

• **Candy thermometer**

• **Metal flame-tamer**

• **Kitchen timer**

• **Kitchen scissors**

• **Bowls:** A set of stainless-steel mixing bowls—3-quart, 2-quart, 1-quart, and 1-pint—and a large bowl—4 quarts or larger for bread dough.

• **Colander and sieve**

Measures

• **Individual measuring cups:** 1-cup, ½-cup, ⅓-cup, ¼-cup.

• **Measuring spoons:** Have two sets, so you don't have to use the same spoon for wet and dry ingredients.

• **Pyrex measures:** A 4-cup and a 2-cup, with lips for pouring.

Pots and Pans

There are now a number of different kinds of pots and pans, many of which I haven't used, on the market. Aluminum should be avoided because it ionizes in boiling water and reacts with acids, and the aluminum particles get into the food. I prefer the enameled cast-iron pots, such as Le Creuset, because they're heavy and retain heat so well. I urge you to rely upon your taste, your pocketbook, and your experience.

• **Large (12-inch), heavy-bottomed nonstick skillet:** This is essential for low-fat cooking. I use mine more than any other pot or pan.

• **Wok:** A very versatile item; with its cover, it can be used for quick stir-fries or slow-cooking soups, stews, and pilafs. You can also use it for sauces. If it doesn't have a wooden handle (or if the handle comes off), you can place it in the oven. I prefer the cast-metal woks to the stainless steel, as they are heavier, and iron is a better heat conductor than stainless steel. Season your new wok by oiling it and heating it on a low flame for half an hour, then wiping it clean. You can wash your wok with soap after you use it, but wipe it dry with a towel and rub oil into it each time until it has a nice oil finish. Woks are not expensive and can be found in cookware stores or department stores as well as Asian import stores.

• **Saucepans:** Three, 1-quart, 2-quart, and 4-quart.

• **Dutch oven or bean pot:** Choose a 5-quart or larger, one that can also go in the oven. I recommend heavy-bottomed equipment, enameled cast iron being my favorite. Heavy stainless steel is also good. Soapstone and earthenware are beautiful, but breakable.

• **Large stockpot:** For boiling water for pasta and corn on the cob, for steaming large amounts of vegetables, for cooking beans, and for incubating jars of yogurt. Thin enamel is fine; it's light and inexpensive.

• **Nonstick omelet pan:** Use a 6- to 7-inch pan for a two-egg omelet, a 9- to 10-inch pan for three eggs, and a 12-inch pan for five. The 6- to 7-inch pan is most useful.

• **Crêpe pan:** Standard 6-inch French, or the inverted American type.

• **Steamer:** Either a metal fold-up steamer that will fit in various-sized pots, or a tiered Chinese bamboo or metal steamer.

• **Chafing dish:** For fondues and table-top cooking.

Baking Dishes

• **Baking pans:** One square or rectangular 2-quart baking pan, either Pyrex, stainless steel, enameled, or, as a last resort, aluminum.

• **Gratin dishes:** A 2- and 3-quart size, either earthenware, Pyrex, or enameled cast iron.

• **Pie pans:** Two, 9- and 10-inch.

• **Tart pans:** One or two 10½-, 12- or 14-inch, either metal, ceramic, or Pyrex.

- **Bread pans:** Two, 8- or $9\frac{1}{2} \times 4\frac{1}{2} \times 2\frac{1}{2}$ inches. Aluminum, tin, nonstick, or dark metal.

- **Baking sheets with rims:** Have two or three; these double as jelly-roll pans.

- **Soufflé dish:** The straight-sided ceramic kind, 2-quart size.

- **Bundt cake pan:** Use a 10-inch size.

- **Springform pans:** For cheesecakes. Have two 8-inch or one 10- or 12-inch.

Serving Utensils and Dishes

- **Large salad bowl and servers**

- **Serving platters:** Have several, in assorted sizes.

- **Bowls:** In assorted sizes, for molding pâtés and presenting spreads and herb butters.

- **Molds:** Have one or two or even more, 2-cup to 1-quart capacity. Your choice of shape.

- **Baskets:** For serving breads.

Electrical Appliances

- **Blender:** For puréeing, for chopping nuts, cracking grains, mixing drinks, and so on. Remarkably low-priced, and worth the money. Don't buy an unfamiliar brand; Osterizer, Kenwood, and Waring make the best. It's difficult to find one without multiple speeds, but the two-speed blenders actually last longer.

- **Hand blender:** Good for puréeing soups right in the pot.

- **Electric mixer:** A time-saver, but not necessary for most of the recipes here. Especially useful in baking and for herb butters. The most versatile and heavy duty are the KitchenAid and Rival.

- **Food processor:** A magic gadget, with uncanny speed and efficiency. Use for pie crusts, mayonnaise, purées, grating cheese, shredding vegetables, on and on.

• **Electric spice mill**: I own two coffee mills, one for grinding spices, the other for grinding coffee beans.

The way you arrange your cookware and utensils depends largely on the size of your kitchen and on how much you cook. I like cookware to be easily accessible, hung on a pegboard or grill, or from a ceiling rack. Measures and utensils can be hung on nails or hooks on pegboards or in small spaces on kitchen walls. Molds look pretty hanging against a wall. My kitchen is very small, especially for a professional kitchen, and I get around my space problem by hanging tiered basket-trays for spices, with hooks on the bottoms for utensils. It depends, of course, on your personal taste; some people like things on display, others don't. The more you work in your kitchen, with your equipment, the more you will know what your requirements are.

SOME SOUND ADVICE: TECHNIQUES AND GENERAL INSTRUCTIONS

I'm not one of those people who believe that long, tedious hours in the kitchen will result in a better meal; for me, the easiest method is usually the best. After all, working against the clock is an integral part of teaching and catering; you must simplify and develop special tricks as you go along. I've learned many techniques from other cooks, and have designed many of my own for the student—for the person who may not feel confident enough with a knife to do the quick chopping we associate with professional cooking. An efficient short-cut reduces kitchen time just as effectively as a quick hand.

This section is not a complete course for the novice cook. It's a list of techniques that will facilitate or clarify instructions that recur throughout the collection.

Cutting and Chopping, Slicing and Seeding

Always use stainless-steel knives for fruits, potatoes, and eggplant. Carbon steel reacts with the acidity and turns the fruit black on the edges, while the fruit or vegetable discolors the knife.

The cell structures of fruits and vegetables are arranged in a definite pattern; you'll notice lengthwise lines in onions and a lengthwise cellular grain in green peppers. All vegetables are constructed this way, but it's more discernible in some than in others. You can dice vegetables easily if you cut first along the grain, then across it.

• **Onions:** To chop or dice onions, cut in half lengthwise (along a line). Cut off the ends and remove the skin from each half. Lay one half flat side down and cut into strips lengthwise along the lines, holding the onion together with your fingers. As the knife nears your fingertips, you will be beset with the problem of steadying the onion without cutting off your fingers. The way to get around this is to turn the onion around, holding onto the cut side, and work again from the other side toward the middle. Once the onion is sliced, turn it a quarter turn and cut across the slices at a right angle to dice. Repeat for the other half.

For onion rings, don't cut the onion in half. Cut the very ends off and remove the skin. If you have trouble peeling the onion, cut a lengthwise slit one layer deep down one side. You can then remove the layer of skin easily, taking with it a layer of onion. Slice rings across the grain, holding onto the onion carefully.

• **Green peppers:** To chop or dice, cut in half lengthwise and gently remove the stem, seeds, and membranes. Proceed as for onions, cutting the pepper into lengthwise strips and then crosswise into dice. For rings, cut the top off crosswise and dig out the seeds with your fingers. Slice rings crosswise, against the grain.

• **Tomatoes, eggplant, turnips:** Treat these and other roundish produce like onions and green peppers, even if you can't recognize the cell structure so easily. To dice, make an extra lengthwise slice or two where you cut the vegetable in half lengthwise. Lay the half vegetable flat side down, as if it were still intact, and proceed as for onions and green peppers.

• **Carrots, zucchini, celery, cucumbers**: This method of slicing applies to long vegetables to be sliced crosswise or on the diagonal. Using a large knife, hold several vegetables side by side on your cutting surface and slice several at once as if they were one item.

• **Avocados**: This eliminates the messy task of peeling. Cut the avocado in half lengthwise. Twist the two halves apart and remove the seed. Hold a half in one hand and, with a sharp knife, cut three or four strips lengthwise through to the skin but not through it; then cut several strips crosswise if you wish to dice the avocado. Take a soup spoon and carefully scoop out the flesh. With this method, you can scoop out precut slices or dice and keep their edges smooth.

• **Cucumbers**: To seed a cucumber, cut it in half lengthwise. Cut in half lengthwise again so that you have spears. Run a sharp knife between the seeds and the cucumber pulp.

• **Pineapples**: To peel, hold the pineapple so that the place where the leafy top joins the fruit is flush with the edge of your table and the leaves extend over the edge. Hold onto the pineapple with one hand and push down on the leafy top with the other; it should break right off. To peel quickly and neatly, use a stainless-steel knife to cut the ends off; cut the pineapple in half lengthwise, then into quarters (quarters are easy to handle). Run a smaller knife down between the skin and the outer edge of the flesh. Now run a knife down between the core and the flesh. For small chunks, cut the now neatly peeled quarters in half or in thirds lengthwise, then dice crosswise.

• **Melons**: Cut in half lengthwise and remove the seeds. Slice in lengthwise strips; cut small crosswise sections down to the skin but not through it, the same way you do with an avocado. Now run a knife along the inside edge of the rind and the pieces will fall right off.

• **Apples**: Cutting the apple straight down each side of the core, make four cuts, and the core will be removed. Then slice or dice each piece. (Place in water with lemon juice to prevent discoloration.)

- **Corn on the cob:** Remove the kernels from the cob by standing the cob upright on a plate and running a knife down between the kernels and the cob.

- **Herbs:** The best way to chop herbs is to cut them with a scissors. Put them in a glass, jar, or measuring cup, point the scissors straight down and cut. The herbs will not bruise if you use this method. If you chop herbs on a board, use quick, rapid strokes. Use a sharp knife; hold the handle in one hand and rest your other hand on top of the blade. Mince rapidly, pushing the herbs back to the center of your surface as they spread out.

- **Nuts:** Don't try to do more than half a cup at a time. Use a cleaver or a large, sharp knife; hold the handle in one hand and the top of the tip down with the other hand. Keeping the tip end down, lift the handle of the knife up and down, pushing the nuts back to the center of the work surface as they spread out. If they begin to fly off the board, work more slowly and deliberately. To chop fine or grind, use a blender, a spice mill, or a food processor; they will grind up in seconds.

Peeling

- **Tomatoes:** Bring a medium or large pot of water to a boil. Drop in the tomatoes. Wait, with the heat still on, for 30 seconds. Drain and run under cold water until cool enough to handle. The skin should peel off easily. You can also place the tomatoes in a bowl and pour on boiling water. Wait 30 seconds and proceed as above.

- **Garlic:** Put the clove on a flat surface. Pound it once with the bottom of a jar or the flat side of a knife or cleaver. The skin should burst and practically pop off, or come away from the clove of garlic enough to allow you to remove it without getting your fingernails full of garlic. If you have a lot of garlic to peel, as you would for a recipe like Sopa de Ajo, garlic soup, you could peel the cloves by pouring boiling water over them, allowing them to sit for 5 minutes, and then rinsing with cold water. The skin should now peel off easily.

• **Almonds**: To "blanch" almonds, bring a pot of lightly salted water to a boil. With the heat still on, drop the almonds in for 1 minute, then drain and rinse under cold water. Pop the skins off, one by one.

• **Oranges** (and other citrus fruits): To remove all the white membranes with the skin, use a very sharp knife (serrated knives work well) to cut the skin off carefully in a spiral, taking with it all the white membranes. The outside edge of the orange will be quite juicy. This is a good method for oranges you would then slice, say, for oranges Grand Marnier. The most efficient way to peel an orange for eating or sectioning is to quarter it just through the skin with a sharp knife. Peel the skin off in neat quarters; it will come off easily.

Blanching and Steaming

• **Eggplant**: Most directions for handling eggplant before cooking involve salting and weighting, and careful rinsing to draw out the liquid. An excellent chef in Austin, the late James Taylor, taught me the following method; essentially it's quick-steaming at very high heat, which is effective not only for drawing out liquid, but also for bringing out the wonderful redolence of eggplant cooked in olive oil.

Preheat the oven to 450 degrees. Cut the eggplant in half lengthwise. With a very sharp knife, make two lengthwise slits in each half, cutting through to the skin but not through it. Oil a baking pan generously. Place the eggplant halves flat side down in the pan and bake for 15 to 20 minutes; remove from the oven. The skin will have shriveled and the eggplant will be soft and fragrant. When it is cool enough to handle, proceed with your recipe.

• **Spinach (and other greens)**: To blanch spinach, wash and stem it. Bring a large pot of lightly salted water to a boil. Drop in the spinach and slowly count to 20. Drain immediately and rinse under cold water to stop the cooking. Alternatively, you can blanch spinach and other greens by washing the leaves and wilting them in a hot skillet using only the water left on the leaves after washing to create steam.

• **Cauliflower, broccoli, carrots, and green beans:** These and other nonleafy vegetables should be left in the boiling water as described above for 1 minute.

• **Vegetables for color:** To steam a vegetable to bring out the color, place on a rack above 1 inch of water in a saucepan. Cover. Bring the water to a boil, and when you see the steam escaping from the pan count 60 seconds. Drain the vegetable and rinse under cold water. Vegetables can be blanched or steamed before you need them, and held in cold water or plastic bags in the refrigerator for up to a day.

If you want the vegetables very crisp, drain and rinse as soon as you see the steam escaping.

Stir-frying

This is quick-frying in a little oil or butter. Always heat the pan first, then add the oil or butter. Add just enough to give the food something to cook in, not to swim in. Don't add the food until the oil is hot, or it will just sit and soak the oil up. Use a paddle or wooden spoon to keep it moving, and don't overcook. You can also keep the food moving by shaking the pan vigorously. Use whichever method you prefer.

Deep-frying

The most important thing here is to heat the oil (which will be at a depth of from 2 to 4 inches, depending on what you are cooking) sufficiently; it should be a constant 370 degrees. Drop your food in; it should float to the top quickly. Remove as soon as it is a golden brown and drain immediately on paper towels.

General Cooking Directions for Grains and Legumes

One part grains cooks up to two and one-half parts. One cup uncooked grains feeds four (allowing ½ cup per person).

• **Brown rice, barley, soy grits:** Use one part grains to two parts water or stock; add ¼ to ½ teaspoon salt per cup of grains.

Combine the grains, water or stock, and bring to a rolling boil. Add the salt, cover, then reduce the heat and simmer for 35 minutes, until most of the liquid is absorbed. Remove the lid and cook, uncovered, for 5 to 10 minutes longer to separate the grains. Soy grits can be cooked combined with other grains.

• **Millet, buckwheat groats (kasha):** Use one part grains to two and one-half parts water or stock. Add ¼ to ½ teaspoon salt for each cup of grains. Cook millet in the same way as brown rice (see above). Cook buckwheat groats as for kasha (see page 30). For a toastier flavor with millet, stir the dry millet over medium heat in a small amount of oil, or in a dry pan, and add boiling stock or water when it begins to smell toasty. Bring back to a boil, reduce the heat, cover, and proceed as above.

• **Wheat berries, whole rye, and soy flakes:** Use one part grains to three parts water; add ½ teaspoon salt for each cup of grains. Soy flakes can be cooked along with wheat berries or whole rye. Cook in the same way as brown rice (see above), but for 1 hour. When the grains are tender, pour off the remaining water.

• **Bulgur:** Use one part bulgur to two parts water, ¼ to ½ teaspoon salt for each cup. Combine the bulgur and salt in a bowl. Bring the water to a boil and pour over the bulgur. Let sit until the water is absorbed and the bulgur is soft and fluffy, not more than 30 minutes. Pour off excess water and squeeze the bulgur in a towel. Bulgur will also soften, in 1 hour, in room-temperature water.

• **Quinoa**: Use two parts water, one part quinoa. Soak the quinoa in a bowl of water to cover for 10 minutes and strain off any impurities that float to the surface. Drain and rinse for a few minutes under cold water. Bring the two parts water to a boil in a saucepan, and add the quinoa and ¼ teaspoon salt per cup of quinoa. Bring back to a boil, cover, reduce the heat, and simmer for 15 to 20 minutes, until the quinoa is tender but still retains some texture. Remove from the heat and pour off any water remaining in the pan.

• **Legumes** (beans of all kinds, including soybeans): Most beans, except lentils and split peas, must be soaked for at least 6 hours. You can soak beans for 2 or 3 days in the refrigerator before you cook them, or freeze them in the soaking water. Consider cooking double what you need and freezing the other half.

Use one part beans to three parts water, with 1 teaspoon salt per cup, or more to taste. Soak the beans in the water for at least 6 hours. Drain and transfer to a pot. Add three to four parts fresh water, making sure the beans are covered by at least 2 inches. Set over a high flame, bring to a boil, cover, reduce the heat, and simmer for 1 hour (45 minutes for lentils and split peas). Add the salt and simmer for another 30 minutes to an hour, until tender. (Salt added too soon will prevent the beans from softening properly.)

To make a more flavorful pot of beans, after soaking the beans, sauté a chopped onion and some garlic in a little oil. When the onion is tender, add the drained beans and water, and proceed as above.

Quantity Cooking Instructions for Grains (Brown Rice and Millet)

For large quantities of rice, you can avoid making pots of mushy, gummy rice if you use the steaming method instead; this will result in a drier, fluffier rice. The same method can be used for millet. Use one part rice or millet to four parts water, with ¼ to ½ teaspoon salt per cup of grains. Combine the grains, water, and salt in a large stockpot and bring to a boil. When the water starts to boil, test the rice for tenderness. If you can bite through the kernel—that is, if the hard center part is somewhat tender—the rice is ready to be steamed. If the kernels are still hard, continue to boil for another 5 to 10 minutes, until you can bite through.

Now place a colander over another large pot. Drain the grains into the colander and place the second pot, now full of hot water, on the stove. Place the colander of grains in the sink. Fill the pot you just drained with cold water and pour over the grains (this will separate any grains that have begun to stick together). Rinse two more times.

Place the colander of partially cooked, rinsed grains over the pot of hot water on the stove. Bring the water to a boil and cover. (If the handles of the colander prevent the lid from fitting tightly, seal the spaces with a towel.) Making sure the colander doesn't touch the boiling water, steam for 30 minutes, or until the grains are tender.

General Cooking Directions for Dried Pasta

You should have a large pot of water simmering. About 10 minutes before serving, bring to a boil, then add a tablespoon of salt and the pasta. Cook for 7 to 10 minutes (see instructions on the package for the different types of noodles). When the pasta is al dente, just about tender, drain.

If you are cooking a large quantity of pasta and need to cook it in shifts (to avoid large clumps of noodles sticking together), have a second pot ready with a colander or strainer resting on it. Pour the pasta into the colander, then place the second pot of already steaming water on the stove. Bring back to a boil and continue to cook the pasta and drain in this fashion.

See page 179 for the cooking directions for fresh pasta.

• **Couscous:** Use equal parts couscous and room temperature or lukewarm stock or salted water. Place the couscous in a bowl. Pour the water over the couscous and let sit for 10 minutes. Fluff with a fork or roll between your fingers. Steam for 10 to 15 minutes in a colander or in the top part of a couscousière.

General Directions for Sprouting

Place 2 tablespoons your choice of alfalfa seeds, mung beans, lentils, adzuki beans, or sunflower seeds in a wide-mouthed pint or quart jar and cover with water; let soak overnight. Cover the jar with cheesecloth, fixing it to the jar with a rubber band (or use one of the special sprouter caps now available in natural foods stores) and pour off the water the next morning. Shake the jar and turn it so that the seeds adhere to the sides; if they are clumped in a layer at the bottom the seeds on the bottom won't get any air and will rot. Wrap the jar in a towel to keep out the light and lay it on its side; place in a cool, dry place.

Rinse the seeds with water and drain twice a day for three days, making sure you shake and turn the jar after you do this. After three days your sprouts will be ready. Place them in the sun for an hour to bring out the chlorophyll, then refrigerate in a sealed plastic bag or container, or in a jar. Sprouts will last for up to a week in the refrigerator if they are kept dry.

Redwood sprouters are now available in many natural foods stores. These are flat perforated trays in a redwood frame. They provide the sprouts with a little "plot" to grow on, so that they grow upward and don't pile on top of each other. If you eat a large amount of sprouts, these pieces of equipment are very worthwhile.

Thickening Soups and Sauces

• **Making a roux:** A roux is a paste made with butter or oil and flour to which liquid is added to make a sauce. Bring the liquid to a simmer in a saucepan. Melt the butter or heat the oil in a heavy-bottomed saucepan over medium-low heat and stir in the flour. Cook together, stirring with a wooden spoon, for a few minutes, and just before the roux begins to brown remove it from the heat and whisk in the liquid all at once. Return to the heat and whisk until the mixture reaches the boiling point, at which point it will thicken. Turn heat to low and simmer, stirring often with a whisk, for 10 minutes, until there is no floury taste.

• **Puréeing**: This is a good method for thickening soups, especially leguminous ones; it makes it unnecessary to cook a soup for hours and hours to obtain a thick consistency. Cook the soup until the beans or vegetables are soft and the broth is flavorful and aromatic. Remove half the beans or vegetables and purée in a blender or food processor, then return to the soup and mix well. Heat through and serve (or chill for cold soups). Add a couple of diced potatoes to the ingredients in puréed soups to obtain a thick consistency. Simmer (as directed) with the vegetables until the potatoes are tender, and purée. No cream will be necessary.

• **Enriching with eggs**: Eggs are often used to enrich a soup or sauce. For a soup, bring the soup to just below the simmer just before serving. Beat the eggs in a bowl (with other ingredients if the recipe calls for them) and carefully stir them into the soup; they should bind in a minute to two. Serve immediately. If you want the eggs to curdle, bring the soup to a simmer or boil. If it is just below boiling you will have a milky broth.

For sauces, beat the eggs and carefully stir into a barely simmering sauce.

• **Adding arrowroot or cornstarch**: Always dissolve the arrowroot or cornstarch in a little liquid before adding it; otherwise it will lump. Add dissolved arrowroot or cornstarch to a hot sauce, soup, or other dish. It will thicken and glaze when it reaches the boiling point.

Miscellaneous Helpful Hints

• **Making cold blender soups**: The most efficient way to make a cold blender soup is to separate your solid and liquid ingredients, placing all the solid ingredients in one bowl and adding them to the blender jar or food processor in batches, with enough of the liquid (and this includes tomatoes, since they liquefy immediately) to make a smooth purée. Pour the purée from the blender into a large bowl, and when all the solids are liquefied add the remaining stock or juice until your soup reaches the desired consistency, then correct the seasoning.

• **Making bread crumbs**: I find that I don't even need dry bread when I use this efficient method. Just put one or two slices of bread, torn up into large chunks, in the blender jar or food processor and blend at high speed. You'll have bread crumbs in no time.

• **Storing herbs**: To store freshly picked herbs or bunches of them bought in the supermarket, place them in a jar with their stems in a little water. Cover with a plastic bag. Attach the plastic bag to the rim of the jar with a rubber band and refrigerate.

• **Covering prepared dishes for storage before baking**: To ensure freshness, and to prevent foil from reacting with the acids in your food, cover first with plastic or waxed paper, then with foil. Always wrap tightly.

• **Whipping cream**: Chill your bowl and beater. If you forget to chill the bowl, place it in a bowl of ice cubes. Add the sweetner or flavoring after the cream is whipped.

• **Separating eggs**: This method presents no threat of jagged eggshell edges breaking the yolk. You have to get your hands slimy, but that usually happens anyway when you're separating eggs. It's easiest to separate eggs when they're cold.

Have three clean, dry bowls. Break the egg carefully into a small bowl. Then carefully lift out the yolk with your hands, letting the white run through your fingers back into the bowl. Place the yolk in one bowl and pour the white into another. (By using three bowls instead of two you won't lose all the separated eggs if one refuses to separate correctly.)

In any recipe calling for eggs, as a matter of fact, you should break each egg into a separate small bowl, then add it to your recipe. Occasionally an egg is rotten; I once had to throw out an entire cake batter because I cracked a rotten egg into it.

• **Making casseroles:** Take time with each element of your casserole. If every part tastes good on its own, your casserole will be outstanding.

Too often one gets overenthusiastic at the beginning of putting a casserole together, only to run out of cheese or tomato sauce before the top layer is reached. So be stingy at first, then be generous. Remember that you'll be serving from the top, and this must look lavish. The sauces on the top will sink down to the bottom, but nothing on the bottom will rise to the top.

THE ART OF ENTERTAINING

A caterer is a professional party giver. My job is to provide not only food (sometimes for hundreds of people) but also excitement; everything must look dazzling. My supper club and catering business have taught me much about orchestrating parties, so that when I give my own—and I do that as often as I can, because giving parties is a passion of mine—I am now quite relaxed.

I am even fairly relaxed now when I am responsible for something like an extravagant wedding reception for 200 people, because I am organized—and that's the key to successfully hostessing (or hosting) a party of any size.

Here is the way I go about planning a private dinner party or a large catering job. First, I choose the menu. If it's a catering job, I meet with clients and we decide together. Often when it's my own dinner party there will be one dish I've been wanting to cook for some time, and I'll plan the menu around that; or I'll have a leftover from a cooking class that needs to be used up, and that gives me a good excuse for entertaining. There are several factors that go into planning a menu, such as the weather, the guests (if you don't know them well, you should choose reliable favorites), the amount of time you have, how to make it easiest on yourself. I think about the entirety of the meal or buffet. If guests eat some of everything, will they have eaten too much? Will they have eaten a preponderance of rich or starchy food? Or will they have gotten enough? Especially with a vegetarian spread, it's important for people to feel completely satisfied, without feeling stuffed. Variety, lightness, and balance of textures, flavors, calories, fat, and protein content, and food you can display beautifully are key factors.

Once my menu is planned, I make shopping lists. First I write down everything I have to buy, then the places I have to go to get them. Included on my lists are paper goods and rentals.

I then make a calendar for shopping and food preparation. The more I can get done in advance the better. This is especially true for large catering jobs, but I do this for small parties as well. If I have people helping me, their jobs are included on the lists. I now know that, no matter how far ahead of the clock I think I am, I will always do some racing at the last minute (I love that "show biz" aspect of entertaining and catering), and the more I've done in advance the less critical this rushing is. I post my lists in the kitchen so that I can check things off and actually see my progress. I try to leave a big space on the last day so that if I've fallen behind I can still get everything done.

Here are examples of a menu and schedule for a large wedding reception held on a Saturday. All the breads were baked on weekends beforehand and frozen; bread is so time-consuming that I put it by whenever I can so I won't have to fit it into a tight catering schedule.

MENU:
Assorted breads and cheeses
Herbed Cream Cheese (page 26)
Extraordinary Chalupas (page 100)
Marinated Vegetables Vinaigrette (page 35)
Vegetable Platter with Assorted Dips (page 40)
Oranges Grand Marnier (page 238)
Wedding cake (subcontracted out)

MONDAY:

Order cheese
Check on rentals (which have been ordered well in
    advance; try to find a rental service that delivers)
Buy paper goods
Start sprouts (I order large quantities from the co-op)

TUESDAY:

Soak beans and refrigerate (can be done Wednesday as
    well)

WEDNESDAY:

Pick up cheese
Buy onions, garlic, lemons, other nonperishables
Make yogurt, mayonnaise, other dips

THURSDAY:

Make radish roses and celery curls (the longer they soak
    in cold water, the more they will open up and curl)
Cook beans
Buy all produce except leaf lettuce
Pick up chalupa shells

FRIDAY:

Make vinaigrette
Buy leaf lettuce, wash, dry, and refrigerate
Purée or refry beans
Herb cream cheese
Vegetable prep
Marinate vegetables for vinaigrette
Thaw bread
Prepare ingredients for salsa

SATURDAY A.M.:

Chop tomatoes
Make Oranges Grand Marnier
Arrange vegetable platters
Slice and rewrap some of the bread
Make guacamole
Make salsa

I also make lists of equipment I will need, things I need to bring to the catering job, and the night before put them all in a box so I don't have to think about them during the final rush. The less you have to think about as "curtain time" approaches, the better. For large buffets I make blueprints of the table arrangements so my help can set them up quickly and easily.

A party in your home is seldom such a production, but I urge that you follow the same principles. Make lists and get as much done as you can ahead of time. One thing to get out of the way early, the night before if possible, is table setting. No matter how frantic things may be in the kitchen, you will at least be reassured to know that the guests will find an air of tranquility in the dining and living area.

I always try to have time to compose beautiful food arrangements. Presentation is one of the most important aspects of entertaining, as well as of good cooking, and the most fun part of the preparation. Entertaining becomes an art when you can give the food this flair (and manage to maintain your composure). Surprise and delight your guests with unexpected touches—Champagne with the hors d'oeuvres, a colorful assortment of vegetables judiciously arranged around a fondue (instead of the usual squares of bread) and garnished with bright, fresh herbs. Arrange your crackers or sliced bread in a nice pattern around cheese, and place radish roses, olives, herbs, and other raw vegetables or sliced apples (dipped in lemon juice so they won't discolor) here and there for color. Place a big wooden bowl of orange wedges on the coffee table to greet your guests in the winter. Mold your hummus or mushroom pâté in a pretty bowl and garnish it with olives, pimientos, cherry tomatoes or radishes, and fresh herbs, or pipe your hummus or baba ghanoush onto squash and cucumber rounds from a pastry bag. Arrange marinated vegetables on a platter over a bright green bed of leaf or Boston lettuce and set them off with black olives. Remove the chokes from your artichokes, place mayonnaise in the middle, and stand up asparagus spears inside. Place scalloped lemons and more mayonnaise around the artichokes.

Surprise your guests again with beautifully garnished bowls of soup and pretty main dishes and salads. For a grand finale I once unmolded a strawberry sherbet into a punch bowl and floated strawberries in Champagne (a semidry dessert Champagne) around it; that was quite a sensation. Recently I delighted my guests by placing chilled ratatouille (left over from my cooking class and the excuse for the dinner party) in a ring on the edge of an elegant china platter, then placing soft Boston lettuce tossed with vinaigrette in the middle under a mound of marinated vegetables. The platter was further garnished with walnuts and herbs. Everything else was simple: artichokes and asparagus prepared as described above for hors d'oeuvres, white wine, cheese soufflé with the ratatouille platter, and a sherbet for dessert. I had had time to compose every part of the meal exactly as I wanted it to be; the soufflé was ready to pop into the preheated oven as soon as we were well into the hors d'oeuvres, and I could come to my party.

Garnish, then, is the key word, and the best ones are leafy lettuce, fresh herbs, vegetables, and flowers. Below are some suggestions for garnishes; further suggestions accompany recipes.

FOR SPREADS AND PÂTÉS:

Sliced olives
Parsley and other fresh herbs
Radishes and radish roses
Pimiento or red pepper strips
Cherry tomatoes and cherry tomato wedges (seeded if
    placed over the top of the pâté)
Cucumber and squash rounds

FOR HORS D'OEUVRE PLATTERS AND SALADS

Bright vegetables, such as briefly steamed broccoli florets
    and asparagus
Cherry tomatoes, carrots, cucumber and squash rounds
Fresh herbs

Black olives
Lemons and limes, sliced or scalloped
Walnuts, almonds
Leaf lettuce
Alfalfa sprouts

FOR SOUPS:

Croutons
Yogurt
Raw vegetables, such as thinly sliced mushrooms
Lemon slices
Grated cheese
Fresh herbs
Sliced apples

FOR MAIN DISHES:

Fresh herbs
Vegetables of contrasting color
Sauces and grated cheese

FOR DESSERTS:

Mint leaves or sprigs
Slivered almonds
Liqueurs for flambés
Yogurt
Thinly sliced fruit

If final meal preparations do require that you be in the kitchen and not with your guests, good wine and beautiful, delicious hors d'oeuvres will relieve you of some of the duties of social director. While people are loosening up with a glass of wine and taking the edge off their hunger with your impressive appetizers, you can retreat to the kitchen and you'll hardly be missed.

Finally, try to work in at least an hour for yourself before your guests arrive. Take a long bath, have a nap, choose your clothes, pamper yourself. Your composure will be contagious.

THANKSGIVING AND OTHER MEATY HOLIDAYS

Thanksgiving is my favorite holiday, as cooking and eating is what this day is all about. But turkey-centered holidays can be difficult for vegetarians. Actually they are most difficult for their families, who don't know what to make for their vegetarian guests. My feeling is that there is so much in the way of wonderful trimmings—the stuffing (some of which can be baked outside of the turkey) and mashed potatoes and/or sweet potatoes, vegetables and salads, the cranberry sauce and desserts—that the bird hardly requires a substitution.

One thing that's fun to do for holiday menus is fit the foods you associate with the meals in where you'd least expect them. Pumpkin, for example, could be served in the form of a gratin, or even more exciting, pumpkin lasagne, a holiday dish if there ever was one. Cranberries could show up in the dessert. When I lived in Austin, Texas, I would often stuff a large squash, and decorate it with feathers. If you go this route, wild rice with chestnuts makes a great stuffing.

If you're agonizing over your next Thanksgiving menu, try this one on for size.

Cream of Raw and Cooked Mushroom Soup (page 62)
Pumpkin Lasagne (page 194)
Steamed Broccoli
Tender Lettuce and Orange Salad (page 220), or Spinach
    and Citrus Salad (page 227)
Pecan Pie (page 257)
Cranberry-Pear Tart (page 263)

THE FINAL TOUCH

The final flavor of a dish depends upon you and your taste buds. No two tomatoes or green peppers are the same; every clove of garlic is a different size. The spices on my shelf may be more aromatic than those on yours, and you may like salt or honey more than I do. You can follow a recipe through to the end, but it is at this point that you must taste it. If the taste of a soup doesn't linger on your tongue, add a little more salt or perhaps a bit more garlic. Learn to recognize the flavors of herbs and spices; a touch more oregano or nutmeg or a dash of lemon juice is often exactly what you need. If you are afraid of overseasoning a dish but feel that it needs more of something, remove a cupful and add a very small amount of the seasoning to see. But a word of warning: Take very small tastes, or even better (making sure that nobody is looking), spit out if you are doing a lot of tasting, and drink water between tastes. If I didn't do it this way I would have no appetite at the table, and I do like to eat with my guests. It is at the table, after all, where you will do the final tasting and make your mental notes on a recipe.

Breads

Bread is miraculous. I've made it week after week for years, and the experience has never been the same, because the dough is alive. Of all cooking activities, bread baking is the most sensual (and bread *eating* may be the most sensual of all eating activities). Each type of dough feels and handles differently; some are heavy, some light, some sticky, some dense. And even the same kind will vary from week to week, because the dough responds to weather conditions, and the quality of your ingredients may vary. Baking is an exhilarating experience for me; I'm so aware of the fact that I'm working with living organisms, which are transforming the raw ingredients into the most basic food of mankind. Working with the dough means working with these ever-multiplying yeasts, and it's so satisfying to manipulate the dough, watch it grow, and make it into bread.

Not only do the breads in this section taste like no other breads in town, but they look divine. The first one, mixed grains bread, is the one I always have on hand. The others are either variations of this or are my own versions of breads you may recognize; they should serve you for many occasions.

Depending on the size of your family and the amount of bread you consume, you may not have to bake too often. Bread freezes well. Wrap your extra loaves tightly in plastic, then seal in plastic bags or foil to freeze. The breads thaw at room temperature in 2 hours, or wrapped in foil in a 350-degree oven in 30 minutes.

Mixed Grains Bread

If I had to choose one bread to have on hand, this would be the one. It's grainy and slightly sweet, nutty, and toasts beautifully.

Step 1. Mixing up the sponge:

In a large mixing bowl, dissolve the yeast in the water. Add the honey and molasses and stir to dissolve. Use water from the bowl to rinse the measuring spoons.

Add both types of flour, a cup at a time, stirring with a whisk or wooden spoon to incorporate the flour into the liquid. The mixture will gradually develop a mudlike consistency. Keep stirring in the flour until you have added all 4 cups.

Now stir the mudlike mixture 100 times. This sounds like a lot of work, but it goes very fast. Make sure you are stirring the batter up from the bottom and center of the bowl. There should be no lumps when you are finished. If there are, stir a little while longer.

Cover the bowl with plastic wrap or a damp towel and set aside in a warm place—over a pilot light, on a heater, in an oven with a pilot light, or in an oven that has been turned on low heat for 10 minutes, then turned off. If your pilot light is very hot, place a baking pan between it and the bread bowl. In the summertime almost any place will suffice, and the pilot light will probably be too hot.

Let the sponge rise for 50 to 70 minutes. At the end of this time it should be bubbling, and you will actually be able to see the mixture expanding.

Step 2. Adding the remaining ingredients; kneading:

Pour the oil onto the sponge and sprinkle on the salt. Incorporate into the sponge by folding the sponge over with a large wooden spoon, turning a quarter turn, folding again, and so on until you no longer see the oil.

continued

FOR THE SPONGE:

1 tablespoon (1 envelope) active dry yeast
3 cups lukewarm water
2 tablespoons mild honey
2 tablespoons molasses (or use ¼ cup honey in all)
2 cups unbleached white flour
2 cups whole-wheat flour

FOR THE DOUGH:

¼ cup canola or vegetable oil
1 tablespoon salt, preferably sea salt
¾ cup rolled or flaked oats
¾ cup cracked wheat (you can crack your own by running wheat berries in the blender, a bit at a time, at high speed), or bulgur
¼ cup chia seeds (optional)
¾ cup finely cracked millet or millet meal (can be done in a blender the same way as cracked wheat)
¾ cup soy flour
2 to 3 cups whole-wheat flour, or more as necessary

FOR THE TOPPING:

Egg wash
¼ cup water
Sesame seeds or poppy seeds

Add the grains, a cup at a time, and fold in just as you folded in the oil and salt: Sprinkle on a cup, fold, turn the bowl a quarter turn, fold again, turn, and so on. Each cup should take about four turns to be incorporated. Start with the oats, then the cracked wheat, then the chia, then the millet.

Add the soy flour, and fold in.

Now begin adding the whole-wheat flour, a cup at a time, and fold in. By the time you begin this the dough should be stiff enough for you to press some of the flour in with your hands from the top, and then fold the dough over with the spoon. It should also become more difficult to work with.

After the first cup of whole-wheat flour, the dough should begin to come away from the sides of the bowl and have some semblance of a lump, though a sticky, formless one. As soon as you see that the dough will stay in one piece, more or less, it is time to dump it out onto your kneading surface. Place a cup of whole-wheat flour on the board or table, spread it around, and turn out the dough. Part of the dough will adhere to the bowl; don't worry, just scrape it out onto the top of the dough that's already on the table.

Now you are ready to go. Your kneading surface should be low, about level with your hips or a little bit lower. *Take your rings off* and flour your hands. To knead, take the far end of the dough, fold it in half toward you; lean into the dough, letting your weight push through the palms of your hands and through your fingertips. Turn the dough a quarter turn, fold toward you, lean into it. Turn, fold, lean; turn, fold, lean. Each time the dough becomes sticky add a small handful of whole-wheat flour to the board; you can also sprinkle some flour on top of the dough. Eventually add flour only to the board. As you continue this process the dough will become stiff and hard to work with, but keep kneading for at least 10 minutes, adding flour—but not too much—whenever it becomes too sticky. After 10 to 15 minutes of kneading, the dough should be stiff, elastic, and heavy; the surface will be smooth but not necessarily glossy.

If you knead for too long it will keep getting sticky, and you will end up adding too much flour. This will result in a heavy bread. Ten to 15 minutes of vigorous kneading is sufficient.

Now the dough is ready to rise. Fold each side toward you and turn without kneading. Pinch the folds together at the bottom so that the dough is formed into a ball. Wash out the bread bowl and oil it well; place the dough in the bowl, round side down, and roll it around to coat with the oil. This will prevent it from getting a dry, crusty shell. Turn the dough over and cover the bowl with plastic or a damp towel. Set in a warm place and let rise 50 to 60 minutes; it should almost double in bulk.

Step 3. Punching down; third rise:

Punch down by gently pushing your fists into the puffed-up dough about 30 times. This is the easiest and probably the most fun part of the whole process. Let the dough rise again, covered, for 45 minutes to an hour. The dough should be very puffed up, doubled in bulk, but much lighter than after the previous rise.

Step 4. Forming the loaves; fourth and last rise:

Remove the dough from the bowl and place it on your kneading surface. If the dough is sticky you will have to flour the surface lightly.

Shape the dough into a ball by folding all the way around in the same manner as in Step 2. Cut this ball into 2 equal pieces with a sharp knife and shape each of these into a ball. (You can weigh the pieces to make sure they're equal.)

Oil 2 bread pans. You can do this by pouring some oil into one pan and turning it upside down on top of another pan so the oil drips into the second one. It is important to oil the pans well so that the bread can be removed quickly and easily after baking. Use your hands or a pastry brush to spread the oil evenly, making sure you coat the corners of the pan as well as the sides and bottom.

continued

Preheat the oven to 350 degrees.

To make the loaves, take each ball, beginning with the one you made first, knead a few times for extra spring, then press out into a rectangle and roll up lengthwise into a log shape; or fold like a business letter. Pinch together firmly along the lengthwise crease; fold the ends over toward the crease and pinch the folds.

Place the loaf creased side up in an oiled loaf pan; gently push it into the pan with the backs of your hands to allow it to be oiled and shaped by the pan. The loaf at this point should be ⅔ to ¾ the volume of the pan. Then turn the loaf so that the smooth side is up, gently press it into shape again, and set aside to rise (covered with a towel if the room is drafty) for 15 to 25 minutes, until the middle of each loaf is a little higher than the edge of the bread pan.

Step 5. Baking, cooling, and storing:

With a very sharp knife, make about three ½-inch-deep slashes across each loaf. This allows air to escape as the bread bakes; otherwise the loaves will tear. (You can slash a design in the loaves, if you prefer.)

Make an egg wash by mixing together the egg and the ¼ cup water. Brush each loaf generously to obtain a rich, shiny brown surface. Sprinkle with sesame seeds or poppy seeds and brush again with egg wash to paste on the seeds.

Bake in the preheated 350-degree oven for 50 to 60 minutes; for extra-shiny, rich brown loaves brush again with the egg wash halfway through baking. The bread is ready when the surface of each loaf is golden brown and it responds with a hollow thumping sound when tapped with the tips of your fingers. Remove from the bread pans immediately and cool on racks. (Sometimes the egg wash will run down the sides of the loaf and cause it to stick to the bottom of the pan. Oiling the pan very well will help prevent this. If you have trouble removing the bread, run a butter knife around the edges of the loaf several times, turn upside down, and shake the pan or beat on the bottom of it.)

Let cool several hours. When *completely* cool, place the loaves in plastic bags and store in your bread box, or freeze the bread (wrapped tightly in foil, then placed in plastic bags or wrapped in foil) and thaw out at a later date. After about 3 days in the bread box, the bread should be stored in the refrigerator to prevent spoilage.

Makes 2 loaves

Brown Rice or Leftover Grains Bread

This is a moist, chewy sponge-type bread, a good way to use up leftover grains.

In Step 2 of the preceding recipe, substitute 1 to 3 cups cooked brown rice or other cooked grains for the cracked wheat and millet. Because the cooked grains contain more water than the raw grains, the dough will be stickier and you will need more whole-wheat flour. The dough will also be lighter and will rise more than the mixed grains dough. Do not be alarmed if the dough is very sticky when you turn it out onto the board to make the loaves. Just sprinkle your board with a small amount of whole-wheat flour to prevent sticking, and handle carefully. Proceed as in the previous recipe.

Makes 2 loaves

Rye-Oatmeal Bread

FOR THE SPONGE:

2½ cups lukewarm water

1 tablespoon (1 envelope) active
 dry yeast

1 tablespoon Postum or instant
 coffee dissolved in ½ cup hot
 water and cooled to lukewarm

¼ cup molasses

2 cups unbleached white flour

2 cups whole-wheat flour

FOR THE DOUGH:

¼ cup canola or vegetable oil

1 tablespoon salt, preferably sea
 salt

2 to 3 tablespoons caraway seeds

1 cup rolled or flaked oats

1 cup rye flakes or 1 more cup
 rolled or flaked oats

½ cup soy flour

2 cups rye flour

2½ cups whole-wheat flour,
 approximately

FOR THE TOPPING:

Egg wash (1 egg beaten with ¼
 cup water)

½ teaspoon Postum (optional)

Caraway seeds (optional)

These moist, savory, hearty loaves are a pleasing variation on mixed grains bread.

Proceed as in Mixed Grains Bread (pages 3–7), adding the Postum mixture to the water and yeast in the sponge before you add the molasses and flour.

To make darker loaves, dissolve ½ teaspoon Postum in the egg wash water before stirring in the egg.

Note: These loaves may be heavier than mixed grains bread, since rye flour has less gluten than whole-wheat flour.

Makes 2 loaves

Black Bread

These sleek black loaves are wonderful for parties, with soups, topped with spreads such as Hummus, Soya Pâté, or Herbed Cream Cheese. They slice nicely.

After dissolving the Postum, set the solution aside to cool to lukewarm.

In a large bowl, dissolve the yeast in the 2 cups lukewarm water. Add the molasses and ginger and stir together. When the Postum mixture has cooled to lukewarm, add it to the yeast mixture.

Now add the bread crumbs and wheat germ, if used, and 2 cups of the unbleached white flour, a cup at a time, to make a sponge. Stir 100 times and set aside in a warm place, covered with plastic wrap or a damp towel. Let rise 50 to 60 minutes.

At the end of the rising time, fold in the oil and salt. Add the rye flour and the soy flour, a cup at a time; the mixture will be very sticky.

As soon as the dough comes away from the sides of the bowl in one lump, place the remaining cup of unbleached white flour on your board and turn the mixture out onto it. Flour your hands generously and begin to knead. Knead very slowly and gently at first, and don't let the moistness of the dough discourage you. The dough will soon start to stiffen up and you can begin to knead more vigorously. Knead for at least 10 minutes, adding unbleached white flour as needed.

When the dough is stiff and smooth (or somewhat smooth; it may still be a little sticky), shape it into a ball. Wash out your bowl and oil it, then place the dough upside down in it first, then right side up. Cover and set in a warm place to rise until doubled in bulk, about 1½ hours.

Preheat the oven to 400 degrees.

Punch the dough down and turn it out onto a lightly floured board. Divide into 2 or 4 equal pieces (weighing the
continued

1 heaping tablespoon Postum dissolved in ½ cup hot water, or ½ cup strong coffee

2 tablespoons (2 envelopes) active dry yeast

2 cups lukewarm water

⅓ cup dark molasses

½ teaspoon ground ginger

2 cups dark or whole-wheat bread crumbs, or 1½ cups bread crumbs plus ½ cup wheat germ

3 cups unbleached white flour, plus more as necessary for kneading

¼ cup canola oil

2 teaspoons salt, preferably sea salt

3 cups rye flour

1 cup soy flour

FOR THE TOPPING:

1 teaspoon Postum

¼ cup hot water

1 egg

Sesame seeds or poppy seeds (optional)

pieces, if you wish, to be sure they're equal) and shape the pieces into 2 long or round loaves or 4 small long or round loaves. Make the loaves high, as the dough will spread out. Brush with oil and place on oiled cookie sheets or in baguette pans, cover with plastic wrap or a damp towel, and let rise again for 30 minutes, until nearly doubled in bulk.

Prepare an egg wash by dissolving 1 teaspoon Postum in ¼ cup hot water and then beating in the egg. Brush the loaves with the egg wash, then, using a sharp knife, make a few slashes across the top of each loaf. Sprinkle with sesame or poppy seeds, if you wish, and brush again.

Bake for 40 to 45 minutes, for extra-shiny loaves brushing again with egg wash halfway through the baking. Remove from the baking sheet and let cool completely on a rack.

Makes 2 large or 4 small loaves

French Bread

These loaves are light and delicate. The wheat germ and whole-wheat flour add a nutty flavor but don't overwhelm the bread or make it "weighty"—and don't worry about this tasting like "health bread." The dough will be much more delicate than others in this section, and when you form the loaves after the final rise it may be sticky. If this is the case, lightly flour your work surface and moisten your hands.

1 tablespoon (1 envelope) active dry yeast
1 tablespoon mild honey
3 cups lukewarm water
5 cups unbleached white flour, plus more as necessary for kneading
1 tablespoon melted butter, olive oil, or canola oil
1 scant tablespoon salt, preferably sea salt
2 cups wheat germ
1 cup whole-wheat flour
Yellow cornmeal
Egg wash (1 egg beaten with ¼ cup water)

Dissolve the yeast and honey in the lukewarm water. Mix in 3 cups of the unbleached white flour, a cup at a time. When the flour is mixed in, stir the batter 100 times. Cover and set in a warm place for 30 minutes.

When the 30 minutes are up, fold in the melted butter or oil and the salt. Then fold in the wheat germ and the whole-wheat flour, a cup at a time. Add 1 cup unbleached flour and fold in. The dough should now be stiff enough to turn onto a board. Place a cup of unbleached white flour on the board and turn the dough out. Begin to knead, adding unbleached white flour as necessary. Knead until the dough is satiny smooth and very elastic, at least 10 minutes.

Shape the dough into a ball and place in the oiled bowl, upside down first, then right side up. Cover with a towel and place in a warm spot until doubled in bulk, about 1 to 1½ hours.

Punch down and let rise again until doubled in bulk, about 1 hour. Meanwhile, butter or oil a baking sheet and sprinkle it lightly with cornmeal.

Turn the dough out onto a lightly floured board. It will be soft and may be sticky. Handle it carefully, but don't let its softness worry you. Add dustings of flour to the board to avoid sticking.

Divide the dough into 3 parts. Roll out each part into a long, wide rectangle, 12 to 14 inches long by about 8 inches wide. Roll this rectangle up tightly lengthwise until it is a long, thin loaf about 2 inches wide. Pinch together at the seam and the ends and place, crease down, on the baking sheet. Brush with the egg wash and slash 3 or 4 times across the top with a sharp knife; set the egg wash aside for use later.

Cover the loaves with a dry towel and let rise until nearly doubled in size, about 30 to 45 minutes.

Meanwhile, preheat the oven to 400 degrees.

Bake for 40 to 45 minutes, spraying the inside of the oven every 10 minutes or so with a fine mist from a spray bottle. Set your timer for 20 minutes at first and brush the loaves with the reserved egg wash. Set it then for 10 minutes, and brush the loaves again. Then set the timer for a final 10 minutes. If the bread is golden brown and responds to the tap of your fingertips with a hollow sound, remove from the oven and cool on a rack. Otherwise, bake another 5 minutes.

Makes 3 long slender loaves

French Herb Bread

To the ingredients for French bread (see preceding recipe), add:

3 garlic cloves, peeled and minced or put through a press

2 teaspoons fresh rosemary or ¾ teaspoon dried

1 tablespoon chopped fresh dill or 1 teaspoon dried

2 tablespoons chopped fresh parsley

1 onion, peeled, minced, and sautéed in 1 tablespoon olive oil until tender

This aromatic bread is especially nice for parties. Of the herbs, I think it is the rosemary that contributes most to its special flavor. You will be following the recipe for my French bread here, and adding the herb-onion mixture to the sponge along with the oil or butter and salt.

Make the sponge, following the recipe for French bread. Let rise for 30 minutes.

Place the garlic, rosemary, dill, and parsley in a mortar and grind together into a paste.

Fold the oil or butter into the sponge. Add the salt, the sautéed onion, and the herb mixture and fold in. Proceed from here as for French bread.

Makes 3 large or 4 smaller loaves

Whole-Wheat–Sesame Pita Bread

2 tablespoons (2 envelopes) active dry yeast

¼ teaspoon mild honey

2 cups lukewarm water

¼ cup olive oil

1 scant tablespoon salt

½ cup sesame seeds

2 cups whole-wheat flour

3 cups unbleached white flour

Cornmeal

Pita bread is Middle Eastern flatbread that puffs up during baking, leaving a nice pouch that you can fill with hummus or with baba ghanoush or anything you would normally use for a sandwich. I love it for sandwiches because it contains the filling so nicely. Torn in strips, pitas make good dippers.

The trick to making pita successfully is not to let it brown too much in the oven. Once it begins to brown it will get crisp, and what you want is a soft, flexible loaf that puffs up during baking, then deflates (sometimes you have to push it down gently, but if it's soft it won't tear). When you tear or cut it open, the inside will be hollow.

When your pita has cooled (it cools quickly), wrap it well in plastic and foil, or put it in plastic bags. Pita freezes well.

Dissolve the yeast and honey in ½ cup of the lukewarm water in a mixing bowl and let sit for 10 minutes to proof (bubble up). Add the remaining water and mix well, then whisk in the oil, salt, and sesame seeds. Stir in the whole-wheat flour, a cup at a time; fold in 2 cups of the unbleached white flour, a cup at a time. Place the remaining cup of unbleached white flour on your board and turn out the dough. Knead vigorously for 10 to 15 minutes, until the dough is smooth and elastic, then shape into a ball and place in an oiled or buttered bowl, upside down first to coat the dough, then right side up. Cover and let rise in a warm place for 1 to 2 hours, until doubled in bulk.

Punch the dough down and turn it out onto your board. Knead 3 or 4 times and allow to rest for 10 minutes, then divide into 8 or 10 equal pieces (depending on how large you want the pitas to be) and shape each piece into a ball. Place the balls on a floured surface, cover with a towel, and let rise for 30 minutes.

Using a well-floured rolling pin, flatten each ball and roll it out into a circle approximately ⅛ inch thick and 8 inches in diameter. Dust two unoiled baking sheets with cornmeal and place two circles on each sheet. Leave the remaining ones on your lightly floured board. Cover and let rise again for 30 minutes. Meanwhile, preheat your oven to 500 degrees.

Place a filled baking sheet on the rack in the middle of your oven and bake for 5 minutes without opening the oven door. Check your loaves, and if they are beginning to brown, remove from the oven. If they still smell yeasty and not like baking bread, leave for another 2 to 5 minutes. (If this is the first time you're making pita, the first loaves will probably be experimental, so you can get an idea of the proper time for your oven.)

Bake all the rounds this way, cool on racks, and wrap well. Keep at room temperature if you're eating them soon, or refrigerate or freeze.

Makes 8 to 10 round pita breads

Challah

1 tablespoon (1 envelope) active
   dry yeast

1½ cups warm water

3 tablespoons mild honey

3 eggs

4 to 5 cups unbleached white
   flour, plus more as necessary
   for kneading

¼ cup canola oil or melted butter

2 teaspoons salt, preferably sea
   salt

1 cup wheat germ

2 cups whole-wheat flour

Egg wash (1 egg beaten with ¼
   cup water)

Poppy seeds

Challah is a traditional braided Jewish bread made with eggs. My version incorporates wheat germ and whole-wheat flour, like my French bread, and has a rich texture and flavor. These braided loaves make delicious presents.

Dissolve the yeast in the water, then add the honey. Beat the eggs well and add them to the yeast mixture. Stir in 3 cups of the unbleached white flour, a cup at a time, to make a sponge. Stir 100 times, then cover and set in a warm place for 1 hour.

When the hour is up, fold in the canola oil and salt, then the wheat germ and the whole-wheat flour. When the dough comes away from the sides of the bowl, place a cup of unbleached white flour on your kneading surface and turn out the dough. Knead until the dough is stiff and elastic and somewhat silky, adding more unbleached white flour as necessary.

Wash out your bowl, oil it, and set the dough in it to rise for 1 to 1½ hours, until doubled.

Punch the dough down and turn out onto your work surface, then divide into 6 equal pieces for 2 braided loaves, or 12 pieces for 4 loaves, weighing the pieces, if desired, to make sure they're equal. Roll each piece out into a rectangle about 9 inches long, then roll up into a tight cylinder. Roll each cylinder on the work surface until it is 12 to 14 inches long. Attach 3 cylinders by pinching the ends together. Fold the pinched part under and make a braid; pinch together at the other end and fold under. Place the braids on an oiled baking sheet and brush with oil. Let rise in a warm place for 30 minutes, while you preheat the oven to 375 degrees.

Brush the braids with the egg wash, sprinkle with poppy seeds, and brush with egg wash again. Bake for 40 to 45 minutes, brushing again with the egg wash halfway through. Cool on a rack.

Makes 2 large or 4 small braided loaves

Boston Brown Bread

This is one of my favorite breakfast breads, especially spread with a little ricotta cheese. It keeps for a couple of weeks if well sealed in the refrigerator, and is moist, rich, sweet, and wholesome. It's a steamed bread, and you can use coffee cans, juice cans, or pudding molds to steam it. Steaming a bread may sound strange to you, but it works, and that's what makes this bread so moist and contributes to its wonderful texture.

1 cup rye flour
1 cup yellow cornmeal, preferably stone-ground
1 cup whole-wheat flour
2 teaspoons baking soda
1 teaspoon salt, preferably sea salt
¾ cup dark molasses
2 cups buttermilk
1 cup raisins

Sift together the rye flour, cornmeal, whole-wheat flour, baking soda, and salt. Stir in the molasses and buttermilk and blend well, then stir in the raisins.

Generously butter two 1-pound coffee or juice cans, or several smaller cans. Fill each can three-quarters full of batter. Butter pieces of foil and cover the cans, sealing well with tape if necessary.

Place the cans in a large pot and pour in water to the depth of 1 inch. Bring the water to a boil on top of the stove. Cover, then reduce the heat and simmer for 3 hours, checking once in a while to make sure the water hasn't boiled off. Remove the cans from the pan, unmold, and cool on a rack. If your bread seems too moist, place in a 375-degree oven for 10 minutes.

Makes 2 large or several smaller loaves

Coffee Cake

This dough is slightly sweet because of the orange juice. You can vary the filling. I first made it to use up several cups of dried fruit compote. You can make the dough the night before you wish to serve it, refrigerate it overnight, and bake the coffee cake the next morning. The finished cake reheats nicely.

FOR THE DOUGH:

1 tablespoon (1 envelope) active dry yeast

½ cup warm water

½ cup orange juice

3 tablespoons mild honey

1 egg, beaten

⅓ cup spray-dried milk

1 tablespoon lemon juice

1 tablespoon grated orange rind

2½ cups unbleached white flour, plus more as necessary for kneading

3 tablespoons melted butter or canola oil

1 teaspoon salt, preferably sea salt

1½ cups whole-wheat flour

FOR THE FILLING:

¼ cup water, more if necessary

1½ cups chopped dried figs, prunes, dates, apricots, raisins, or a mixture

½ cup finely chopped almonds

1 teaspoon ground cinnamon

¼ teaspoon freshly grated nutmeg

1 tablespoon grated orange rind

¼ cup mild honey

1 teaspoon vanilla extract

1 teaspoon rum (optional)

Pinch of salt, preferably sea salt

FOR THE TOPPING:

Egg wash (1 egg beaten with ¼ cup water)

½ cup slivered almonds

¼ to ½ cup mild honey heated in ½ cup water

First prepare the dough. Dissolve the yeast in the water in a large bowl. Heat the orange juice in a small pan and stir in the honey, then remove from the heat and let cool to lukewarm. Add to the yeast mixture; stir in the egg, spray-dried milk, lemon juice, and orange rind. Stir in 1½ cups of the unbleached white flour and stir 100 times for the sponge. Cover and set in a warm place for 1 hour.

When the hour is up, fold the butter or oil and salt into the sponge; fold in the whole-wheat flour and remaining cup of unbleached white flour. Turn out onto a floured work surface and knead until smooth and elastic, adding more unbleached white flour as necessary. Wash out your bowl, oil it, and place the dough in it; let rise 1 hour.

Meanwhile, combine the ingredients for the filling in a saucepan. Simmer, adding a little more water if necessary, until the fruit is softened and the mixture thick.

Punch the dough down, turn out onto your work surface, and roll out to a rectangle about 12 × 14 inches. Spread with the fruit mixture and roll up lengthwise, like a jelly roll. Place on an oiled baking sheet and join the ends by pinching them together. Using kitchen shears or a sharp knife, cut slits halfway through the dough, 1 inch apart. Let rise for 30 to 45 minutes, while you preheat the oven to 350 degrees.

Brush the dough with egg wash, sprinkle with the slivered almonds, and brush again with egg wash. Bake for 40 minutes, until golden brown.

Meanwhile, heat honey and water. Drizzle the syrup over the warm cake.

Serve warm.

Makes 1 ring-shaped loaf

Corn Bread

This is a rich, moist bread with a grainy texture.

Preheat the oven to 450 degrees.

Sift together the cornmeal, flour, salt, baking powder, and baking soda in a large bowl. Beat together the yogurt, milk, honey, and eggs in another bowl.

Put the butter in a heavy-bottomed 9 × 9-inch baking dish, a 2-quart gratin dish, or a 9-inch cast-iron skillet and place it in the oven for about 3 to 4 minutes, until the butter melts. Remove from the heat, brush the butter over the sides and bottom of the pan, and pour the remaining melted butter into the yogurt and egg mixture. Stir together well, then fold the liquid mixture into the dry mixture (or vice versa). Do this quickly, being careful not to overwork the batter. A few lumps are okay.

Pour the batter into the hot, buttered pan, place it in the oven, and bake 30 to 40 minutes, until the top is golden brown and a toothpick inserted comes out clean. Let the loaf cool in the pan, or serve it hot.

Makes 1 loaf, serving 8 to 10

1 cup stone-ground cornmeal
½ cup whole-wheat flour
¾ teaspoon salt
1 tablespoon baking powder
½ teaspoon baking soda
1 cup plain low-fat yogurt
½ cup milk
1 tablespoon mild honey
2 eggs
3 tablespoons unsalted butter

Sesame Crackers

1½ cups whole-wheat flour
¼ cup soy flour
¼ cup sesame seeds
¾ teaspoon salt, preferably sea salt
¼ cup canola or vegetable oil
⅓ cup cold water (more as
 needed)

These are always a hit at a party, with their rich, nutty flavor. There's something impressive about making your own crackers, too, and these are very easy. Make sure you roll them out thin enough, and don't overbake.

These crackers cut well with a cookie cutter. My catering logo is a crescent moon and star, and I've spent many an afternoon making dozens of lunar sesame crackers.

Preheat the oven to 350 degrees.

Stir together the flours, seeds, and salt. Add the oil and blend well by rolling the mixture briskly between the palms of your hands. Add enough water to create a dough the consistency of pie pastry.

Gather the dough into a ball and roll it out to a thickness of ⅛ inch on a well-floured board, or between 2 pieces of waxed paper. Cut the dough into squares, rectangles, sticks, or cookie-cutter shapes and place on an oiled baking sheet.

Bake until crisp and golden, about 20 minutes. Be careful not to let the crackers get too brown, or they will taste bitter.

Makes 3 to 4 dozen

Garlic Croutons

Several ½-inch thick slices bread
 of your choice
1 garlic clove, cut in half lengthwise
2 tablespoons olive oil (optional)

Use these as a garnish for soups or an addition to salads, or spread with one of the spreads or pâtés on pages 21–26.

Toast the bread in an oven or in a toaster until it just begins to color. Remove from the heat and rub with the cut clove of garlic. Brush with olive oil if you wish. Cut into ½- or 1-inch squares. Store in a jar, a plastic container, or a plastic bag.

Cocktail Snacks and Hors d'Oeuvres

The most gracious way to receive company is with a glass of good wine and a beautiful and tempting appetizer. No matter how elaborate the rest of my menu may be, I never leave out this course. James Beard called it a "rite;" often the mere display of hors d'oeuvres will ensure an animated party. A bountiful platter of crudités around a piping hot chafing dish of fondue, a loaf of homemade bread on a board with a pâté or a nice cheese will dazzle your guests' eyes, then their palates, and will take the edge off their hunger. Pour the wine and relax with your guests. Once you see that people are eating you can retreat to the kitchen to tend to the soup. You needn't feel that you are abandoning your company. If they have nothing else in common, the food itself will stimulate conversation.

Cocktail snacks and hors d'oeuvres are what I do most as a caterer. At wedding receptions I set long skirted tables with colorful vegetable platters, aromatic chafing dishes, and elaborate boards of cheeses and homemade breads. Throughout the event we never stop refilling chafing dishes, slicing more bread, smoothing out pâtés, and replenishing cheeses. People congregate around the food, and the better it looks and tastes, the more successful the party.

My own dinner parties aren't quite as frenetic. Before a dinner party, one or two, or at most three, items will suffice; my hors d'oeuvres are sometimes as simple as olives and crudités. But I always give myself time to decorate whatever I'm serving, whether it's simple or elaborate.

The choice of hors d'oeuvre and the amount of preparation time it demands should be determined by the remainder of the menu. If there's bread in your soup or if your main dish is heavy, don't offer bread before dinner; serve crudités or marinated vegetables. Stuffed mushrooms are almost always appropriate. Cheese hors d'oeuvres can provide the protein you may fear is lacking in the rest of the meal, if it's a light one.

In any case, whatever the occasion, always have hors d'oeuvres ready and waiting when your guests arrive. They will feel well looked after, and you will all be put at ease.

Hummus

Hummus, one of my very favorite foods, is a Middle Eastern chick-pea and sesame spread flavored with garlic, lemon juice, and olive oil. You can mold it into a bowl or onto a plate and garnish it with fresh parsley, cherry tomatoes cut in wedges, olives, and radishes; you can spread it on bread or crackers for canapés, or pipe it from a pastry bag onto sliced rounds of cucumbers or squash. It can be made up to two days in advance and stored, tightly covered, in the refrigerator. It makes a wonderful sandwich spread as well, on whole-wheat bread or pita (Middle Eastern flat bread), with lettuce or sprouts and tomatoes.

I have lightened my original hummus recipe, cutting down on olive oil and sesame butter and substituting yogurt to smooth out the spread. This recipe will feed from six to twelve people if you aren't serving a number of other hors d'oeuvres, and up to twenty people if it is one of many.

2¼ cups cooked chick-peas (1 cup dried; see page xxxvi), drained (save some of the liquid), or one 15-ounce can, drained (save some of the liquid)

2 large garlic cloves

¼ cup lemon juice

2 tablespoons olive oil

3 tablespoons sesame tahini

¼ cup plain low-fat yogurt (or as needed)

½ teaspoon ground cumin

Salt, preferably sea salt, to taste (you'll need a generous amount)

If you want a textured hummus, keep out half the chick-peas and mash them in a bowl with a potato masher.

Turn on a food processor fitted with the steel blade and drop in the garlic. When the garlic is finely chopped, turn off the machine and add the chick-peas. Process for about half a minute, until the chick-peas are chopped and mealy, and add the lemon juice, olive oil, tahini, half the yogurt, the cumin, and the salt with the machine on. Process until the mixture is smooth. Thin out as desired with the remaining yogurt. The hummus should be smooth but not runny. From time to time, scrape the sides of the processor bowl. If the purée seems dry, add a bit of liquid from the beans, or a bit more olive oil or yogurt.

Remove the mixture from the food processor and combine with the mashed chick-peas if using. Taste and adjust salt.

Note: You can also make hummus in a blender or with a mortar and pestle. If you use a blender, you will have to stop and start the machine often, and stir the chick-pea mixture.

Makes 3 cups

Soya Pâté

2 garlic cloves
2 cups cooked soybeans (1 scant
    cup dried; see page xxxv), or 2
    cups cooked soy flakes (1 cup
    raw; see page xxxv)
2 eggs
⅓ cup milk
2 tablespoons brandy
2 teaspoons Marmite or Savorex
2 teaspoons tamari or Kikkoman
    soy sauce
½ teaspoon dried thyme
⅛ teaspoon ground allspice
⅛ teaspoon ground ginger
¼ teaspoon salt, preferably sea salt
¼ teaspoon freshly ground pepper
½ onion, chopped and sautéed in
    2 teaspoons canola or vegetable
    oil until tender

Soya pâté is a marvelous vegetarian staple. It lasts for up to a week in the refrigerator, is extremely high in protein and B vitamins, and it's delicious. It's also cheap and easy to make, filling and low in calories. With a flavor that is somewhat reminiscent of liverwurst, it's definitely one of those "vegetarian-but-you'd-never-know-it" dishes. The secret to this pâté is the Marmite or Savorex. It occurred to me one day that I could combine soya with the yeast extract to achieve a liverlike flavor. Then it was just a question of working out the seasonings, and a study of traditional liver pâté recipes helped me in this. A friend once remarked that this had all the attractive qualities of a pâté without the heavy, fat-laden sensations. That said, this pâté is filling, and a little goes a long way. It makes a tasty and attractive hors d'oeuvre and a fine sandwich spread. For hors d'oeuvres I mold it in a mound and cover it with sliced olives and pimientos, and surround it with deep-green parsley and other herbs. Hard-boiled eggs make a nice garnish too. The pâté goes beautifully with mayonnaise or mustard, and on whole-grain bread it's a meal in itself.

As with hummus, you can cook the soybeans up to two days in advance and keep them in the refrigerator until you're ready to make the pâté. Remember to soak the beans before you cook them.

Preheat the oven to 350 degrees. Oil or butter a 1-quart pâté tureen, a bread pan, or a small casserole or soufflé dish.

Turn on a food processor fitted with the steel blade and drop in the garlic. When it is finely chopped, add the soybeans and grind with 10 pulses of the machine. Add the remaining ingredients, except the onion, turn on the machine, and blend until smooth. Make sure your mixture is completely smooth; it takes over a minute of grinding in the food processor. (If using a blender, place all the ingredients except the onion and soybeans in the blender jar and turn on at low speed. Increase the speed and gradually pour in the cooked soybeans. Blend until the mixture is completely smooth, stopping and stirring occasionally if necessary.) Stir in the onion.

Pour the pâté into the prepared baking dish. Cover tightly with foil or a lid, and bake in the preheated oven for 45 to 50 minutes, until set and beginning to brown on the top. Remove from the oven, allow to cool, and refrigerate. Do not eat until completely chilled

Note: For a creamier pâté, use ½ cup milk.

Makes 3 cups

Baba Ghanoush (Middle Eastern Eggplant Spread)

Baba ghanoush is a garlic-flavored, lemony spread from the Middle East. It sometimes incorporates the charred skin of the baked or broiled eggplant, which gives it a roasted flavor. This dish can be made one or two days before you plan to serve it.

Preheat the oven to 450 degrees. Cut the eggplants in half and score the cut sides with a sharp knife down to the skin but not through it. Place the eggplants cut sides down on an oiled baking sheet and bake for 20 to 30 minutes, until charred and shriveled. Remove from the heat and allow to cool.

You may leave the eggplant skin on if you like the charred taste. Otherwise, remove it. Discard the seeds, and blend together the eggplant, lemon juice, garlic, olive oil, yogurt, tahini, and optional cumin in a food processor, or purée using a mortar and pestle. Season to taste with salt and pepper. Stir in the tomato and bell pepper.

Transfer the purée to a bowl and sprinkle on the parsley. Serve with croutons, pita bread, and/or crudités.

Makes 2 cups

2 pounds eggplant
Juice of 1 to 2 lemons, to taste
2 garlic cloves, minced or put through a press
2 tablespoons olive oil
2 tablespoons plain low-fat yogurt
2 tablespoons sesame tahini
¼ to ½ teaspoon ground cumin, to taste (optional)
Salt, preferably sea salt, to taste
Freshly ground pepper, to taste
1 medium tomato, chopped
1 green or red bell pepper, minced
2 tablespoons chopped fresh parsley

Mushroom Pâté

½ cup toasted almonds

2 tablespoons olive oil

½ cup chopped onion

1 pound fresh cultivated mushrooms, trimmed and cleaned

2 large garlic cloves, minced or
put through a press

1 teaspoon fresh thyme leaves, or
½ teaspoon dried thyme

Salt, preferably sea salt, to taste

Freshly ground pepper, to taste

2 tablespoons dry vermouth

1 teaspoon finely grated lemon
zest (optional)

Chopped fresh parsley or sage
leaves for garnish

This is a wonderful combination of savory, aromatic mush-rooms, and crunchy ground almonds. Since these mushrooms will be cooked and blended, you needn't look for the most beautiful ones you can find (as you would for stuffed or mari-nated mushrooms). In fact, you can even use just the stems, if you have enough. When I serve Marinated Vegetables Vinaigrette (page 35), I use the stems for mushroom pâté. This is easy to make and keeps for five days, well covered, in the refrigerator.

Set aside 2 tablespoons of almonds for garnish, and grind the rest in a blender or food processor. Place the ground almonds in a mixing bowl and set aside.

Heat the olive oil in a large, heavy-bottomed nonstick skillet over medium heat and add the onion. Cook, stirring, until tender, about 5 minutes, and add the mushrooms, garlic, thyme, salt, and freshly ground pepper. Cook uncov-ered over medium heat, stirring often, until the mush-rooms are tender and aromatic, about 15 to 20 minutes. Add the vermouth and cook for 3 more minutes.

Purée the mushrooms in a blender or food processor fitted with the steel blade. Pour into the bowl with the ground almonds and stir the mixture together. Taste and adjust salt and pepper to taste. If you wish, add the finely grated lemon zest.

Transfer to an attractive bowl, cover, and refrigerate for several hours. Serve garnished with the almonds you have set aside, and the chopped parsley or sage leaves.

Makes 2 cups

Herb Butter

I use herb butter very sparingly. You only need to spread a tiny amount of this on a piece of bread to get a big, wonderful taste. Herb butter is best if served soon after it is made. The herbs will be very fresh, and the garlic and onions sweet. Make sure that you let the butter soften before you make this. You will be able to proceed much faster if you do, whether you use a food processor, a wooden spoon, a whisk, or a hand mixer. If you are using a food processor, use the steel blade only for chopping the herbs, and be very careful to chop them with a minimum of one-second bursts. The green from the herbs and green onion (as well as the bitter juice from the onion) is quickly released by the steel blade, and if you aren't careful you'll have green herb butter. (I once had to serve some that my processor had made green, and guests piled it onto their bread, thinking it was guacamole. What a shock when they bit into all that butter!)

This can be molded and garnished with parsley and other herbs.

¼ pound (1 stick) butter, softened
1 garlic clove, minced or put through a press
1 green onion, both white part and green, finely minced, or 1 tablespoon chopped fresh chives or shallots
1 tablespoon chopped fresh parsley
1 teaspoon chopped fresh dill (omit if fresh is unavailable)

If you are not using a food processor, put the softened butter in a small bowl and whip with a whisk, a wooden spoon, or an electric mixer. Stir in the remaining ingredients and mix well. If you are using a food processor, insert the steel blade and chop the herbs with a very few one-second bursts. Remove them and wipe out the bowl, then replace the steel blade with the plastic blade. Make sure the butter is softened, and mix the herbs, onions, and garlic together with the butter, using the plastic blade.

Place the herb butter in a butter dish or mold, cover well, and chill until serving time.

Note: I use lightly salted butter for my herb butter. If you are using unsalted butter, you might want to add a little salt to taste.

Makes approximately ½ cup

Herbed Cream Cheese

8 ounces cream cheese or low-fat cream cheese, softened

3 to 4 green onions (both white part and green), chopped

2 small or medium garlic cloves, minced or put through a press

½ teaspoon dry mustard

½ teaspoon Worcestershire sauce

¼ cup chopped fresh parsley

¼ cup chopped fresh dill (omit if fresh is unavailable)

2 to 4 tablespoons chopped fresh basil (optional)

¼ cup chopped ripe olives (optional)

1 to 2 tablespoons lemon juice

Salt, preferably sea salt, to taste

Freshly ground pepper, to taste

Like herb butter, a little of this glorious mixture goes a long way. It is bursting with the fragrance of fresh herbs, and can be made in a lower fat version (see following variation).

I like to mold this in a ring, then shortly before serving unmold it onto a platter and garnish with additional herbs and fresh vegetables. To unmold, dip the mold in warm water for 10 seconds and invert onto your platter. Refrigerate immediately to stop the surface from melting.

This is easier to make with a mixer than with a food processor, since the juices of the herbs and onions are released by the action of the steel blade (see the headnote for the preceding recipe), and if you aren't careful to clean the bowl and replace the steel blade with the plastic one you'll have green herbed cream cheese.

In a large mixing bowl, whip the softened cream cheese and add the other ingredients. Mix well, adding salt and pepper to taste. Mold in a bowl or ring, or in a mound on a platter. Cover and refrigerate, or serve immediately (although if it is runny or too soft, 15 minutes in the refrigerator will stiffen it up), garnished with fresh herbs and vegetables.

Makes 1½ cups

Herbed Cottage Cheese

This is a lower-fat version of the above recipe, one I am more likely to make today.

For the recipe above, substitute 1½ cups nonfat cottage cheese and ⅓ cup plain low-fat yogurt for the cream cheese. Blend together the cottage cheese and yogurt until smooth, then stir in the remaining ingredients.

Makes 1½ cups

Quichettes

There are two ways to make "quichettes." You can make little crusts in tart pans and fill them, or you can make a big quiche, allow it to cool, and cut it into neat little squares. I prefer the latter. The little tart pans are expensive, and you need a number of them, and making all those little pastries is very time-consuming. It depends upon how much you like working with pastry. I usually assemble and bake my quiche several hours or a day in advance and allow it to cool and set; then I cover it with plastic wrap and refrigerate it. You can make your pie crust well in advance and freeze it, or up to three days in advance and refrigerate it, making sure it is well sealed.

See the recipe for Spinach and Onion Quiche (page 105). Instead of a pie pan, use a rectangular pan (8 × 10 inches); you need only cover the bottom with your crust. Beat an egg and brush the crust with it before prebaking; this will keep the crust from getting soggy. Fill the prebaked crust with the spinach and onion filling, or onion alone, or onion and 2 cups sliced mushrooms, sautéed until soft and fragrant in a little butter and olive oil with 1 minced garlic clove, and salt and pepper.

Proceed as in the quiche recipe. Allow to cool, cover, and refrigerate. When you are sure the quiche has set, cut it into 2-inch squares. Warm in a 250-degree oven on buttered baking sheets, remove to a platter or plate, and serve. You can also keep these warm in a chafing dish. Garnish with tomato wedges or radish flowers, or parsley and sliced oranges.

If you are using little tart pans, you will need 8 to 10 of them. Brush the pastry shells with egg and prebake, then fill with the quiche mixture, but bake only 25 minutes (check then, and continue to bake if necessary until firm).

6 to 10 servings

Stuffed Mushrooms

1 pound large, firm, fresh mush-
    rooms (or enough to allow 2 to
    3 per person)
1 tablespoon olive oil
1 garlic clove, minced or put
    through a press
Salt
Freshly ground pepper
¼ teaspoon dried thyme
Filling of your choice (pages
    29–31)

I have made the fillings for stuffed mushrooms a day in advance and stored them, tightly covered, in the refrigerator. The flavors mature and are actually more savory. I do think it is best, however, to do the step of preparing the mushrooms themselves and filling them on the day you wish to serve them. This way they will not lose their shape or become soggy.

Stuffed mushrooms also make an excellent side dish at a meal, and jumbo mushrooms can be filled and served as a main course, garnished with chopped fresh parsley.

Thinking in terms of 2 to 3 mushrooms per person, choose the largest, firmest mushrooms you can find; they will shrink when cooked. A fresh mushroom is closed up to the stem on the underside; don't choose those whose caps are accordionlike underneath.

Clean the mushrooms and cut or twist the stems off at the cap; if you can twist them off, you will have a bigger space to fill. Set the stems aside to use in the filling.

Heat the olive oil in a large, heavy-bottomed nonstick skillet or wok over medium-high heat and add the garlic. Cook for about 1 minute, until the garlic just begins to color, and add the mushroom caps, salt, pepper, and thyme. Sauté gently just until they begin to soften up and become aromatic, 3 minutes. Give them another stir and drain on paper towels.

Preheat the oven to 325 degrees.

Stuff with the filling of your choice. Even small mushrooms will hold a certain amount: press the mixture in with the back of a spoon. The filling should make a little mound over the top of the mushroom.

Place the mushrooms, filled side up, in an oiled baking dish, cover with foil to prevent drying out, and bake for 20 minutes. Serve hot.

Serves 6 to 8

WILD RICE FILLING

Bring the stock or water to a boil in a saucepan. Wash the rice and slowly pour it into the boiling liquid. Add ½ teaspoon salt, reduce the heat, and cover. Cook for 40 minutes, then remove the lid and cook for another 10 minutes, or until the rice is tender; pour off the excess liquid.

Heat the oil over medium heat in a large, heavy-bottomed nonstick frying pan and sauté the onion until it is soft, about 5 minutes. Add the garlic, the mushroom stems, and the almonds and sauté a few minutes more. Add the cooked wild rice, sherry, parsley, thyme, and seasonings and stir together. Cook over a low flame for 5 to 10 minutes, stirring occasionally, until the mushroom stems are cooked through and the mixture is nice and aromatic. Correct the seasoning, adding a little tamari if you wish, and perhaps more garlic. Remember, if you are making the filling for the next day, that the flavors will mature overnight.

Store, covered, in the refrigerator, or fill the mushrooms, bake, and serve.

Note: You may have more filling than you need for the mushrooms. In this case, surround the filled mushrooms with a ring of filling, or keep it in the refrigerator for up to three days and serve it as a side dish.

Makes enough to fill 30 mushrooms, or 1 pound

1 cup Vegetable Stock (page 49) or water
⅓ cup wild rice
Salt, preferably sea salt, to taste
1 tablespoon olive oil
½ cup finely chopped onion or shallots
1 garlic clove, minced or put through a press
⅓ cup finely minced mushroom stems
¼ cup finely chopped almonds
2 tablespoons dry sherry
1 tablespoon chopped fresh parsley
½ teaspoon fresh thyme leaves or ¼ teaspoon dried thyme
Pinch of freshly grated nutmeg
Freshly ground pepper, to taste
Tamari, to taste (optional)

1 tablespoon olive oil

½ small onion, chopped

1 garlic clove, minced or put
through a press

Stems from the mushrooms,
chopped fine

½ cup finely chopped almonds
(you can do this quickly in a
blender)

1 medium carrot, grated

¼ cup freshly grated Parmesan
cheese

2 tablespoons chopped fresh
parsley

Salt, preferably sea salt

Freshly ground pepper, to taste

Tamari, to taste (optional)

1 egg

½ cup buckwheat groats (kasha)

1¼ cups boiling Vegetable Stock
(page 49) or water

½ onion, chopped

½ carrot, chopped

½ stalk celery, chopped

Stems from the mushrooms,
chopped fine

½ teaspoon salt, preferably sea
salt, or to taste

Freshly ground pepper, to taste

SAVORY ALMOND FILLING

Heat the oil over medium heat in a large, heavy-bottomed nonstick frying pan and sauté the onion, garlic, and mushroom stems until the onion is tender. Add the almonds and cook a few minutes longer. Add the remaining ingredients, stir together, and cook, uncovered, over a low flame for 5 more minutes, stirring occasionally. Check the seasoning and remove from the heat.

Store, covered, in the refrigerator, or fill the mushrooms, bake, and serve.

Makes enough to fill 30 mushrooms, or 1 pound

KASHA FILLING

Beat the egg in a bowl. Combine with the buckwheat groats and stir together until all the grains are coated with egg.

Heat a heavy pan over moderate heat and pour in the groats/egg mixture. (You are pouring this into a dry pan, which may puzzle you, but the mixture will not stick if the heat is moderate and you continue to stir it.) Keep stirring the mixture with a wooden spoon until the egg is absorbed and the grains begin to toast; it's important that the egg be absorbed completely or you will have unattractive strings of cooked egg in the kasha. This step gives the dish its toasty aroma.)

Immediately pour in the boiling stock or water. Add the onion, carrot, celery, mushroom stems, and salt and bring to a second boil. Lower the heat, cover, and cook slowly for 35 minutes, then remove the lid and continue cooking until the liquid is absorbed. Season to taste with more salt, if desired, and pepper.

Cover, refrigerate, and store overnight, or fill the mushrooms, bake, and serve.

Makes enough to fill 30 mushrooms, or 1 pound

HERBED BREAD CRUMBS FILLING

Sauté the green onions and garlic gently in the olive oil for 3 minutes. Add the bread crumbs and herbs and sauté, stirring, until the bread crumbs are toasted. Add the Parmesan; stir together and remove from the heat. Correct the seasoning. Cover, refrigerate, and store overnight, or fill the mushrooms, bake, and serve.

Makes enough to fill 30 mushrooms, or 1 pound

4 green onions (both white part and green), minced

1 to 2 garlic cloves, minced or puréed

1 tablespoon olive oil, or more if necessary

1 cup bread crumbs, preferably whole wheat

¼ cup chopped fresh parsley

1 teaspoon chopped fresh tarragon, or ½ teaspoon dried tarragon

¾ teaspoon chopped fresh oregano, or ¼ teaspoon dried oregano

¼ cup freshly grated Parmesan cheese

Tiropites (Greek Filo Turnovers)

½ pound filo dough
¼ cup olive oil
2 tablespoons melted butter
Filling of your choice (pages
 33–34)

Tiropites are triangular turnovers made with filo dough. You can make the fillings and assemble the tiropites a day in advance, but bake them just before serving to be sure they are crisp. To store, place on an oiled baking sheet, cover with plastic, and refrigerate or freeze.

You needn't restrict yourself to the fillings that follow. Use your imagination—and your leftovers—to fill the tiropites with anything you think would contrast nicely with the crisp filo.

Preheat the oven to 350 degrees. Remove the filo dough from the package and unfold it carefully. Take one sheet at a time, and keep the rest of the dough wrapped in a towel so it doesn't dry out. Lay the sheet of filo across a cutting board and cut down the shorter length into strips about 2½ inches wide for small triangles.

Put the olive oil and butter in a small saucepan and heat over very low heat until the butter melts. Brush a strip of filo lightly with the olive oil and butter mixture. Place a teaspoon of the filling on the right side of one end of a strip of pastry, about ½ inch down from the end. Fold the left-hand corner of the pastry diagonally over the filling so that the filling is inside the triangle. Fold the triangle over at the bottom and continue folding the pastry over itself until you reach the end. Place on a nonstick or lightly oiled baking sheet. Continue with the remaining strips of filo, working with one sheet at a time and keeping the remaining dough wrapped in the towel.

Bake the pastries for 30 minutes, or until golden brown. Serve hot. If you have frozen the tiropites, do not thaw but transfer directly from the freezer to the oven. They may require an extra 5 or 10 minutes of baking.

Makes 60, serving 15

GREEK SPINACH FILLING

This filling may be made a day in advance and stored in a covered container in the refrigerator. Stir it up before you fill the tiropites.

Heat the olive oil in a heavy-bottomed nonstick skillet over medium heat and add the onion. Sauté, stirring, until tender, about 5 minutes. Add the spinach and stir. Remove from the heat. In a medium-sized mixing bowl, beat the eggs and crumble in the feta. Add the spinach and onion and the remaining ingredients, and stir together. Taste and adjust seasonings. Store, refrigerated, or use right away.

1 tablespoon olive oil
1 small onion, minced
1 pound spinach, stemmed, cleaned, blanched, drained, and chopped, or 1 package (10 ounces) frozen spinach, thawed, squeezed dry, and chopped
2 eggs, beaten
4 ounces feta cheese
¼ cup freshly grated Parmesan cheese
Pinch of freshly grated nutmeg
1 teaspoon chopped fresh rosemary, or ½ teaspoon dried rosemary
½ teaspoon oregano
Salt, preferably sea salt, to taste (remember that the cheeses are very salty)
Freshly ground pepper, to taste

MEXICAN FILLING

This filling should not be made in advance unless you are filling the tiropites with it and then storing them. Grated cheese tends to clump together and dry up, and it'll be hard to work with if kept too long.

Combine all the ingredients and mix well.

8 ounces Monterey Jack or Cheddar cheese, grated
1 cup low-fat ricotta
2 eggs, beaten
¼ cup finely chopped fresh or canned jalapeño peppers
½ to ¾ teaspoon cumin, or more to taste
¼ cup chopped cilantro
Salt, preferably sea salt, to taste

1 tablespoon olive oil

½ cup chopped onion

2 eggs

4 ounces feta cheese

12 ounces low-fat ricotta

2 tablespoons chopped fresh parsley or dill

Freshly ground pepper, to taste

¼ cup grated Parmesan cheese

RICOTTA FILLING

This filling may be made a day in advance and stored in a covered container in the refrigerator. Stir it up before you fill the tiropites.

Heat the oil over medium heat in a heavy-bottomed nonstick skillet and add the onion. Sauté, stirring, until tender. Remove from the heat and set aside.

In a medium-sized bowl, beat the eggs, then crumble in the feta. Add the remaining ingredients, including the sautéed onion, and mix well.

Marinated Vegetables Vinaigrette

This, always a crowd-pleaser, makes a stunning platter. Don't feel compelled, however, to serve all of these vegetables at once. One or two alone always works. For instance, you may just want to start a meal off with marinated mushrooms and cucumbers, or potatoes and cauliflower. Use your imagination for different combinations.

Prepare all the vegetables; separate the leaves of lettuce, wash and dry them, and hold for garnish, along with the radish flowers and olives.

Make a marinade by combining the lemon juice, vinegar, garlic, mustard, and seasonings. Stir in the olive oil and yogurt and blend well.

Toss the vegetables and herbs with the marinade and refrigerate for several hours, tossing them every once in a while to distribute the marinade evenly.

When ready to serve, cover a serving platter with the lettuce leaves. Drain the vegetables but retain the marinade. Arrange the vegetables in a nice design, perhaps with the mushrooms in a mound in the middle, surrounded by the cucumber, squash, and onion. Here and there scatter tomatoes. Place the green peppers over the other vegetables and scatter the olives and radishes throughout. Ladle ¼ cup of the retained marinade over the vegetables.

Serve with toothpicks, either stuck into the vegetables or in little cups near the platter. Have napkins close by.

Note: You can use the drained marinade as a salad dressing.

Serves 6 to 10

FOR THE VEGETABLE PLATTER:
4 tomatoes, cut in wedges, or a
    ½-pint box cherry tomatoes,
    stems removed and halved
2 green peppers, or 1 red pepper
    and 1 green pepper, seeded and
    sliced crosswise
½ pound fresh mushroom caps
½ head cauliflower, broken into
    florets and steamed for
    5 minutes
1 cucumber, peeled if waxed or bit-
    ter, and sliced (score the skin with
    a fork if not waxed or bitter)
1 yellow squash, sliced
3 red or new potatoes, steamed
    until crisp-tender and sliced
1 Bermuda onion, sliced in thin
    rounds
½ cup chopped fresh herbs, such
    as tarragon, basil, dill, parsley,
    chives, marjoram
1 head Boston or leaf lettuce
Radish flowers for garnish (see
    page 41)
½ cup pitted ripe or imported
    black olives

FOR THE MARINADE:
Juice of 1 lemon
½ cup wine vinegar or cider vinegar
2 large garlic cloves, minced or
    put through a press
2 teaspoons Dijon mustard
Salt, preferably sea salt, to taste
Freshly ground pepper, to taste
½ cup olive oil
1 cup plain low-fat yogurt

Nachos with Black Bean Topping

FOR THE BEANS:

1 cup dried black beans, washed
    and picked over

2 quarts water

2 tablespoons canola oil

1 medium onion, chopped

3 large garlic cloves, minced or
    put through a press

Salt, preferably sea salt, to taste

2 tablespoons chopped cilantro

1 teaspoon ground cumin, or
    more as necessary

1 teaspoon chili powder

FOR THE NACHOS:

1 package nacho chips, or 9 corn
    tortillas, cut in quarters

Canola oil for frying

4 ounces (1 cup) strong white
    Cheddar cheese or Monterey
    Jack, grated

6 fresh jalapeño peppers or 1
    small can (4 ounces) jalapeños,
    sliced in rounds

No matter where I am, the flavor of the black beans in this dish always carries me back to Mexico. The nachos are easy to assemble, and the beans can be soaked, cooked, and refried up to two days in advance. The amount of time this recipe takes will depend on whether or not you use prepared nacho crisps. Using the prepared ones, with my beans ready and cheese grated, I once assembled four hundred of these for a wedding, and did it in three hours!

Do note that the beans have to be soaked overnight, or for at least six hours, before you can prepare them—and that the preparation itself will take a couple of hours.

Wash and pick over the beans, and soak them overnight or for at least 6 hours in one quart of the water. Drain.

Heat 1 tablespoon of the oil in a large, heavy-bottomed saucepan or dutch oven and sauté the onion with one of the garlic cloves until the onion is beginning to soften, about 3 minutes. Add the beans, the remaining quart of water, and another clove of garlic and bring to a boil. Reduce the heat, cover, and simmer 1 hour. Add salt to taste, the rest of the garlic, and the cilantro, and continue to simmer until the beans are soft and the liquid thick and aromatic, about 1 more hour. Adjust seasonings and remove from the heat.

Allow the beans to cool a while, then drain off about half the liquid, retaining it in a separate bowl to have on hand later if you need to moisten the refried beans. Mash half the beans coarsely in batches in a food processor or with a potato masher. Stir back into the unmashed beans.

Heat the remaining tablespoon of oil in a large, heavy-bottomed nonstick skillet over medium-high heat and add the cumin, chili powder, and a pinch of salt. Stir for about half a minute, until the spices begin to sizzle, and add the beans. (This can be done in batches if your skillet is too small to accommodate all the beans.) Fry the beans, stirring often, until they begin to get crusty and aromatic. If they seem too dry, add some of the reserved cooking liquid. Mash and stir the beans as they cook. They should bubble, thicken, and cook down, forming a thin crust on the bottom, which you should stir back into the beans. Remove from the heat after about 20 minutes. The mixture should be thick and aromatic.

Preheat the oven to 350 degrees.

If you are using tortillas, cut them into quarters. Heat 1 inch of canola oil in a skillet, wok, or saucepan to 370 degrees, and quickly deep-fry the tortillas, turning once. Remove from the oil with a slotted spoon and drain on paper towels. Toss with salt.

Spread a layer of the refried bean mixture on each nacho chip. Top with grated cheese, then with the sliced jalapeños. Place on baking sheets and heat through in the oven until the cheese melts, about 15 minutes. Serve hot, with Fresh Tomato Salsa (page 201).

Makes 3 dozen nachos

Marinated Broccoli Stems

3 to 4 broccoli stems
½ teaspoon salt, preferably sea salt
1 garlic clove, crushed
1 tablespoon white wine vinegar
   or cider vinegar
1 tablespoon olive oil

Here is a brilliant way to use your trimmed broccoli stems. I always felt so wasteful throwing them away before. This serves as a tasty hors d'oeuvre, a side dish, or a great addition to green salads. You'll be pleased to see how easy it is to peel the stems.

Peel the broccoli stems, slice diagonally ⅛ inch thick, and place in a jar. Add the salt, then cover the jar, shake, and place in the refrigerator overnight, or for several hours at least.

In the morning, or after several hours, drain the liquid from the jar. Add the crushed garlic, vinegar, and oil, shake well, and refrigerate for several hours longer.

Makes about 1 cup

Marinated Vegetables à la Grecque

FOR THE MARINADE:

2 cups water, or more if necessary
½ cup dry white wine, or more if
   necessary
⅓ cup red wine vinegar or cider
   vinegar, or more if necessary
½ cup olive oil, or more if necessary
2 garlic cloves, minced or put
   through a press
1 dozen whole black peppercorns
2 bay leaves
1 teaspoon whole fennel seed or
   aniseed

The flavors of many different spices make this a sensational dish; fennel or anise adds an exceptional touch. In addition to the vegetables I've mentioned here, squash, eggplant, and cucumber are nice for this dish. You will want to use different ones according to what's available. My favorite vegetables in this recipe are the carrots; they turn out delicate but still crunchy.

This is a dish that must be made the day before you wish to serve it, or very early that morning. However, it keeps well in the refrigerator, so you can make it several days before-hand.

Combine all the ingredients for the marinade in a large, heavy saucepan. Bring to a simmer, cover, and continue to simmer for 10 to 15 minutes to combine and bring out the flavors. You can be preparing the vegetables in the meantime.

Drop the pearl onions into the simmering liquid and cook for 10 minutes. Add the brussels sprouts and cauliflower and cook for 5 minutes. Next add the carrots and cook 5 minutes. Add the mushrooms and cook 5 minutes, then add the green beans. Make sure all the vegetables are submerged in the liquid; if they are not, add more water, wine, vinegar, and olive oil in their original proportions. Now cook all the vegetables, uncovered, for 5 to 10 minutes, until tender but not too soft. Add the artichoke hearts and simmer for another 5 minutes. Add the cherry tomatoes and coriander seeds.

Remove from the heat and allow the vegetables to cool in the marinade. Then place the entire contents of the saucepan, the vegetables still covered with the marinade, in wide-mouthed jars or a bowl and cover tightly. Refrigerate overnight.

Strain the vegetables, reserving the marinade, and arrange on a large platter in an attractive pattern—the green beans and cauliflower in the middle, perhaps, surrounded by the rest of the vegetables. Insert toothpicks in the vegetables, or provide them nearby.

Transfer the marinade to a saucepan and bring to a boil. Reduce by half, and pour over the vegetables. Garnish with cilantro or parsley, and serve.

Note: You may also serve these vegetables on individual salad plates, as a first course.

Serves 6

1 teaspoon chopped fresh thyme, or ½ teaspoon dried thyme
4 sprigs fresh parsley
½ teaspoon mustard seed
Salt, preferably sea salt, to taste
1 onion, sliced
¼ cup currants

FOR THE VEGETABLE PLATTER:

12 whole pearl onions, peeled
1 box brussels sprouts (about 2 cups) trimmed (optional)
½ head cauliflower, cut into small florets (about 2 cups)
½ pound carrots, quartered if very large or halved if small, and cut into 3-inch sticks (about 2 cups)
12 medium-sized whole mushrooms, stems cut level with the caps
½ pound green beans, ends cut off (about 2 cups)
1 small jar (6 ounces) artichoke hearts or bottoms
½-pint box cherry tomatoes (about 18)
1 tablespoon cracked coriander seeds
Sprigs of cilantro or parsley for garnish

Vegetable Platter with Assorted Dips

For this dish you can use whatever vegetables are in season. The important thing to use is your imagination. The variety of colors you get from the different vegetables makes this a dramatic hors d'oeuvre. Give yourself enough time to make a nice arrangement; you'll be creating a garden on a platter. Be fanciful and have fun.

Your dips can be simple or elaborate. Plain homemade mayonnaise, always popular, or low-fat commercial mayonnaise is a good place to begin. Both mayonnaise and yogurt serve as the bases for many of the dips listed below.

The amount of servings will depend on the quantity of vegetables you use.

SUGGESTED DIPS

Food Processor Mayonnaise (page 203)
Tofu Mayonnaise (page 204)
Curry Dressing (page 208)
Russian Dressing Dip (page 42)
Green Dressing (page 209)
Sunflower Seed Dressing (page 210)
Avocado Dip (page 43)
Tahini Dressing (page 211)

SUGGESTED VEGETABLES

Asparagus
Broccoli
Carrots
Cauliflower
Celery
Cucumbers
Black olives (whole, with pits)
Red and green bell peppers
Radishes
Yellow squash
Cherry tomatoes

Break the tough stems off the asparagus and, as for broccoli, steam until bright green, immediately cooling under cold water.

Break the broccoli into florets and steam until bright green. Immediately run under cold water to stop the cooking.

Cut carrots into sticks, or cut curls with a vegetable peeler (this is tedious work). Place in cold water in the refrigerator for at least a day.

Break the cauliflower into florets and either blanch them or leave raw (I leave them raw).

You can either cut celery into sticks or, a few days beforehand, make celery curls. Cut off the leafy ends and carefully quarter the stalks lengthwise from the base. Slice each quarter into thin lengthwise sections, leaving them connected at the base. Submerge these sections in cold water and refrigerate for a few days. They will curl during this time.

Score and slice cucumbers.

Seed and slice red and green bell peppers crosswise.

Make radish flowers a few days beforehand. Cut four "petals" by running the knife down from the top just on the inside of the skin on all 4 sides, stopping just short of the base of the radish. Place the radishes in cold water and refrigerate for a few days; the "petals" will curl out. If you are able to get the tiny French radishes, leave them whole.

Cut squash in rounds or in 2-inch spears. Blanch or leave raw.

Remove the stems from the cherry tomatoes; if the tomatoes are very large, cut them in half.

You can prepare the vegetables that need not spend a few days in the refrigerator, and the dips, a day in advance if you refrigerate them tightly covered or sealed well in plastic bags. Submerge carrots and celery in water to prevent them from drying out.

Preparing the platter: After you have prepared your vegetables and made your dip comes the fun part. Choose a large round or oval platter. Toward the center make a circle

continued

of broccoli and cauliflower, leaving a space inside; in this space stand the asparagus upright in a pretty wide-mouthed glass jar or ceramic container. Surround the broccoli and cauliflower with alternating rounds of cucumber and yellow squash, and surround these in turn with carrots and celery. Scatter sliced peppers here and there, and place tomatoes inside the pepper rounds; scatter radishes and olives throughout. Garnish with parsley.

Of course, this is just a suggestion. You may want to incorporate the dip into the arrangement, and you may want to create other designs. Have fun with it; you can't lose, as the materials with which you are working are so beautiful.

1 cup Food Processor Mayonnaise (page 203) or low-fat commercial mayonnaise
1 to 2 teaspoons prepared horse-radish
2 green onions (both white part and green), minced
¼ cup chili sauce or salsa

RUSSIAN DRESSING DIP

Stir all the ingredients together. Store, refrigerated, in a well-sealed jar. This will keep for 2 days, tightly covered, in the refrigerator.

Makes about 1½ cups

1 avocado
½ cup plain nonfat yogurt, home-made (see page 202) or commercial (more if desired)
Juice of ½ lemon
Salt, preferably sea salt, to taste
Ground cumin, to taste (optional)
Chili powder, to taste (optional)

AVOCADO DIP

Peel and seed the avocado and purée with the yogurt in a blender. Add the lemon juice, salt, and the optional spices. Add more yogurt, if you wish. Chill, if desired, before serving, or serve immediately. This will keep for a day in the refrigerator, tightly covered.

Makes about 1½ cups

Fresh Fruit and Nuts

This is a refreshing appetite-whetter. Choose fruits in season—in the fall and winter, pears, oranges, and apples (toss the pears and apples with lemon juice to prevent discoloration); in the spring and summer, melon, figs, pineapple, strawberries, berries, and peaches.

Cut melon and pineapple into bite-sized chunks and serve with toothpicks. Arrange all the fruit on a platter, paying attention to color, and garnish with wedges of fresh lime. Or fill a large bowl with the cut fruit and scatter lime wedges throughout.

Fill bowls with nuts—almonds, cashews, hazelnuts, walnuts, pecans—or place them on the platter with the fruit.

Egg Rolls or Spring Rolls

2 tablespoons peanut oil or canola oil, plus as needed if deep-frying

2 tablespoons grated fresh ginger-root

1½ cups chopped green onions, both white part and green

2 garlic cloves, minced or put through a press

½ pound firm tofu, cut in small dice

2 tablespoons tamari, or to taste

½ pound carrots, shredded

½ head green cabbage, shredded

1 cup chopped mung bean sprouts

1 green or red pepper, seeded and minced

3 tablespoons sesame seeds

½ cup chopped cilantro

20 to 25 egg roll wrappers or dry round rice-flour wrappers about 6 inches in diameter

1 tablespoon arrowroot or corn-starch

There's no mystery to egg rolls, and they make a great hors d'oeuvre, first course, or side dish. Obviously the deep-fried variety is also the high-fat version, but if you keep the oil at 370 degrees the egg rolls won't absorb too much of it. You can also use spring roll wrappers for these, in which case there is no frying involved. I'm giving you both versions here.

These egg rolls are vibrant and bounteous; the filling is crunchy and saladlike. The recipe makes a large amount of filling—enough for an entire 1-pound package of egg roll or spring roll wrappers (about twenty to twenty-five; they are sold in the produce section of many supermarkets, and in Asian food stores). If you don't plan to make this many, you can freeze the extra skins (wrapped tightly in plastic, then placed in bags or wrapped in foil), or store spring roll wrappers in a cool, dry place. Cut the filling quantities in half. If you still have leftover filling, it makes a great salad.

You can assemble these several hours ahead of serving and keep them in the refrigerator. But if you're deep-frying, they should be cooked shortly before serving or they'll become soggy. If you are holding the assembled egg rolls, keep them on lightly floured waxed paper.

Heat the oil in a wok or a large, heavy-bottomed nonstick skillet over medium heat and add the ginger. Cook about 30 seconds, just until it begins to color, and add the onions. Cook, stirring, for a couple of minutes, until they begin to soften, then add the garlic and tofu. Cook, stirring, for a couple of minutes, then stir in the tamari, the remaining vegetables, and the sesame seeds. Stir together, and remove from the heat. Add the cilantro, and adjust seasonings, adding salt to taste.

To make a neat egg roll:

Place a wrapper on your work surface diagonally, so it appears diamond-shaped rather than square. Place 2 tablespoons of the filling in the center, slightly closer to the bottom edge of the wrapper, nearest you. Fold the sides in over the filling about an inch from the corners, then fold the bottom or top edge over this and roll up tightly. This makes a compact egg roll that will fry quickly without absorbing too much oil. Seal each egg roll with arrowroot or cornstarch dissolved in a little water.

To make small spring rolls:

One at a time, place a wrapper in a bowl of hot water for about 30 seconds, until tender. Remove from the water, drain on a kitchen towel, and lay out on the towel. Place a heaped tablespoon of the filling in the middle of the wrapper, slightly closer to the bottom edge. Fold the sides of the wrapper over the filling and roll up tightly. The spring roll should be about 2 inches long. You can also use larger wrappers, filling them with 2 tablespoons of filling. Arrange on a platter, cover with plastic wrap, and refrigerate. Serve cold.

To deep-fry:

Heat peanut oil or canola oil to a depth of 4 inches in a wok or deep-fryer to 370 degrees. Deep-fry the egg rolls until golden brown, turning them so that they brown evenly. Remove from the oil with a deep-fry skimmer and drain on paper towels.

Serve with Sweet and Sour Sauce (page 202).
Makes 20 to 25 rolls

Roasted Soybeans

1 cup dried soybeans
3 cups water
Salt, preferably sea salt

A good way to introduce soybeans into your diet, and to use up extra cooked soybeans, these make a terrific crunchy snack or party nibble. Unlike commercially roasted soybeans, they are not oily and need not be salty. Crack them in a blender and use them as you would bacon bits; they make a great sandwich with tomato, lettuce, and low-fat or homemade mayonnaise (see Food Processor Mayonnaise, page 203).

Soak the soybeans overnight or for several hours. Drain and combine with the 3 cups water in a large bean pot or dutch oven. Bring to a boil, reduce the heat, cover, and simmer 30 minutes. Add 1 teaspoon salt and continue to simmer another 30 minutes. Drain.

Preheat the oven to 325 degrees.

Spread the beans on a cookie sheet or in a baking pan and salt them, then place in the oven and bake for about 1 to 1½ hours, turning every 15 minutes and checking carefully when the soybeans begin to smell toasty; they will sometimes smell done before they are crunchy all the way through, so be careful not to remove them from the oven prematurely. To test for doneness, remove one from the pan, let cool, and bite through to see. If it is not crunchy, leave the beans in about 10 to 15 minutes longer. (Be careful at this stage, because the roasted soybeans will burn quickly once they are done.) Remove from the oven when they are ready and allow to cool in the pan. Store in a covered jar (these keep very well if covered tightly).

Makes 1 cup

Soups

When I ran my "supper club" back in the seventies, the soups were always the most talked-about part of the menu. In the wintertime a hot, soothing bowl of nourishing soupe au pistou, a thick puree of white bean soup, or a creamy raw and cooked mushroom soup—and in the summer a serving of crisp, cool blender gazpacho, tangy egg-lemon soup, or fruity purée of strawberry—along with a bread and salad, will often suffice for a meal.

Garnish can turn a good bowl of soup into a brilliant one. For me, part of the ritual of giving dinner parties is the serving and garnishing of this course. We used to have a "soup assembly line" at the club. When enough people had arrived, I would call upon some friends to help. One person would ladle the soup into bowls, another might add a dollop of yogurt, another sprinkle on croutons or sunflower seeds, while the next might top it with alfalfa sprouts. The last person in the line would deliver the bowls to the table.

There are so many food items you can sprinkle or spread over a soup to give it body, texture, creaminess, or "zip." A savory cheese soup served with garlicky croutons is like a splendid fondue, as the bread becomes coated with the soup but stays crisp. Croutons also add a great touch to puree of white bean soup; in fact, you should always hold onto stale bread for croutons. Sprouts and sunflower seeds always surprise and please my guests; the seeds become coated with soup and the sprouts become enmeshed in it. Sunflower seeds provide a welcome crunch to purées like chilled avocado-tomato soup. Yogurt and tofu not only enliven a soup, but also add to the protein content.

If soup is to be a first course, ladle out small servings so you and your guests won't get full right off the bat. I have changed my cooking methods since the first edition of this book, and don't use buttery roux to thicken my soups. Rather, I add a potato to the ingredients, and thicken the soup by puréeing in a blender or through a food mill. The soups here are rich but not heavy.

Most of the recipes here call for vegetable stock or tamari-bouillon broth. Use the tamari-bouillon broth whenever you're short on time; it's perfectly acceptable. And always have tamari and vegetable bouillon cubes on hand. Garlic broth also makes a lovely stock.

Many of these soups are quite substantial when served with a salad and bread.

The menu suggestions listed here are just a few possibilities. Use your imagination to combine hors d'oeuvres, breads and soups, salads, and desserts for some outstanding meals. And remember that a simple meal—soup, salad, bread—is often the best.

Stocks and Broths

Most people set aside at least a day for making traditional meat-based stocks so they can make huge amounts. But the stocks and broths here are easy; there is no endless simmering of soup bones and skimming off of fat. In fact, it rarely takes me longer than 10 minutes to do the preparation for any of these. The recipe for garlic broth may look tedious, but if you use the garlic-peeling trick it will go quickly.

These can all be made up to three days in advance and kept refrigerated. They may also be frozen for several months.

VEGETABLE STOCK

Combine all the ingredients in a large stockpot. Bring slowly to a gentle boil, then reduce the heat and simmer, uncovered, for 1 to 2 hours, until you have a nice, aromatic broth. Correct the seasoning.

Strain and discard the vegetables and whole seasonings. Use this stock for soups (you may have to add more water to get the amount called for) and sauces.

This stock freezes well.

Makes 1¾ quarts

2 quarts water
2 medium onions, quartered
2 medium carrots, coarsely
   chopped
2 stalks celery, coarsely chopped
2 to 3 medium potatoes,
   unpeeled, cut in large pieces
2 leeks, white part only, washed
   well and coarsely chopped
6 garlic cloves, peeled
4 sprigs fresh parsley
1 bay leaf
2 sprigs fresh thyme, or
   ¼ teaspoon dried thyme
4 whole black peppercorns
1 tablespoon tamari (optional)
2 teaspoons Marmite or Savorex
   (optional)
Salt, preferably sea salt, to taste
3 vegetable bouillon cubes
   (optional)

6 cups water

4 vegetable bouillon cubes

3 garlic cloves, minced or put
through a press

⅓ cup tamari

Salt, preferably sea salt, to taste

Freshly ground pepper, to taste

2 heads garlic, separated into
cloves and peeled (see page
xxxii)

2 quarts water

1 tablespoon olive oil

1 bay leaf

2 sprigs fresh thyme, or ¼ teaspoon dried thyme

4 sprigs fresh parsley

Pinch of dried leaf sage

2 teaspoons salt, preferably sea
salt, or to taste

TAMARI–BOUILLON BROTH

Combine all the ingredients in a stockpot. Bring to a boil, then reduce the heat and simmer gently for 30 minutes. Make sure bouillon is dissolved.

Makes 1½ quarts

GARLIC BROTH

This has the rich, soothing flavor of a chicken broth with none of the fat. Guests sometimes don't believe it doesn't contain meat.

Combine all the ingredients in a stockpot. Bring to a gentle boil, then cover and reduce the heat. Simmer for 1 to 2 hours. Strain.

This is excellent as a starting stock for soups and some sauces, and it can be frozen.

Makes 1¾ quarts

Egg Drop Soup

This easy soup has a delicate, silky texture and a warming, chicken soup–like broth. Authentic egg drop soup is a simpler soup, but I like the addition of the mushrooms and the white parts of the onions here. It's important to serve this soup right after the eggs bind or the vegetables will cook too much.

Combine the stock, the chopped white part of the green onions, the ginger, garlic, and mushrooms in a soup pot or dutch oven and bring to a simmer. Simmer 10 minutes, until the mushrooms are just beginning to be tender. Add the optional tamari and snow peas and simmer another 3 to 5 minutes, until the peas are crisp-tender. Add pepper to taste.

Make sure the soup is at a bare simmer. Beat the eggs in a bowl. Hold the bowl about 8 inches above the surface of the soup and slowly stream into the soup through the back of a fork, moving the fork around so that the beaten egg covers the entire surface of the soup. When all of the egg has been added, cover the soup tightly and let set off the heat for 1 minute.

Sprinkle on the green part of the onions and the cilantro or parsley. Stir the soup three times. Taste and adjust salt, and serve.

Serves 4 to 6

1½ quarts Vegetable Stock (page 49)

1 bunch green onions, both white part and green, chopped separately

One ¼-inch-thick slice of gingerroot, chopped

1 garlic clove, minced or put through a press

8 fresh mushrooms, sliced

2 tablespoons tamari (optional)

½ pound fresh snow peas, strings removed

Freshly ground pepper

2 eggs, beaten

3 tablespoons chopped fresh cilantro or parsley

Salt, preferably sea salt, if necessary

SUGGESTED MENUS
Egg Rolls or Spring Rolls (page 44)
Egg Drop Soup
Stir-fry Chinese Tofu and Vegetables (page 144)
Cooked Brown Rice or Millet
Apple Pie (page 255) or Peaches Marsala (page 240)

Hummus (page 21)
Egg Drop Soup
Brown Rice Salad (page 225)
Fresh fruit (page 234)

Ratatouille

1 large eggplant, prepared as
    directed on page xxxiii

2 tablespoons olive oil

2 medium onions, sliced

4 to 6 large garlic cloves, to taste,
    minced or put through a press

1 medium green bell pepper,
    seeded and sliced

1 medium red bell pepper, seeded
    and sliced

1 pound zucchini, sliced ¼ inch
    thick (or use half zucchini, half
    yellow squash)

Salt, preferably sea salt, to taste

6 medium tomatoes, peeled and
    sliced

1 cucumber, peeled, seeded, and
    chunked (optional)

1 bay leaf

1 to 2 teaspoons dried oregano, or
    to taste, or a mixture of thyme
    and oregano

Freshly ground pepper, to taste

2 tablespoons chopped fresh basil

Chopped fresh parsley for garnish

Vinaigrette, if serving cold
    (optional)

Ratatouille is actually a vegetable stew, but I usually serve it as a first course, so I'm including it in this soup chapter. It goes beautifully with cheese dishes such as quiche or soufflé, and as a filling it makes an omelet or crêpe truly distinctive. It is wonderful hot or cold, and it keeps well.

After the eggplant has been "steamed" and is cool enough to handle, dice it, skin and all, and set it aside.

Heat 1 tablespoon of the olive oil over medium heat in a heavy-bottomed stockpot, a large, lidded nonstick frying pan, or a wok, and sauté the onions until tender and translucent, about 5 minutes. Add half the garlic and all of the peppers, and cook, stirring, another 5 minutes. Add the remaining tablespoon of oil, the zucchini, and the eggplant, salt lightly, and continue to cook, stirring, for another 5 to 10 minutes, until the vegetables have begun to soften. Add half the tomatoes, the cucumber, bay leaf, oregano and/or thyme, salt, and pepper, stir together, reduce the heat to low, cover, and simmer 30 minutes, stirring often. The vegetables should be cooked through and the broth fragrant. Add the remaining garlic and tomatoes, and the basil, taste and adjust salt, cover and simmer another 20 minutes.

Remove the ratatouille from the heat. Place a colander in a bowl, and drain the ratatouille into the colander. Let drain for 15 minutes, then return the ratatouille to the cooking pot and transfer the drained liquid to a saucepan. Heat the liquid to a boil over high heat and reduce it by about half. Stir back into the ratatouille. Taste and correct salt and pepper. Allow the ratatouille to cool, cover and refrigerate overnight, if possible. If serving hot, reheat gently in a casserole, stirring often. Sprinkle with parsley and serve. If serving cold, remove from the refrigerator 30 minutes to an hour before serving so it isn't too cold. Douse with vinaigrette if you wish, and sprinkle with parsley.

Serves 6

SUGGESTED MENUS
Vegetable Platter (page 40) with Tofu Mayonnaise (page 204)
Ratatouille
Spinach and Onion Quiche (page 105)
Mixed Green Salad (215)
Pears Poached in Red Wine with a Touch of Cassis (page 236)

Stuffed Mushrooms (page 28)
Ratatouille
Cheese Soufflé (page 109)
Mixed Green Salad (page 215)
Bananas Poached in White Wine (page 235)

Stracciatella

3 garlic cloves, minced or put
    through a press
1½ quarts Tamari-Bouillon Broth
    (page 50), Garlic Broth (page
    50), or Vegetable Stock (page
    49)
Salt, preferably sea salt, to taste
1 pound fresh spinach, washed
    and stems removed
2 eggs, beaten
¼ cup whole-wheat bread crumbs
¼ cup freshly grated Parmesan
    cheese

This is a light, delicate soup, so it's perfect with substantial Italian dishes such as eggplant parmesan or lasagne. It's really an Italian version of egg drop soup.

You can prepare all the ingredients beforehand, have the stock made and the spinach stemmed and washed, the cheese grated, and the bread crumbs ready. But the final steps are a last-minute operation, and the soup must be served immediately.

Combine the garlic and broth or stock in a stockpot and simmer for 20 minutes. Season with salt to taste, then add the spinach and simmer for 30 seconds.

In a medium bowl, mix together the beaten eggs, bread crumbs, and cheese. With the stock at a bare simmer, slowly stir in the egg mixture, stirring the mixture through the soup with a fork. The eggs should bind in a few seconds.

Serve immediately.

Serves 4 to 6

SUGGESTED MENUS
Orange wedges in a bowl
Stracciatella
Eggplant Parmesan (page 132)
Mixed Green Salad (page 215)
Mediterranean Fruit Compote (page 237)

Marinated Vegetables Vinaigrette (page 37)
Stracciatella
Lasagne (page 192)
Tender Lettuce and Orange Salad (page 220)
Fresh fruit (page 234) or Bavarian Crème au Café (page 244)

Fruit Soup

Served hot in the winter, this is a very warming soup. It's also one of the most refreshing cold soups you can make in the summer. I usually eat the leftovers for breakfast. Fruit soup gets sweeter every day in the refrigerator, but the fruit will not retain its lovely appearance after the first day. Fruit soup also makes a wonderful dessert.

Combine the dried fruits and the water in a stockpot. Bring to a boil and simmer over low heat until tender, about 30 minutes.

Add the fresh fruit, except for berries, and cook for 5 minutes. Add the berries and cook for 5 minutes more.

Remove from the heat and add the lemon juice, honey, nutmeg, and brandy and stir well.

Adjust the sweetness to taste, then serve hot or well chilled, topped with a dollop of yogurt and a sprinkling of slivered almonds.

Serves 6

1 pound mixed dried fruit, such as pears, peaches, apples, apricots, raisins, figs
2 quarts water
2 pounds mixed fresh fruit (apples, bananas, pears, peaches, berries)
⅓ cup fresh lemon juice
Mild honey, to taste
Freshly grated nutmeg, to taste
1 tablespoon brandy (optional)
Plain low-fat yogurt, homemade (page 202) or commercial, for topping
2 tablespoons slivered almonds for garnish (optional)

MENU SUGGESTIONS
Fruit Soup
Vegetable Shish Kebab with cooked grains (page 143)
Dessert soufflé (pages 247–249)

Spring Rolls (page 44)
Fruit Soup
Curried Tofu and Vegetables over Millet or Bulgur (page 148)
Gingerbread Soufflé (page 248)

Soupe au Pistou
(Provençal Vegetable Soup)

FOR THE SOUP:

2 medium onions, chopped

2 medium carrots, sliced

3 medium potatoes, unpeeled,
    diced

4 to 6 garlic cloves, to taste,
    minced or put through a press

1 teaspoon salt, preferably sea salt,
    or to taste

Freshly ground pepper, to taste

1 bay leaf

2 quarts water

1 small zucchini, sliced

1 cup fresh or frozen green peas

1 cup cooked white beans (½ cup
    dried; see page xxxvi)

½ cup broken dry spaghetti

¼ teaspoon saffron threads
    (optional)

½ teaspoon dried thyme, or a few
    sprigs of fresh thyme

Pistou is a hearty soup, and it's a favorite with my students and my catering clients. There are many versions, some "green" and some with tomatoes, of which this is one. Like ratatouille, it goes well with cheese dishes, but it's substantial enough to be served with just a nice salad and bread.

The first hour of cooking can be done in advance, as can the "pesto." You will also have to remember to soak and cook the white beans, which are an important ingredient. The other vegetables may be prepared in advance, but don't add them to the soup until shortly before serving. This will give the soup a nice variety of textures, and the vegetables will still be very much alive.

Combine the onions, carrots, potatoes, garlic, salt, pepper, bay leaf, and water in a large stockpot and bring to a boil. Reduce the heat and simmer, uncovered, for 1 hour. Meanwhile, prepare the remaining vegetables and set them aside, along with the white beans and broken spaghetti.

In a food processor fitted with the steel blade, or in a mortar and pestle, blend together the garlic, basil, tomato, and salt. Slowly add the olive oil and blend until smooth. Stir in the Parmesan. Set the pesto aside.

About 20 minutes before serving, have the stock at a gentle simmer and add the saffron, thyme, zucchini, peas, and white beans. Simmer gently until the vegetables are cooked through but the zucchini and peas are still bright green, and stir in the spaghetti. Continue to simmer until the spaghetti is cooked al dente, firm to the bite, about 8 to 10 minutes. Adjust seasonings, adding salt to taste and lots of freshly ground pepper. Carefully stir in the pesto. Blend thoroughly to dissolve the pesto and serve, topping each serving with Parmesan and chopped parsley.

Alternatively, you can ladle the soup into bowls and

place a tablespoon of pesto in each serving, and either stir to dissolve or have your guests stir to dissolve. This method makes a more intense bowl of soup.

Serves 6

SUGGESTED MENU

This soup makes a meal in itself, with a green salad, good bread, and fruit for dessert. But if you do want a more elaborate meal, follow the menu suggestions for Ratatouille (page 53).

FOR THE PISTOU (PESTO):

4 garlic cloves, minced or put through a press
2 cups fresh basil leaves
1 medium tomato, peeled and seeded
¼ cup good-quality olive oil
Salt, to taste
½ cup freshly grated Parmesan cheese

FOR THE GARNISH:

¼ cup freshly grated Parmesan cheese
¼ cup chopped fresh parsley

Purée of White Bean Soup

2 cups dried white beans, washed

3 quarts water (Method 1) or
   1½ quarts water (Method 2),
   or more if necessary

2 medium onions, chopped

5 large garlic cloves, minced or
   put through a press

1 bay leaf

2 teaspoons salt, preferably sea
   salt, or more if necessary

Freshly ground pepper

Milk, as needed

1 tablespoon olive oil

Juice of 1 lemon

2 tablespoons chopped fresh
   parsley

1½ cups Garlic Croutons (page
   18)

This simple, elegant soup is touched up just before serving with a little bit of olive oil, lemon juice, garlic croutons, and chopped fresh herbs. There are two methods you can use to cook the beans: You can soak them and cook them according to Method 1, or if you don't have time for soaking you can use Method 2. Whichever method you use, this part of the recipe can be done a day in advance and kept in the refrigerator. But the beans should be puréed on the day you are serving the soup, and the final enrichment should be done shortly before serving. The bay leaf here is essential—it brings out the delicate flavor of the white beans.

Method 1:

Wash the beans and soak them overnight or for at least 6 hours in the 1½ quarts water. Drain and combine with 1½ quarts fresh water, the onions, and 2 of the garlic cloves in a stockpot or dutch oven. Bring to a boil and add the bay leaf, then reduce the heat, cover, and simmer for 1 hour. Add the salt and 2 more garlic cloves, and simmer for another hour, until the beans are thoroughly tender.

Method 2:

If you haven't soaked the beans, combine them with the 1½ quarts water and onions and bring to a boil. Boil for 2 minutes, then cover tightly and turn off the heat. Allow to sit 1 hour, covered. Add 2 cloves of the garlic and the bay leaf, and bring to a boil again, then reduce the heat and simmer, covered, for 1 hour. Add the salt and 2 more garlic cloves, and simmer another hour, until the beans are tender. (You may have to add more liquid during this time.)

When the beans are tender and the broth is aromatic, place a colander over a bowl or pot and drain the beans, saving the liquid. Discard the bay leaf, return the liquid to the soup pot, and purée the beans, in batches, in a blender or through a food mill (use some of the broth if necessary).

Return the purée to the soup pot, mix together with the stock, and bring back to a simmer. Taste and adjust salt, and add freshly ground pepper. Thin out with some milk if it's too thick.

Mix together the olive oil, lemon juice, and the last clove of garlic, and drizzle over the soup. Sprinkle on the parsley and serve, garnishing each bowl with garlic croutons.

Serves 4 to 6

SUGGESTED MENU
Purée of White Bean Soup
Mixed Green Salad (page 215) or Beet and Endive Salad
    (page 227)
Fruit and cheese or Oranges Grand Marnier (page 238)

Tortilla Soup

6 cups Garlic Broth (page 50)

1 tablespoon olive oil

½ onion, minced

1 garlic clove, minced or put through a press

1 pound (4 medium) tomatoes, peeled, seeded, and puréed

1 tablespoon tomato paste

12 corn tortillas, cut in strips

Canola or vegetable oil (optional)

2 to 3 tablespoons chopped fresh cilantro, plus additional for garnish

Salt, to taste

Freshly ground pepper, to taste

½ cup grated Gruyère cheese

2 eggs, beaten

This is a hearty, warming soup, good on a cold night. Serve it with a light main course and a salad. The tasty tomato-garlic broth is enriched with crisp tortilla strips, and the combination is unforgettable.

The garlic broth may be made in advance, but the rest of the soup is best made on the day you plan to serve it.

After preparing the garlic broth, strain and discard the garlic, bay leaf, parsley, and thyme.

Heat the olive oil over medium-low heat in a stockpot and add the onion. Sauté, stirring, until the onion is tender, about 5 minutes, and add the garlic. Stir together for about a minute, just until the garlic begins to color, and add the tomato purée and tomato paste. Cook over a low flame, stirring, for 8 to 10 minutes. Add the garlic broth and stir well, then cover and let simmer for 30 minutes over very low heat.

Meanwhile, either toast the tortilla strips in a medium oven until just about crisp, or heat ¼ inch of canola oil in a frying pan and sauté the tortilla strips in batches (do not crowd the pan), stirring or turning, for about 3 minutes; do not allow them to get too crisp. Drain on paper towels, then add to the soup and cook for 3 minutes, until soft. Add the cilantro and cook for 1 minute. Taste the broth and season to taste with salt and pepper.

Put some grated Gruyère in each soup bowl.

Bring the soup to a boil and stir in the eggs; they should cook at once. Immediately spoon the soup into the bowls, over the cheese, and serve garnished, if desired, with more cilantro.

Serves 4 to 6

SUGGESTED MENUS
Tortilla Soup
Black Bean Enchiladas (page 97)
Avocado and Citrus Salad (page 217)
Strawberry and Cassis Sherbet (page 261)

Nachos with Black Bean Topping (page 36)
Tortilla Soup
Mixed Green Salad (page 215) or Spinach Salad (page 216)
Pineapple with Kirsch (page 241)

Cream of Raw and Cooked Mushroom Soup

1½ pounds fresh mushrooms, ends trimmed

1 tablespoon olive oil

1 small onion or 2 shallots, chopped

4 garlic cloves, minced or put through a press

3 tablespoons dry sherry

2 teaspoons soy sauce

1 teaspoon fresh thyme leaves, or ½ teaspoon dried thyme

5 cups Vegetable Stock (page 49) or water

2 medium potatoes, peeled and diced

1½ cups low-fat milk

Salt, to taste

Freshly ground pepper, to taste

¼ cup slivered fresh sage leaves or chopped fresh parsley for garnish

Mushrooms become very aromatic as they cook, and they make an exceptional broth, so it's no wonder that mushroom soup is so popular. This lovely version adds the fresh, unique texture of raw mushrooms as garnish. The fresh sage is a wonderful touch.

If you use a food processor to purée the mushrooms for this soup, the puree will have a somewhat grainy texture. I like this (and so do my guests), but you may want a creamy texture. If so, use a blender or sieve for the purée. The stock can be made a day or two in advance.

Wash all the mushrooms and set aside about 6 to be used as garnish. That's the "raw" part of this soup. Cut the rest in half, or if they are very large, quarter them.

Heat the oil over medium heat in a heavy-bottomed soup pot or dutch oven and add the onion or shallots. Cook, stirring, until tender, about 5 minutes. Add the halved or quartered mushrooms and cook, stirring, for 10 minutes, until they begin to cook through and release their liquid. Add the garlic and 2 tablespoons of the sherry, the soy sauce, and the thyme, and stir together for a few minutes. Add the stock and the potatoes, bring to a boil, reduce the heat, cover, and simmer 1 hour.

Purée the soup in a blender or food processor, or put through a sieve. Return it to the pot and stir in the milk and the remaining 1 tablespoon sherry. Heat through, add salt and freshly ground pepper. Slice the reserved raw mushrooms and garnish each bowl of the hot soup with a few of the mushroom slices and a sprinkling of slivered fresh sage or chopped fresh parsley.

Serves 4 to 6

SUGGESTED MENUS
Vegetable Platter with Assorted Dips (page 40)
Cream of Raw and Cooked Mushroom Soup
Stir-fry Chinese Tofu and Vegetables (page 144) with
    cooked grains
Bavarian Crème au Café (page 244)

Tiropites with Greek Spinach Filling (pages 32–33)
Cream of Raw and Cooked Mushroom Soup
Potatoes Gruyère (page 152)
Beet and Endive Salad (page 227)
Light Cheesecake (page 250)

Sopa de Ajo (Garlic Soup)

2 heads garlic, separated into
 cloves and peeled (see page
 xxxii)

2 quarts water

2 teaspoons salt, preferably sea
 salt

Freshly ground pepper, to taste

2 whole cloves

½ teaspoon dried leaf sage, or 2
 teaspoons slivered fresh sage

¼ teaspoon dried thyme, or 2
 sprigs fresh thyme

1 bay leaf

4 sprigs fresh parsley

1 tablespoon olive oil

½ cup macaroni shells

2 eggs, beaten

6 whole-wheat Garlic Croutons
 (page 18)

½ cup grated Gruyère cheese

¼ cup chopped fresh parsley

6 poached eggs (optional)

This is a good soup for a cold, as garlic is reputed to be a cura-tive. Restorative powers or not, your kitchen will certainly smell heavenly as the soup simmers. Float a poached egg in it and you have a soup-and-main-dish.

Combine the garlic, water, salt, pepper, cloves, sage, thyme, bay leaf, parsley sprigs, and oil in a large soup pot. Bring to a gentle boil, then cover and simmer for 1 hour. Strain and discard the garlic, cloves, bay leaf, and parsley.

About 20 minutes before serving, add the macaroni shells. When the shells are cooked through but still firm to the bite (al dente), beat the eggs in a bowl and stir in a ladle of hot soup. Slowly stir this back into the soup; do not let it boil.

Place a crouton in each bowl and sprinkle with some of the grated cheese. Ladle the soup over this, garnish with chopped parsley, and serve.

For a heartier meal, place a poached egg in each bowl of soup.

Serves 6

SUGGESTED MENUS
Sopa de Ajo
Extraordinary Chalupas (page 100)
Guacamole (page 221)
Strawberry and Cassis Sherbet (page 261)

Sopa de Ajo
Black Bean Enchiladas (page 97)
Spinach Salad (page 216)
Oranges Grand Marnier (page 238)

Sopa de Ajo, with poached egg
Spinach and Citrus Salad (page 228)
Strawberry and Cassis Sherbet (page 261)

Leek, Potato, and Cheese Soup with Garlic Croutons

This is a great dish for a cold evening. Be careful not to boil the soup once the cheese and eggs have been added, or else the mixture will curdle. The stock can be made in advance, the cheese grated, and the croutons prepared.

Combine the stock, bouillon, or water, the leeks, potatoes, garlic, wine, thyme, and Worcestershire sauce in a large, heavy-bottomed soup pot or dutch oven. Bring to a boil, and if using water, add salt (at least 1 teaspoon, more to taste). Reduce the heat, cover, and simmer 45 minutes, until the vegetables are tender and the broth fragrant.

Remove the soup from the heat and purée in batches in a food processor or blender, or through the medium blade of a food mill, and return to the pot. (If you have a hand blender, purée the soup in the pot.)

Beat the eggs in a medium bowl and stir in the cheeses. Heat the soup to a simmer and stir about 3 ladlefuls into the egg/cheese mixture. Stir until the cheese has begun to melt, and pour the mixture back into the soup pot.

Heat through, stirring over medium-low heat and taking care not to let the broth boil (or the eggs will curdle), until the cheese has melted. Taste and adjust salt, stir in lots of freshly ground pepper, and stir in the sage or parsley.

Serve, topping each bowl with a handful of garlic croutons.

Serves 4 to 6

1½ quarts Vegetable Stock (page 49), bouillon, or water
4 leeks, white part only, cleaned well and sliced
1 pound (4 medium) potatoes, peeled and diced
4 large garlic cloves, peeled
1 cup dry white wine
1 teaspoon dried thyme
1 teaspoon Worcestershire sauce
Salt, preferably sea salt, to taste
2 eggs, beaten
½ cup grated Parmesan cheese
1 cup grated white sharp Cheddar cheese
Freshly ground pepper
¼ cup slivered fresh sage leaves or chopped fresh parsley
4 to 6 Garlic Croutons (page 18), cut or broken into small pieces

SUGGESTED MENUS
Cucumber Salad (page 222)
Leek, Potato, and Cheese Soup with Garlic Croutons
Soufflé Omelets with Savory Mushroom Filling (page 115)
Mixed Green Salad (page 215)
Pineapple with Kirsch (page 241)

Leek, Potato, and Cheese Soup with Garlic Croutons
Spinach Salad (page 216)
Peaches Marsala (page 240) or Peach Pie (page 255)

Fresh Pea Soup

1 tablespoon olive oil

1 medium onion, chopped

4 cups fresh shelled peas (about 4 pounds unshelled), or 1 pound frozen peas

2 medium potatoes, peeled and diced

5 cups Vegetable Stock (page 49) or water

Salt, preferably sea salt, to taste

Freshly ground pepper, to taste

2 sprigs parsley

1 cup low-fat milk

Chopped fresh mint for garnish

½ cup plain nonfat yogurt for garnish (optional)

This soup is completely different from the split-pea soup with which you're familiar. It's a beautiful spring green color—one of the most beautiful soups I've ever seen—and has the overwhelming sweetness of fresh garden peas (even if you use frozen ones!). Fresh pea soup can be made a day in advance and kept in the refrigerator. Reheat over a low flame and serve piping hot or cold.

Heat the oil over medium-low heat in a heavy-bottomed soup pot or dutch oven and add the onion. Cook, stirring, until the onion is tender, about 5 minutes, and add the peas, potatoes, stock or water, salt and pepper, and parsley sprigs, and bring to a boil. Reduce the heat, cover, and simmer 30 minutes, until the potatoes and peas are tender. Purée in a blender or a food processor fitted with the steel blade. Return to the pot and stir in the milk. Heat through and adjust seasonings. Serve, garnishing each bowl with chopped fresh mint, and a dollop of yogurt if you like.

Serves 4 to 6

SUGGESTED MENUS

Fresh Pea Soup

Squash Soufflé (page 116), Cheese Soufflé (page 109), or Piperade (page 117)

Tomatoes and Fresh Herbs (page 226) or Mixed Green Salad (page 215)

Pineapple with Kirsch (page 241)

Fresh Pea Soup, chilled

Hummus (page 21)

Tabouli (page 218)

Bananas Poached in White Wine (page 235)

Cream of Wheat Berry Soup

This is a wonderful winter soup—thick, savory, and earthy.

Place the dried mushrooms in a bowl and pour on the boiling water. Let sit 30 minutes. Drain into a bowl through a strainer lined with cheesecloth, and rinse the mushrooms thoroughly in several changes of water. Squeeze dry and chop. Add the mushroom soaking liquid to the stock or broth.

Heat the oil in a large, heavy-bottomed soup pot or dutch oven over medium-low heat and add the onion. Cook, stirring, until the onion begins to soften, and add the carrots and celery. Cook, stirring, for about 5 minutes (do not brown), and stir in the garlic, thyme, and the mushrooms. Stir together for about a half minute, then stir in the wheat berries. Add the stock or water, salt, and pepper, and bring to a boil. Reduce the heat, cover, and simmer 1 hour, until the wheat berries are tender. Remove 2 cups of the soup and purée in a blender or a food processor fitted with the steel blade. Stir the purée back into the soup, along with the sherry. (Alternatively, you can blend partially with a hand blender). Add salt to taste and lots of freshly ground pepper. Heat through, taste, and adjust seasonings. Sprinkle on the parsley and serve.

Serves 4 to 6

½ cup dried porcini mushrooms
Boiling water to cover
6 cups Vegetable Stock (page 49)
    or Tamari-Bouillon Broth
    (page 50), or water
1 tablespoon olive oil or canola oil
1 medium onion, chopped
2 medium carrots, chopped
1 stalk celery, chopped
2 to 3 garlic cloves (to taste),
    minced or put through a press
1 teaspoon fresh thyme leaves, or
    ½ teaspoon dried thyme (more
    to taste)
1½ cups wheat berries
Salt, preferably sea salt, to taste
Freshly ground pepper, to taste
2 tablespoons dry sherry
3 tablespoons chopped fresh
    parsley

SUGGESTED MENUS
Salade Niçoise (page 218)
Cream of Wheat Berry Soup
Strawberry and Cassis Sherbet (page 261)

Soya Pâté (page 22)
Cream of Wheat Berry Soup
Watercress and Mushroom Salad (page 226)
Fresh fruit (page 234)

Purée of Asparagus Soup

2 pounds asparagus, trimmed and
  cut in 1½-inch pieces
1 tablespoon olive oil or vegetable
  oil
1 medium onion, chopped
2 medium potatoes, peeled and
  diced
5 cups water or Vegetable Stock
  (page 49)
2 sprigs parsley
Salt, preferably sea salt, to taste
Freshly ground pepper, to taste
1 cup low-fat milk

*It's hard to beat the taste of asparagus, which is practically all
you need for this thick soup that contains no cream at all. A
couple of potatoes and lots of asparagus account for its rich
texture.*

Set aside 1 cup of the asparagus tips for garnish.

Heat the oil in a large, heavy-bottomed soup pot over
medium heat and add the onion. Sauté, stirring, until the
onion begins to soften, about 3 minutes, and add the
asparagus, potatoes, water or stock, the parsley, salt, and
pepper. Bring to a boil, reduce the heat, cover, and simmer
20 to 30 minutes, until the potatoes are tender. Remove
from the heat.

Purée the soup using a hand blender, a food processor,
or a blender, or put it through the medium blade of a food
mill. Return it to the pot, and stir in the milk. Heat through
and adjust seasonings.

Steam the asparagus tips that you set aside for 5 to 8
minutes, until just tender and still bright green. Garnish
each bowl of soup with a few of the tips and serve.

Note: The soup can also be served cold. At the end of Step 3, after
reheating, cool and chill several hours. Serve as directed.

Serves 4 to 6

SUGGESTED MENUS:
Purée of Asparagus Soup
Vegetable Paella (page 142)
Mixed Green Salad (page 215)
Watermelon–Fruit Extravaganza (page 239)

Herbed Cottage Cheese (page 26)
Sesame Crackers (page 18) or Mixed Grains Bread (page 3)
Purée of Asparagus Soup
Chick-pea Salad (page 231)
Raspberries in Red Wine (page 240)

Leek Soup

I first had this simple, elegant soup while living in a little Mexican weaving village near Oaxaca. The Indian family I lived with thought that Americans were unable to digest anything other than soups or eggs, so they fed me many wonderful soups for breakfast, lunch, and dinner. This soup is so simple that you will be amazed at how rich and soothing it is.

Heat the oil over medium-low heat in a large, heavy-bottomed soup pot or dutch oven and add the leeks and a little salt. Cook gently, stirring often, for 5 to 10 minutes, until the leeks are thoroughly tender and fragrant. Add the garlic and continue to cook, stirring, for another minute, until the garlic begins to color. Add the stock or water, pepper, thyme, and bay leaf, bring to a boil, reduce the heat, cover, and simmer for 1 hour. Taste and adjust seasonings. Remove the bay leaf.

Pour the soup into bowls, sprinkle each serving with a tablespoon of the grated cheese, if desired, and serve.

Serves 4 to 6

1 tablespoon olive oil
4 medium leeks, white part only, cleaned well and sliced
Salt, preferably sea salt, to taste
2 to 4 garlic cloves (to taste), minced or put through a press
1½ quarts Vegetable Stock (page 49) or water
Freshly ground pepper, to taste
1 teaspoon fresh thyme leaves, or ½ teaspoon dried thyme
1 bay leaf
6 tablespoons freshly grated Parmesan cheese (optional)

SUGGESTED MENUS
Leek Soup
Chick-pea and Bulgur Gratin with Garlicky Tomato Sauce (page 136)
Spinach and Citrus Salad (page 227)
Bavarian Crème au Café (page 244)

Tiropites with the filling of your choice (page 32)
Leek Soup
Chick-pea Salad (page 231)
Fresh fruit (page 234)

Egg–Lemon Soup
(Avgolemono Soup)

3 eggs

½ cup fresh lemon juice, or more
    to taste

1½ quarts Garlic Broth (page 50)

2 cups broccoli florets

1½ cups cooked long-grain brown
    or white rice (3/4 cup raw; see
    page xxxv)

Salt, preferably sea salt, to taste

Freshly ground pepper, to taste

Paper-thin lemon slices for
    garnish

This remarkable soup, which can be served hot or chilled, comes from the Middle East. It's a favorite among my students and catering clients, whose eyes light up when they taste the delicate, lemony broth. The broccoli adds a nice touch of color.

Beat together the eggs and lemon juice. Bring the garlic broth to a simmer in a stockpot or large saucepan.

If serving hot:

About 3 minutes before serving, add the broccoli florets to the broth. Then remove 1 cup of the broth and stir into the egg-lemon mixture.

Have the broth just barely simmering, or "just smiling" (barely trembling at the surface but not bubbling). Slowly pour the egg mixture into the soup pot, stirring constantly. When the eggs are bound—it should only take a minute or so—spoon 2 or 3 tablespoons of rice into each serving bowl and ladle in the soup. Add a bit more lemon juice if it isn't lemony enough for you, and season to taste.

Serve, garnishing each bowl with a thin slice of lemon.

If serving cold:

Steam the broccoli florets separately until bright green, cool, and hold. Follow the directions for the hot egg-lemon soup, but chill after the eggs are set, and add the broccoli and rice to each bowl or to the soup just before serving.

Serves 4 to 6

SUGGESTED MENUS
Egg–Lemon Soup
Spanokopita (page 118)
Mixed Green Salad (page 215) or Tomatoes and Fresh Herbs
    (page 226)
Pears Poached in Red Wine with a Touch of Cassis (page
    236)

Hummus (page 21)
Baba Ghanoush (page 24)
Egg–Lemon Soup
Mixed Green Salad (page 215)
Fresh fruit (page 234)

Potato–Cheese Soup

During the winter I get many requests for this thick, hearty soup. It's good with a salad and black bread, or with a vegetable-oriented main dish.

Heat the oil over medium-low heat in a heavy-bottomed soup pot or dutch oven and add the leeks or onion. Cook, stirring, until tender, about 5 minutes. Add the potatoes, stock or water, and salt. Bring to a boil, reduce the heat, cover, and simmer for 30 minutes, until the potatoes are tender.

Add the milk, caraway seeds, and pepper. Let simmer another 15 to 20 minutes; the soup should become thick and the potatoes should begin to fall apart. Using a wooden spoon, mash some of the potatoes against the side of the pot. Add the dill or sage, stir in the cheeses, and allow them to melt. Taste, adjust the seasoning, and serve piping hot.

Serves 4 to 6

SUGGESTED MENUS
Potato–Cheese Soup
Mixed Green Salad (page 215) or Watercress and Mushroom Salad (page 227)
Apple Pie (page 255) or Baked Apples (page 242)

Potato–Cheese Soup
Picante Zucchini Gratin (page 138)
Mixed Green Salad (page 215)
Fresh fruit (page 234)

1 tablespoon olive oil
3 leeks or 1 large onion, sliced
2½ pounds (5 large or 10 medium) waxy potatoes, scrubbed and diced
1 quart Vegetable Stock (page 49) or water
Salt, preferably sea salt, to taste
2 cups low-fat milk
½ teaspoon caraway seeds
Freshly ground pepper, to taste
2 tablespoons fresh dill or slivered fresh sage
3 ounces (¾ cup grated) Gruyère cheese
2 tablespoons freshly grated Parmesan cheese

Potato—Tomato Soup

1 tablespoon olive oil

2 medium onions, sliced

4 large garlic cloves (or more to taste), minced or put through a press

1 pound (2 large or 4 medium) potatoes, scrubbed and sliced about ¼ inch thick

5 cups water or Vegetable Stock (page 49)

Salt, preferably sea salt, to taste

2 teaspoons fresh thyme leaves, or 1 teaspoon dried thyme (or more to taste)

Bouquet garni made with a bay leaf, a few sprigs of parsley, and a few sprigs of thyme

2½ pounds (6 large or 10 medium, or drained from two 28-ounce cans) tomatoes, peeled, seeded, and sliced

Freshly ground pepper, to taste

¼ cup freshly grated Parmesan cheese for topping

¼ cup chopped fresh basil or parsley for topping

This is a comforting soup at any time of year (in the winter you'll have to use canned tomatoes). It's easy to make and makes a great lunch or supper with a green salad and good bread.

Heat the oil in a heavy-bottomed soup pot or dutch oven over medium heat and add the onions. Sauté, stirring, until the onions are just about tender, about 5 minutes, and add half the garlic. Stir together for about 30 seconds and add the potatoes, water or stock, the salt, thyme, and bouquet garni. Bring to a boil, reduce the heat, cover, and simmer 30 minutes.

Add the tomatoes, pepper, and the remaining garlic. Bring back to a boil, cover, and simmer 45 minutes. Taste and adjust seasonings, adding more garlic, thyme, salt, or pepper if you wish.

Serve, garnishing each serving bowl with a spoonful of Parmesan and a sprinkling of chopped fresh basil or parsley.

Serves 4 to 6

SUGGESTED MENUS
Potato—Tomato Soup
Mixed Green Salad (page 215)
Fresh fruit (page 234) and cheese or Mediterranean Fruit Compote (page 237)

Potato—Tomato Soup
Spinach and Onion Quiche (page 105)
Mixed Green Salad (page 215) or Spinach Salad (page 216)
Orange Dessert Crêpes (page 243)

Cabbage–Cheese Soup

This is a creamy, heavenly soup. With bread and salad it is a complete meal.

Heat the oil or butter in a large, heavy-bottomed soup pot or dutch oven over medium heat and add the onion. Sauté, stirring, until the onion is tender, about 5 minutes, and add the grated potato and the shredded cabbage. Stir together for about a minute (the potatoes will begin to stick to the bottom of the pot fairly quickly), and add the stock, salt, and pepper. Bring to a boil, reduce the heat, cover, and simmer 20 to 30 minutes, or until the vegetables are tender and the broth aromatic.

Stir in the milk and bring back to a simmer. Stir in the cheeses and continue to stir until they melt into the soup. Taste, adjust salt and pepper, and serve.

Serves 4 to 6

SUGGESTED MENU
Cabbage–Cheese Soup
Omelet (pages 120–124)
Tomatoes and Fresh Herbs (page 226)
Apple Pie (page 255)

1 tablespoon olive oil, canola oil, or butter
1 medium onion, chopped
1 large potato, peeled and grated
½ pound white cabbage (about ½ medium head), shredded
5 cups Vegetable Stock (page 49), bouillon, or water
Salt, to taste
Freshly ground pepper, to taste
2 cups low-fat milk
4 ounces Gruyère cheese, grated (1 cup grated)
1 ounce Parmesan cheese, grated (¼ cup grated)

Minestrone

1 tablespoon olive oil

1 large onion, chopped

4 to 6 garlic cloves (more to taste), minced or put through a press

1 cup dried navy beans, kidney beans, or garbanzo beans (navy beans recommended), washed, picked over, soaked overnight or for at least 6 hours in 1 quart water, and drained

2 quarts, in all, water, Vegetable Stock (page 49), or Garlic Broth (page 50)

1 bay leaf

Salt, preferably sea salt, to taste

2 leeks, white part only, cleaned well and sliced thin

2 medium carrots, sliced

2 stalks celery, sliced

6 medium tomatoes, peeled and sliced

3 medium potatoes, unpeeled and diced

1 cup shredded cabbage

1 teaspoon fresh thyme leaves, or ½ teaspoon dried thyme

1 teaspoon dried oregano

1 large or 2 medium zucchini, sliced thin

1 cup fresh green beans, ends cut off and halved, or 1 cup fresh or frozen peas

1 cup broken dry spaghetti

Freshly ground pepper, to taste

Minestrone means "big soup." Irma Goodrich Mazza, in her delightful Herbs for the Kitchen *(Arco, 1973), says it's closest to the heart of her household: "A plate of this potage topped with grated Romano cheese, served with crisped and garlicked French bread, a salad and a glass of wine, and we have dined." Mine is tomatoey and thick, full of fresh vegetables, rich with beans and pasta and Parmesan cheese. Serve piping hot for a hearty winter meal; in the summer, serve it at room temperature in smaller bowls.*

For this soup you'll need to remember to soak the beans. If you can find no fresh green beans or peas, use frozen peas. The soup is even better one day after it's made. If you make it ahead, hold the fresh vegetables and the pasta. The next day, bring the soup to a simmer and proceed as in the recipe, adding the vegetables and pasta 15 minutes before serving the soup and simmering until they are cooked through but still colorful and crisp.

Heat the oil over medium-low heat in a soup pot or dutch oven and add the onion. Cook, stirring, until the onion begins to soften, about 3 to 5 minutes, and add 2 cloves of the garlic. Cook another minute, until the garlic begins to color, and add the beans and 1 quart of the water or stock. Bring to a boil. Add the bay leaf, reduce the heat, cover, and simmer 1 hour.

Add the remaining stock or water, salt (at least 1 teaspoon), half the remaining garlic, the leeks, carrots, celery, tomatoes, potatoes, cabbage, thyme, and oregano, and bring to a boil. Reduce the heat, cover again, and simmer 1 hour. Add the remaining garlic, the zucchini, beans or peas, the broken spaghetti, and lots of freshly ground pepper. Simmer 15 minutes, until the vegetables are tender but still bright green and the spaghetti is just tender to the bite. Stir in the basil and 2 tablespoons parsley, taste and adjust seasonings, adding more salt, pepper, or garlic if you wish.

Spoon into wide soup bowls, topping each bowlful with a heaped spoonful of grated Romano or Parmesan and a sprinkling of parsley.

Serves 6

SUGGESTED MENUS
Stuffed Mushrooms (page 28)
Minestrone
Tender Lettuce and Orange Salad (page 219)
Fresh fruit (page 234)

Minestrone
French Bread (page 10) or French Herb Bread (page 12)
Herb Butter (page 25)
Mixed Green Salad (page 215)
Light Cheesecake (page 250)

1 to 2 tablespoons chopped fresh basil, to taste
2 tablespoons chopped fresh parsley, plus additional for garnish
½ cup freshly grated Romano or Parmesan cheese

Vichyssoise

1 tablespoon olive oil

3 leeks, white part only, cleaned well and then sliced

1 onion, chopped

2 pounds potatoes, peeled and diced

Salt, preferably sea salt, to taste

1 quart Vegetable Stock (page 49) or water

2 cups milk

Freshly ground pepper, to taste

¼ cup chopped fresh chives for garnish

This isn't as heavy as the traditional vichyssoise because it calls for milk instead of cream. It still has a very rich and satisfying flavor.

Heat the oil over medium-low heat in a heavy-bottomed soup pot or dutch oven and sauté the leeks and onion until tender, about 5 to 8 minutes. Add the potatoes, salt, and stock or water. Bring to a boil, then reduce the heat, cover, and simmer 30 minutes to 1 hour, until the potatoes are tender and beginning to fall apart. Purée in a blender or put through the medium blade of a food mill. Return the purée to the pot and stir in the milk. Heat through and adjust seasonings, adding salt and freshly ground pepper to taste.

Remove the soup from the heat, allow to cool, and chill several hours. Serve cold, garnishing each bowl with chopped fresh chives.

Serves 4 to 6

SUGGESTED MENU
Vichyssoise
Omelet (pages 120–124)
Spinach Salad (page 216) or Mixed Green Salad (page 215)
Pears Poached in Red Wine with a Touch of Cassis (page 236) or Fresh fruit (page 234)

Dill Soup

This soup is marvelous hot or cold. Make it a day in advance if you plan to serve it chilled. If you're serving it hot and wish to prepare it ahead, you should make it only through the purée step and add the egg, yogurt, and dill just before you heat it through before serving.

Combine the water, salt, bouillon cube, bay leaf, potatoes, carrots, onion, garlic, and celery in a stock pot or dutch oven and bring to a boil. Reduce the heat, cover, and simmer for 1 to 2 hours; the vegetables should be very tender. Remove the bay leaf.

Purée the soup using a hand blender, an electric blender, a food mill, or a food processor; if you use a food processor, use the grater blade, not the steel blade (otherwise you'll get a very sticky paste). The soup should retain some texture. Return to the pot and add a generous amount of pepper (8 to 10 twists of the pepper mill, or more to taste).

In a bowl, beat the eggs and mix with the dill and yogurt. Ladle some soup into the bowl and mix well, then pour the mixture back into the soup. Heat through gently, stirring; do not allow to boil.

Serve hot, garnishing each bowl with a sprig of dill and garlic croutons. Or on a hot day heat through, cool, and chill. Serve garnished with sliced cucumbers, dill sprigs, and yogurt.

Serves 6

1½ quarts water

1 teaspoon salt, preferably sea salt, or to taste

1 vegetable bouillon cube

1 bay leaf

5 medium waxy potatoes, peeled and diced

2 medium carrots, coarsely sliced

1 medium onion, quartered

3 large garlic cloves, peeled

2 ribs celery, coarsely sliced

Freshly ground pepper, to taste

2 eggs

½ cup chopped fresh dill

1 cup plain nonfat yogurt, homemade (page 202) or commercial

Dill sprigs and Garlic Croutons (page 18) for garnish

SUGGESTED MENUS
Hummus (page 21) with Assorted Breads (pages 3–15)
Dill Soup
Cucumber Salad (page 222)
Fresh fruit (page 234)

Dill Soup
Tomato Quiche (page 107)
Watercress and Mushroom Salad (page 226)
Watermelon–Fruit Extravaganza (page 239)

Tomato–Rice Soup

1 tablespoon olive oil

1 medium onion, chopped

4 garlic cloves, minced or put
    through a press

1 rib celery, sliced

1 carrot, sliced

¾ cup raw brown rice

3 pounds fresh tomatoes, peeled,
    chopped, and mashed, or two
    28-ounce cans crushed toma-
    toes, chopped and mashed

1 tablespoon tomato paste

Salt, preferably sea salt, to taste

Freshly ground black pepper, to
    taste

1 teaspoon oregano

1 tablespoon chopped fresh basil,
    or 1 teaspoon dried basil

1 quart Vegetable Stock (page 49),
    Garlic Broth (page 50), or
    water

1 bay leaf

A crisp tossed salad, a good loaf of bread, and tomato-rice soup can make a marvelous meal.

Heat the oil over medium heat in a heavy-bottomed soup pot or dutch oven and sauté the onion until it is tender. Add 1 clove of the garlic, the celery, and carrot and sauté for another 5 minutes. Add the rice and sauté, stirring, until the rice is beginning to smell toasty, about 5 minutes. Add the tomatoes, tomato paste, the remaining garlic, salt, pepper, oregano, and dried basil, if using (but not fresh; that will be added later), the stock, broth, or water, and the bay leaf. Bring to a boil, reduce the heat, cover and simmer for 1 hour, or until the rice is done. If using fresh basil, stir it in now. Remove the bay leaf. Taste and adjust seasonings. Serve hot.

Note: For a thicker soup, purée 2 cups of the soup in a blender or food processor and stir back into the rest of it.

Serves 4 to 6

SUGGESTED MENU
Tomato–Rice Soup
Squash Soufflé (page 116) or Stuffed Eggplant (page 134)
Mixed Green Salad (page 215)
Baked Apples (page 242)

Sesame–Spinach Soup

Ginger, tamari, and sherry give this soup its Chinese character. It's quick and easy, yet elegant. You can have the stock simmering and the spinach stemmed in advance; then it's a last-minute operation.

Heat the oil over medium heat in a heavy-bottomed soup pot or dutch oven and sauté 1 teaspoon of the ginger and the 2 tablespoons of sesame seeds for 3 minutes, or until the sesame seeds begin to smell toasty. Add the stock or broth and bring to a simmer.

Combine the tamari and sherry with the remaining ginger and the garlic, mustard, and arrowroot or cornstarch. Add to the stock and simmer for 15 to 30 minutes.

Five minutes before serving, or less, add the spinach and stir until it is just cooked through. Serve immediately, topping each serving, if you wish, with more sesame seeds and chopped fresh chives or green onion tops.

Serves 4 to 6

SUGGESTED MENUS
Sesame–Spinach Soup
Couscous with Vegetables (page 154)
Mixed Green Salad (page 215)
Soufflé Grand Marnier (page 249)

Spring Rolls (page 44)
Sesame–Spinach Soup
Baked Beans with Fruit and Chutney (page 151)
Couscous with Fruit (page 251) or Buckwheat Cake (page 260)

1 tablespoon canola oil or peanut oil

2 teaspoons freshly grated gingerroot

2 tablespoons sesame seeds, plus additional for garnish, if desired

6 cups Vegetable Stock (page 49) or Tamari-Bouillon Broth (page 50)

¼ cup tamari, if using vegetable stock (omit if using tamari-bouillon broth)

¼ cup dry sherry or sake

2 garlic cloves, minced or put through a press

¼ teaspoon dry mustard

1 tablespoon arrowroot or cornstarch

10 ounces fresh spinach, washed well and stemmed

¼ cup chopped fresh chives or green onion tops for garnish

Tamari–Noodle Soup
with Green Beans

6 cups Vegetable Stock (page 50)

½ cup tamari

½ pound buckwheat noodles (soba)

½ pound green beans, ends snapped off, washed, then sliced if desired

This, simple, light, pleasing soup couldn't be easier to throw together.

Bring the stock and tamari to a simmer in a large saucepan or stockpot. About 10 minutes before serving, add the noodles and green beans to the stock. Serve when the noodles are tender.

Serves 4 to 6

SUGGESTED MENUS

Tamari–Noodle Soup with Green Beans

Baked Beans with Fruit and Chutney (page 151) or Cheese Soufflé (page 109)

Mixed Green Salad (page 215)

Bananas Poached in White Wine (page 235)

Tamari–Noodle Soup with Green Beans

Spinach and Mushroom Omelet (page 123)

Mixed Green Salad (page 215)

Tomatoes and Fresh Herbs (page 224)

Apricot Soufflé (page 247)

Corn Chowder

Corn chowder is rich and creamy, a perennial favorite made with corn, milk, and potatoes. The green pepper lends a nice crunch, and the kernels of corn are bursting with juicy sweetness that flows into the creamy stock. This is a protein-rich soup, good to serve with bean and vegetable dishes. Preparation goes fairly quickly. You can easily remove the corn from the cob by running a knife down between the kernels and the cob; you'll be amazed at how much corn you can get.

Heat the olive oil over medium-low heat in a stockpot or dutch oven and sauté the onion until tender, about 5 minutes. Add 1 of the garlic cloves and the green pepper and cook, stirring, for 5 minutes, until the pepper has softened slightly. Add the remaining garlic, the corn kernels, potatoes, stock, milk, thyme, salt, and pepper. Bring to a simmer, reduce the heat to low, cover and simmer 30 minutes, or until the potatoes are tender, stirring from time to time.

Purée 2 cups of the soup and stir back into the pot. Taste and adjust seasoning. If you are using the cheese, add it to the soup, stir until it melts, and serve.

Serves 6

1 tablespoon olive oil

1 onion, chopped

2 garlic cloves, minced or put through a press

1 green pepper, seeded and diced

2 cups fresh corn kernels (from 2 to 4 ears of corn)

1 pound (4 medium) potatoes, scrubbed and diced

2 cups Vegetable Stock (page 49) or Garlic Broth (page 50)

1 quart milk, enriched with 3 tablespoons spray-dried milk

2 teaspoons fresh thyme leaves, or 1 teaspoon dried thyme

Salt, preferably sea salt, to taste

Freshly ground pepper, to taste

½ cup grated Cheddar or Gruyère cheese (optional)

MENU SUGGESTIONS
Corn Chowder
Baked Beans with Fruit and Chutney (page 151)
Mixed Green Salad (page 215)
Orange Dessert Crêpes (page 243)

Corn Chowder
Winter Squash Gratin (page 171)
Beet and Endive Salad (page 227)
Gingerbread Soufflé (page 248)

Noodle–Bean Soup

2 tablespoons canola oil or vegetable oil

2 onions, chopped

3 garlic cloves, minced or put
through a press

⅔ cup dried kidney beans,
washed, picked over, and
soaked overnight or for 6
hours in 2 cups water

⅔ cup dried black beans, washed,
picked over, and soaked
overnight or for 6 hours in 2
cups water (or you may use 1⅓
total cups dried kidney beans,
soaked in 1 quart of water)

2 quarts water, or 1 quart water
and 1 quart Vegetable Stock
(page 49) or Tamari-Bouillon
Broth (page 50)

1 teaspoon salt, preferably sea salt,
or more to taste

3 green onions, both white part
and green, chopped separately

1 cup tofu, cut in slivers

1 cup matchstick-cut carrots

1 cup matchstick-cut turnips

1 tablespoon cider vinegar

2 tablespoons tamari (omit if
using tamari-bouillon broth)

¼ teaspoon chili powder

¼ teaspoon freshly ground
pepper

8 ounces flat buckwheat (soba) or
other whole-grain noodles

1 tablespoon miso paste

1 cup Bibb or romaine lettuce,
torn in pieces

The combination of whole-grain noodles, beans, and miso not only gives this delightful soup an Asian character—they also combine to make this quite a high-protein soup. You must remember to soak and cook the beans in advance; they will keep for two days in the refrigerator with no problem.

Heat 1 tablespoon of the oil over medium heat in a heavy-bottomed soup pot or dutch oven and sauté 1 of the onions and 2 of the garlic cloves until the onion is tender, about 5 minutes. Drain the soaked beans and add to the pot, along with 1 quart of water. Bring to a boil, reduce the heat, cover, and simmer for 1 hour. Add salt and continue to simmer for 30 minutes to 1 hour, until the beans are tender but not mushy and the broth is aromatic. Place a colander or strainer over a large bowl or another pot and drain the beans. Measure out the liquid and add enough vegetable stock, tamari-bouillon broth, or water to make 7 cups.

Wash out your stockpot and dry it, then heat the rest of the oil in it and sauté the remaining onion and garlic until the onion is tender. Add the chopped white part of the green onions, the tofu, ¼ cup each of the carrots and turnips, the beans and their 7 cups of liquid, vinegar, tamari, chili powder, freshly ground pepper, and a little salt. Bring to a gentle boil, then cover, reduce the heat, and simmer for 30 minutes.

Fifteen minutes before serving, add the noodles, and 5 minutes later add the remaining turnips and carrots.

Remove a cup of liquid from the pot and add the miso paste; stir well to dissolve. Pour back into the pot and add the lettuce and the chopped green part of the green onions. Heat through, without boiling, for 3 to 4 minutes, then correct the seasonings. Make sure the noodles are cooked through and serve.

Serves 4 to 6

SUGGESTED MENUS

Egg Rolls or Spring Rolls (page 44)
Noodle–Bean Soup
Stir-fry Chinese Tofu and Vegetables (page 144), with bulgur, millet, or rice
Apricot Soufflé (page 247) or Gingerbread Soufflé (page 248)

Noodle–Bean Soup
Spicy Tofu Salad (page 222)
Gingered Broccoli (page 167)
Fresh fruit (page 234)

Thick Cabbage Soup

1 tablespoon canola oil

1 onion, chopped

3 tablespoons sesame seeds

7 cups shredded cabbage (about ½ large head)

2 tomatoes, chopped

2 slices whole-wheat or rye bread, diced

6 cups Vegetable Stock (page 49) or Tamari-Bouillon Broth (page 50)

Salt, preferably sea salt, to taste

3 tablespoons soy sauce, or to taste (omit if using tamari-bouillon broth)

⅛ teaspoon cayenne pepper

½ teaspoon caraway seeds (optional)

A wonderful, easy soup, one of my favorites. Sesame seeds are a nice touch, adding texture and nuttiness to a thick soup with a dark and fragrant broth. A little bit of cayenne goes a long way here; it's an important ingredient that enhances the character of the soup.

Heat the canola oil over medium heat in a heavy-bottomed stockpot and sauté the onion until it begins to soften, about 3 minutes. Add the sesame seeds and cabbage and continue to cook, stirring, over low heat, for about 10 minutes, until the cabbage has cooked down.

Stir in the remaining ingredients, bring to a boil, reduce the heat, cover, and simmer for 45 minutes. Taste and adjust seasonings. Serve hot.

Serves 4 to 6

SUGGESTED MENU
Thick Cabbage Soup
Whole-Grain Pasta with Olive Oil and Herbs (page 164)
Baked Acorn Squash (page 168)
Mixed Green Salad (page 215)
Orange Dessert Crêpes (page 243)

Black Bean Soup

Black bean soup is a Cuban dish traditionally made with lots of meat. But this vegetarian version is not just a pot of beans. What distinguishes it is the sherry and the lemon juice, which give it a nice tartness.

You must remember to soak the beans in advance. The soup can be made a day before serving; store it, covered, in the refrigerator.

Heat the oil over medium heat in a large, heavy-bottomed soup pot or dutch oven and add the onion, celery, and half the garlic. Cook, stirring, until tender, about 5 minutes. Drain the soaked beans and add them to the pot, along with the stock or water, and bring to a boil. Reduce the heat, cover, and simmer 1 hour. Add the remaining garlic and the salt, and continue to simmer another hour, until the beans are tender.

Remove half the beans from the pot and purée in a blender with enough soup liquid to cover. Return the purée to the pot and reheat, stirring, until the soup thickens slightly. Stir in the lemon juice and sherry, and lots of freshly ground pepper. Taste and adjust seasonings, adding salt or garlic if you wish.

Serve garnished with lemon slices and, if desired, chopped hard-boiled egg.

SUGGESTED MENUS
Black Bean Soup
Omelet (pages 120–124)
Mixed Green Salad (page 215)
Pineapple with Kirsch (page 241)
Marinated Vegetables Vinaigrette (page 35)

Black Bean Soup
Brown Rice Salad (page 225)
Oranges Grand Marnier (page 238)

1 tablespoon canola oil
1 onion, chopped
1 rib celery, with leaves, chopped
4 garlic cloves, minced or put through a press
2 cups dried black beans, washed, picked over, and soaked overnight or for several hours
6 cups Vegetable Stock (page 50) or water
2 teaspoons salt, preferably sea salt, or to taste
Juice of 1½ lemons
3 to 4 tablespoons dry sherry, to taste
Freshly ground pepper, to taste
Paper-thin lemon slices
1 hard-boiled egg, chopped (optional)

Lentil Soup

1 tablespoon olive oil

1 onion, chopped

2 to 3 garlic cloves, minced or put through a press

¼ teaspoon chili powder or ⅛ teaspoon cayenne pepper

½ teaspoon ground cumin

2 cups dried lentils, washed

1 carrot, sliced

2 ribs celery, sliced

1 bay leaf

2 quarts water

2 teaspoons salt, preferably sea salt, or to taste

Freshly ground pepper, to taste

The bay leaf is a key herb here; it brings out the best in lentils. This easy recipe makes a rich but not heavy pot of soup.

Heat the oil over medium heat in a heavy-bottomed soup pot or dutch oven and add the onion. Sauté until the onion begins to soften, 3 to 5 minutes, and add half the garlic and the spices. Continue to cook, stirring, until the onion is soft, another 3 to 5 minutes, and stir in the lentils, carrot, celery, bay leaf, and water. Bring to a boil, reduce the heat, cover, and simmer 30 minutes. Add the salt and the remaining garlic, and continue to simmer another 30 minutes to an hour, until the lentils are tender and the broth fragrant. Remove the bay leaf, add pepper to taste, correct the seasoning, and serve.

Serves 4 to 6

SUGGESTED MENU
Lentil Soup
Omelet (pages 120–124)
Spinach Salad (page 216)
Peach Pie (page 255)

Curry-flavored Lentil Soup

This subtle, delicate soup is one of my favorites. Only half the lentils are puréed, so you'll have a thick soup with lots of whole lentils to bite into.

Heat the oil over medium-low heat in a heavy-bottomed soup pot or dutch oven, and sauté the onion until it begins to soften, about 3 minutes. Add half the garlic and the spices and continue to cook another 3 minutes, until the onion is tender. Add the lentils and water or stock and bring to a boil, then cover, reduce the heat, and simmer 30 minutes. Add the remaining garlic, the salt, and the pepper and continue to simmer until the lentils are tender, about 30 minutes to an hour.

Remove half the lentils from the pot and mash or purée in a blender or food processor. Return them to the pot and heat through. Correct the seasoning and serve, garnishing each bowl with chopped fresh cilantro.

Serves 4 to 6

SUGGESTED MENU
Vegetable Platter with Assorted Dips (page 40)
Curry-flavored Lentil Soup
Brown Rice Salad (page 225)
Strawberry and Cassis Sherbet (page 261)

1 tablespoon peanut or canola oil
1 onion, chopped
2 garlic cloves, minced or put
    through a press
¼ teaspoon chili powder
2 teaspoons curry powder (or
    more to taste)
½ teaspoon ground cumin
½ teaspoon ground coriander
2 cups dried lentils, washed
2 quarts water or Vegetable Stock
    (page 50)
2 teaspoons salt, preferably sea
    salt, or to taste
Freshly ground pepper, to taste
3 tablespoons chopped fresh
    cilantro for garnish

Curried Eggplant Soup

Salt, preferably sea salt, to taste

2 pounds (2 large) eggplant, peeled and diced

1 tablespoon canola or peanut oil

1 onion, chopped

2 garlic cloves, minced or put through a press

2 teaspoons freshly grated ginger-root, or ½ teaspoon ground ginger

½ teaspoon crushed cuminseed or ground cumin

½ teaspoon ground coriander

2 teaspoons curry powder, or to taste

6 cups Vegetable Stock (page 50) or water

2 medium potatoes, peeled and diced

Freshly ground pepper, to taste

1 cup low-fat milk or plain, non-fat yogurt

Cayenne pepper to taste

Plain, nonfat yogurt, grated orange peel, and chopped fresh cilantro for garnish

A perfect marriage of eggplant and curry, this pleasing soup is elegant served hot or cold.

Salt the eggplant generously and let sit for 30 minutes. Rinse and set aside.

Heat the oil over medium-low heat in a heavy-bottomed soup pot or dutch oven and sauté the onion gently until it begins to soften, about 3 minutes. Add the garlic, ginger, and spices and continue to cook, stirring, another 30 seconds to a minute, until the spices and garlic begin to stick to the bottom of the pan. Add the eggplant, stock or water, and potatoes, and bring to a boil. Add salt and pepper to taste, reduce the heat, cover, and simmer 1 hour.

Purée the soup in batches in a blender or food processor, or with a hand blender. Return to the pot or a bowl and stir in the milk or yogurt and the cayenne. Adjust the seasoning and chill for several hours, or heat through but do not boil, and serve hot.

Garnish each portion with a dollop of yogurt, a sprinkling of grated orange peel, and chopped cilantro.

Serves 4 to 6

SUGGESTED MENU

Curried Eggplant Soup

Tabouli (page 218) or Curry Salad (page 150)

Bavarian Crème au Café (page 244) or Pears Poached in Red Wine with a Touch of Cassis (page 236)

Blender Gazpacho

There are probably as many recipes for gazpacho as there are villages in Spain. I prefer this one because it's so easy. It's like a liquid salad with an array of garnishes.

This gazpacho keeps for about four days. It's a convenient item to have on hand for a quick, healthy, and delicious meal.

Place the tomatoes in one bowl, all the other vegetables and herbs in another bowl, the lemon juice and olive oil together in another bowl, and the stock in another (or leave the V-8 in its can).

Purée the vegetables in a blender or food processor with the stock, lemon juice, and olive oil, according to the directions for cold blender soups on page xxxix. Pour each batch off into a large container, and then, when all the vegetables have been puréed, stir together well and adjust the seasoning with salt and pepper. For a richer tomato taste, and to thin out to desired consistency, add some V-8, then cover and chill for several hours.

Serve the soup, and pass the garnishes you've selected in separate bowls.

Serves 4 to 6

SUGGESTED MENUS
Blender Gazpacho
Almond–Cheese-stuffed Crêpes (page 127)
Spinach Salad (page 216)
Strawberry and Cassis Sherbet (page 261)

Blender Gazpacho
Omelet (pages 120–124), or Spinach and Onion Quiche
    (page 105), or Black Bean Enchiladas (page 97)
Spinach Salad (page 216)
Peaches Marsala (page 240)

FOR THE SOUP:

4 ripe tomatoes, peeled
2 garlic cloves, peeled
1 small onion, chunked
1 carrot, coarsely chopped
1 cucumber, peeled and coarsely
    chopped
1 green pepper, seeded and quar-
    tered
2 sprigs fresh parsley
¼ cup chopped fresh basil
¼ to ½ cup fresh lemon juice, or
    to taste
3 tablespoons olive oil
3 cups cold Vegetable Stock (page
    50) or V-8 juice
Salt, preferably sea salt, to taste
Freshly ground pepper, to taste
Additional V-8 juice as necessary

FOR THE GARNISH (CHOOSE AS
MANY AS YOU WISH):

1 cup cubed tofu
½ cup grated carrot
¼ cup minced green pepper
¼ cup minced cucumber
1 tomato, chopped
½ cup alfalfa or mung bean
    sprouts
¼ cup sunflower seeds
Plain low-fat yogurt, homemade
    (page 202) or commercial

Chilled Avocado–Tomato Soup

1 quart V-8 juice or tomato juice,
  preferably V-8
1 tomato, peeled and quartered
1 small onion, quartered
1 green pepper, seeded and
  coarsely chopped
2 to 3 ripe avocados, peeled, pitted, and sliced thick
¼ cup fresh lemon juice
Salt, preferably sea salt, to taste
1½ cups plain nonfat yogurt,
  homemade (page 202) or commercial
Sunflower seeds for garnish
  (optional)

This rich soup tastes like a cross between gazpacho and gua-camole. It keeps well in the refrigerator for up to three days. It's been a cooking class favorite for years.

Liquefy all the ingredients except the yogurt and garnish in a blender or food processor until smooth, following the directions for cold blender soups on page xxxix. Stir in 1 cup of the yogurt; chill well.

Serve, topping each bowl with a dollop of yogurt and a sprinkling of sunflower seeds.

Serves 4 to 6

SUGGESTED MENU
Chilled Avocado–Tomato Soup
Black Bean Enchiladas (page 97)
Spinach Salad (page 216)
Oranges Grand Marnier (page 238)

Bulgarian Cucumber Soup

This soup is almost a salad, bursting as it is with cucumbers steeped in a vinaigrettelike marinade with an abundance of dill, and then tempered with creamy yogurt. It's a terrifically refreshing and exciting summer soup.

Combine the lemon juice and vinegar in a 2- or 3-quart bowl. Stir in the garlic, salt, pepper, and dill. Whisk in the olive oil. Add the onion, walnuts, and cucumbers, then toss and let marinate, covered, in the refrigerator, for several hours.

Pour off some of the liquid and add the quart of yogurt. Toss well; add more yogurt, if you desire. Place an ice cube in each soup bowl, ladle in the soup, and serve.

Serves 4 to 6

SUGGESTED MENU
Bulgarian Cucumber Soup
Stuffed Zucchini (page 157)
Mixed Green Salad (page 215)
Strawberry and Cassis Sherbet (page 261)

Juice of 1 large lemon
¼ cup vinegar
1 garlic clove, minced or put
    through a press
½ teaspoon salt, preferably sea salt
¼ teaspoon freshly ground pepper
¼ cup chopped fresh dill
2 tablespoons olive oil
1 Bermuda onion, thinly sliced
¼ cup finely chopped walnuts
3 cucumbers, peeled, seeded, and
    diced
1 quart or more plain low-fat
    yogurt, homemade (page 202)
    or commercial
6 ice cubes

Turkish Cucumber Soup

1 to 1½ quarts plain nonfat yogurt, homemade (page 202) or commercial

3 cucumbers, peeled, seeded, and coarsely chopped

Juice and grated rind of 1 or 2 lemons, to taste

1 tablespoon chopped fresh dill

1 to 2 garlic cloves, to taste

1 teaspoon dill seeds (optional)

1 teaspoon chopped fresh mint leaves, plus additional for garnish

½ teaspoon salt, preferably sea salt, or more if necessary

Paper-thin lemon and cucumber slices for garnish

A cooling, salady soup, high in protein and very easy to make. This differs from the Bulgarian cucumber soup in that all of the ingredients are liquefied.

Liquefy all the ingredients except the garnishes in a blender or food processor until smooth, following the directions for cold blender soups on page xxxix.

Correct the seasoning, then chill and serve garnished with mint, lemon slices, and cucumber slices.

Serves 4 to 6

SUGGESTED MENUS
Turkish Cucumber Soup
Hummus (page 21)
Tabouli (page 218)
Light Cheesecake (page 250)

Turkish Cucumber Soup
Curry Salad (page 150)
Watermelon–Fruit Extravaganza (page 239)

Purée of Strawberry Soup

This is a sweet and refreshing summer soup. It's a wonderful starter for a brunch or luncheon, and even makes a good dessert. It can be made a day in advance.

Set aside 6 of the strawberries and slice, for garnish. Purée the rest in a blender or food processor with the orange juice, mint, cinnamon, and allspice. Taste for sweetness, and if you wish add a little honey.

Pour the strawberry purée into a bowl or other nonreactive container and add the grated lemon peel, lemon or lime juice, and buttermilk or yogurt; stir together well. Taste and add more lemon or lime juice, if desired. Chill for a few hours or serve immediately, garnished with the reserved sliced strawberries, and with mint leaves and thin slices of lemon or lime.

Note: An exciting way to serve this is to cut cantaloupes in half, scoop out some of the fruit, scallop the edges, and serve the strawberry soup in the cantaloupe "bowls." You can serve the scooped-out melon along with the soup, or as part of the dessert. This will make a more filling soup.

Serves 4 to 6

SUGGESTED MENU
Purée of Strawberry Soup
Cheese Soufflé (page 109)
Mixed Green Salad (page 215)
Peaches Marsala (page 240)

2 pint boxes fresh strawberries in season, washed and stemmed

1½ cups freshly squeezed orange juice

¼ cup fresh mint leaves

⅛ teaspoon ground cinnamon

⅛ teaspoon ground allspice

Mild honey to taste (optional)

1 teaspoon grated lemon peel

2 tablespoons fresh lemon or lime juice, to taste

2 cups buttermilk or plain, nonfat yogurt

Thin slices of strawberries, fresh mint leaves, and lemon or lime sliced for garnish

Main Dishes

When I was once in Brazil, where there are few vegetarians, I gave a dinner party. Later I found out that the guests had come reluctantly, expecting bread and water, or at best boiled vegetables, beans, and rice. Imagine their surprise when they were served a glorious ratatouille and big, beautiful slices of savory spinach and onion quiche.

Actually, I haven't had to try hard to avoid the predictable repertoire of typically vegetarian dishes, that "hair shirt" fare that seems to apologize for its absence of meat by masking vegetables with thick sauces and cheese or by employing meat "substitutes." You won't find that every dish here tastes like tamari, nor will every one contain nuts and raisins.

There's something for everybody in this chapter. When I give a dinner party and don't know all of my guests well, and certainly when I cater, I choose dishes that I know everyone will like. Some people are averse to sweet foods in a main dish, for instance, or don't like nuts or certain spices like caraway or ginger. So, when I suspect that there might be a few of these people at my table, I avoid dishes like fruited baked beans with chutney.

The most reliable dishes for skeptical dinner guests and large crowds are those featuring cheese or eggs (there are at least twenty here) like quiches, soufflés, omelets, and crêpes; or Italian and Mexican food—eggplant Parmesan, lasagne, or black bean enchiladas.

If you or your guests prefer light dishes, there are plenty to choose from: Chinese and Japanese vegetable dishes with marvelous sauces, Indian curries with chutneys and raitas, satiny couscous with vegetables.

Some of these entrées are visually quite spectacular; they make great party fare. Soufflés puff up dramatically, as does spanokopita, the Greek spinach strudel, which also bakes to the most beautiful golden brown. Vegetable shish kebab displays a kaleidoscope of colors, the vegetables skewered over saffron-colored rice. Vegetable paella, especially when served in a wok or paella pan, is another gorgeous one, with bright green peas, red peppers, and black olives on saffron rice.

Some entrées here are perfect for cold winter nights— bean dishes, crêpes with rich fillings, grain dishes. Airy soufflés, curries, marinades, and stir-fries are good in the summertime. Complement rich soups with light main dishes, and prepare something more substantial if you plan to serve a light soup or starter, or if the main dish is your only course.

Black Bean Enchiladas

Black bean enchiladas are one of my favorites for entertaining a crowd; I often make them for catered dinners. The first of the casserole-type dishes in this section, they are a perfect model for my first casserole rule, which is this: If every part of a casserole tastes great alone, the casserole will be smashing.

In this recipe we start with a very tasty pot of beans, season it with chili powder and cumin, and use top-quality Cheddar cheese. The tortillas are a far cry from the ordinary bland enchilada tortillas; these are first softened in a spicy tomato sauce. Delicious!

My other casserole rule is to start skimpy and end generous. That is, don't be overenthusiastic in the beginning with your cheese and black bean filling, or you'll run out of it before you've filled the last enchiladas. Remember that you'll begin serving from the top. That's the part everyone will see, and it should look lavish.

You'll have to start thinking about this dish a bit in advance, as you first have to soak and cook the beans. The cooked beans will last up to three days in the refrigerator. Putting the enchiladas together will go smoothly if you are organized: Have your ingredients next to each other in bowls, the beans in the pan, and the tortillas on their paper towels. As with any casserole, this stage is "assembly line" work, and the less distance you and your hands have to move, the better it will go.

If you make the enchiladas a day in advance, be sure to cover them well, or they will dry out. After baking, keep them well covered until you're ready to serve.

Tortillas may be frozen, wrapped in plastic. Even if they're kept for several weeks, they will be revitalized when you prepare them for the enchiladas.

Soak the beans in 6 cups water overnight, or for several hours. Drain.

Heat 1 tablespoon of the oil over medium heat in a large, heavy-bottomed soup pot or dutch oven and sauté

FOR THE BLACK BEANS:

2 cups dried black beans, washed

12 cups water, in all

2 tablespoons canola oil or vegetable oil

1 onion, chopped

4 garlic cloves, or more to taste, minced or put through a press

2 to 3 teaspoons salt, preferably sea salt, to taste

2 tablespoons chopped fresh cilantro

1 tablespoon cumin powder, or to taste

1 tablespoon chili powder, or to taste

FOR THE ENCHILADAS:

Approximately 1 tablespoon canola oil or vegetable oil

Salt, cumin, and chili powder as needed

1½ cups puréed tomato or canned tomato sauce

18 corn tortillas

6 ounces medium or sharp Cheddar cheese, grated (about 1½ cups grated)

½ to ¾ cup very finely minced onion (optional)

2 tablespoons chopped fresh cilantro

the chopped onion until it is tender, about 5 minutes. Add half the garlic and continue to cook for another minute, until the garlic begins to color. Add the beans and 6 cups of fresh water and bring to a boil. Reduce the heat, cover, and simmer 1 hour. Add the remaining garlic, the salt, and the cilantro, cover, and simmer for another hour, until the beans are soft and their liquid is thick and soupy. Taste and adjust salt. Remove from the heat.

Drain off about half the liquid from the beans, reserving it in a separate bowl to use later for moistening the beans, should they dry out. Mash half the beans coarsely in a food processor or with a potato masher. Don't purée them, however. You want texture. Stir the mashed beans back into the pot.

Heat the remaining tablespoon of oil over medium heat in a large, heavy-bottomed nonstick frying pan and add the cumin and chili powder. Cook, stirring, over medium heat, for about a minute, until the spices begin to sizzle, turn the heat to medium-high, and add the beans (this can be done in batches, in which case cook the spices in batches as well). Fry the beans, stirring and mashing often, until they thicken and begin to smell aromatic and get crusty on the bottom. Stir up the crust each time it forms, mixing it in with the beans. Cook for about 15 minutes. The beans should be thick but not dry. Add a small amount of liquid you saved from the beans if they seem too dry. Taste the refried beans and adjust the salt.

You are now ready to start assembling the enchiladas.

In a heavy-bottomed skillet, heat ½ teaspoon of oil over medium heat and add a pinch each of salt, cumin, and chili powder. Add about 3 tablespoons tomato purée, and as soon as it bubbles, take a couple of tortillas at a time and heat them through quickly, turning once. The tortillas should be soft and pliable, but if you saturate them too much with the tomato purée they'll fall apart when you try to manipulate them. Set them aside on paper towels and continue until all the tortillas have been taken care of, adding oil, tomato sauce, and seasonings as needed (this step is one of the keys to flavorful enchiladas.)

Set aside 1⅓ cups of refried black beans, ½ cup of the grated cheese, and ¼ cup of the finely minced onion.

Oil a large (3-quart) baking dish. Preheat the oven to 350 degrees. To assemble the enchiladas, spread a large spoonful of black beans over each tortilla, then a layer of grated Cheddar and a thin layer of minced onion. Roll up and place, seam side down, in the baking dish. (You can seal the enchilada by "pasting" it with black bean sauce if the tortilla won't stay closed.) When all the tortillas have been filled, pour on the reserved black bean sauce and sprinkle with the remaining cheese and onions.

If you fill up the pan and need to make a second layer of enchiladas, top the first layer with some of the reserved sauce, cheese, and onion (save some for the second layer); oil some foil on both sides and place it on top of the first layer, then proceed with the second layer, topping it with the remaining sauce, cheese, and onion.

Cover the top of the dish tightly with foil and bake in the preheated oven for 30 minutes, until the cheese is bubbling. Remove the foil, garnish with the chopped cilantro, and serve, passing a bowl of salsa for those who like their Mexican food more picante.

Note: The enchiladas become very soft when they bake, and you will need to use two spatulas to prevent them from falling apart when you serve. If they should fall apart, don't worry. Your guests, already overwhelmed by the aroma, will be impatient to cut into them and won't even notice.

Serves 6

MENU SUGGESTIONS

Hors d'oeuvres: Guacamole (page 221) with tortilla chips, Marinated Vegetables Vinaigrette (page 35)

Soups: Sopa de Ajo (page 64), Chilled Avocado–Tomato (page 90), or Blender Gazpacho (page 89)

Salads: Spinach (page 216), Spinach and Citrus (page 227), or Guacamole (page 221)

Desserts: Oranges Grand Marnier (page 238), Pineapple with Kirsch (page 241)

Extraordinary Chalupas

2 cups dried black beans, washed and picked over

12 cups water, in all

2 tablespoons canola oil

1 onion, chopped

5 garlic cloves, or more to taste, minced or put through a press

2 to 3 teaspoons salt, preferably sea salt, or more as necessary

2 tablespoons chopped cilantro

1 tablespoon plus ¼ teaspoon ground cumin

1 tablespoon plus ¼ teaspoon chili powder

1 or 2 avocados, depending on size

1 medium-size tomato

1 additional small garlic clove, minced or put through a press

Juice of 1 large lemon

½ cup low-fat ricotta

½ cup plain yogurt, homemade (page 202) or commercial

1 quart canola oil, vegetable oil, or peanut oil if deep-frying the tortillas

1 dozen corn tortillas or prepared chalupa crisps

4 ounces Cheddar cheese, grated

2 cups sprouts (alfalfa, mung bean, or lentil, or a mixture) or shredded lettuce

1½ cups Fresh Tomato Salsa (page 201)

½ cup coarsely chopped toasted almonds

The standard Tex-Mex chalupa consists of a crisp tortilla, refried pinto beans, shredded iceberg lettuce, guacamole, grated longhorn cheese, and chopped tomatoes. These "extraordinary" chalupas are a departure from the Tex-Mex variety. They consist of layer upon layer of delight, with some special surprises: I use black beans, sprouts doused with vinaigrette, good Cheddar cheese, yogurt enriched with ricotta, and—to set off the luscious guacamole and tomatoes—crunchy roasted almonds.

These chalupas are always a great hit at large catered events. Scores of people move through the buffet lines, remarking that they've never seen some of these foods before, "but they sure are good, and they sure are pretty!"

If you don't want to make your own tortilla crisps, chalupa shells are available in many supermarkets.

Soak the beans in 6 cups water overnight, or for several hours. Drain.

Heat 1 tablespoon of the oil over medium heat in a large, heavy-bottomed soup pot or dutch oven and sauté the chopped onion until it is tender, about 5 minutes. Add half the garlic and continue to cook for another minute, until it begins to color. Add the beans and 6 cups of fresh water and bring to a boil. Reduce the heat, cover, and simmer 1 hour. Add the remaining garlic, the salt, and the cilantro, cover, and simmer for another hour, until the beans are soft and their liquid is thick and soupy. Taste and adjust salt. Remove from the heat.

Drain off about ⅔ of the liquid from the beans, retaining it in a separate bowl to use later for moistening the beans should they dry out. Mash half the beans coarsely in a food processor or with a potato masher. Don't purée them, however; you want texture. Stir the mashed beans back into the pot.

Heat the remaining tablespoon of oil over medium heat in a large, heavy-bottomed nonstick frying pan and add 1 tablespoon each of the cumin and chili powder. Cook, stirring over medium heat, for about a minute, until the spices begin to sizzle, turn the heat to medium-high, and add the beans (this can be done in batches, in which case cook the spices in batches as well). Fry the beans, stirring and mashing often, until they thicken and begin to get aromatic and crusty on the bottom. Stir up the crust each time it forms, and mix in with the beans. Cook for about 15 minutes. The beans should be thick but not dry. Add a small amount of liquid you saved from the beans if they seem too dry. Taste the refried beans and adjust the salt. Set aside.

In a separate bowl, peel, seed, and mash the avocados; peel the tomato and mash it with the avocado. Add the small clove of garlic. Season with the lemon juice, salt to taste, and part or all of the remaining cumin and chili powder, to taste; set this guacamole aside.

Whip the ricotta in a blender, with a mixer, or with a whisk, and stir in the yogurt. (Don't use the blender or mixer for this or the mixture will become too runny.) Set aside.

Have all the ingredients, in their separate bowls, within easy reach.

If you are making your own chalupa crisps, heat 1 quart canola oil, vegetable oil, or peanut oil to 370 degrees in a wok or a large saucepan and deep-fry the tortillas in batches until golden. Drain on paper towels in a colander.

Now assemble your chalupas. Spread a spoonful of black beans over each tortilla crisp. Top this with a layer of the yogurt-ricotta mixture, then a layer of the guacamole. Over this sprinkle some grated Cheddar cheese, and top with the sprouts or lettuce. Next spoon on some salsa, and sprinkle on some chopped toasted almonds.

Serves 6
continued

MENU SUGGESTIONS
Hors d'Oeuvres: Stuffed Mushrooms (page 28)
Soups: Sopa de Ajo (page 64), Tortilla Soup (page 60)
Salads: Spinach (page 216), Spinach and Citrus (page 227)
Desserts: Fresh fruit (page 234), Oranges Grand Marnier
    (page 238), or Strawberry and Cassis Sherbet (page 261)

Whole-Wheat Pie Crust

1 cup whole-wheat pastry flour
½ cup unbleached white flour
½ cup wheat germ (or use 1 cup
    unbleached white flour in all)
½ teaspoon salt, preferably sea salt
¼ pound (1 stick) plus 2 table-
    spoons cold butter
3 to 4 tablespoons ice-cold water,
    or as needed

You'll find the crust here is a vast improvement over the usual bland pie pastry—it has a buttery, nutty taste that is truly scrumptious. It can be made up to three days in advance and refrigerated, or it can be frozen (a frozen crust can go directly into the oven for prebaking). This recipe will make two 9-inch crusts, so you can use one now and freeze the other for a later date. It will also make one 12- to 14-inch crust, for use in such recipes as tomato quiche.

Making the crust by hand:

In a large bowl, combine the flours, wheat germ, and salt. Quickly cut in the butter and roll briskly between the palms of your hands to make sure that the butter is evenly distributed. Add the water, a tablespoon at a time, and blend with a fork until you can gather the dough into a mass. Divide evenly into 2 balls.

Place a ball of dough on a piece of lightly floured waxed paper. Press it down with your hand and place another piece of lightly floured paper on top. Roll the dough out with a rolling pin; peel off the top paper, turn the crust into a buttered pie plate, and then peel off the other paper. Press the dough into the pie pan and pinch a pretty scalloped edge around the rim. Repeat with the other ball of dough; then refrigerate both crusts for 2 hours, covered with plastic wrap, or freeze (to freeze, cover with plastic and place in plastic bags or wrap in foil).

Making the crust with a food processor:

The action of the food processor makes the dough very moist, and it's easier to press it into the pie pan than roll out, as it tends to stick to the waxed paper. Place the flours, wheat germ, and salt in the container of your food processor, fitted with the steel blade. Flick on 4 times to combine the ingredients. Cut the butter into tablespoon-sized pats and place in the bowl. Pulse on and off 10 times. With the machine running, add the water a tablespoon at a time. As soon as the dough comes together on the blade of the machine, stop the machine and remove the dough. Divide into 2 balls. Butter a piepan and press one ball flat between the palms of your hands. Place in the center of the pie pan, and then, working from the center out, press out the dough. Push from the heel of your palm out toward your fingertips, and keep spreading out the dough, turning the pan with your other hand, so that it spreads up the sides of the pan evenly all the way around. Pinch a pretty scalloped edge around the rim. Repeat with the other ball of dough; refrigerate or freeze as described above.

Completing both methods:

Preheat the oven to 350 degrees. Pierce the bottom of each crust with a fork or weigh it down with dried beans on a piece of foil (to keep it from buckling). Prebake in the preheated oven for 7 minutes; cool before filling.

Two 9-inch crusts or one 12- to 14-inch crust

Yeasted Olive Oil Pastry

1 teaspoon active dry yeast

5 tablespoons lukewarm water

1 large egg, at room temperature

3 tablespoons olive oil

1 scant cup whole-wheat pastry flour

1 scant cup unbleached white flour

½ to ¾ teaspoon salt (depending on your taste for salt)

This is an extremely easy-to-work-with, low-fat crust. It's perfect for savory tortes, like the deep-dish vegetable torte.

Dissolve the yeast in the water and let sit 5 to 10 minutes. Beat in the egg and the olive oil. Combine the flours and salt, and stir in (this can be done in an electric mixer; combine the ingredients using the paddle, then switch to the kneading hook). Work the dough until it comes together in a cohesive mass, knead for a few minutes, and shape the dough into a ball. Place in a lightly oiled bowl, cover with plastic wrap, and let rise in a warm spot for 2 hours or a little longer. It will not rise too much, but it will expand and soften.

When the pastry has risen and softened, punch it down gently and divide into 2 unequal pieces for a torte, with 1 piece just slightly smaller than the other. Shape each piece into a ball, cover with plastic wrap, and let rest 10 minutes. Butter or oil a 10- to 12-inch tart pan or springform pan, and roll out the dough to fit the dish. Roll it very thin, about ⅛ inch thick, and line the dish. Cover loosely with a dish towel and let rest 20 to 30 minutes. Don't roll out the top piece of dough until you have filled the torte.

Fill with the filling of your choice. Roll out the top piece of dough and place over the filling. Join the edges. Bake at 400 degrees, following specific recipe instructions in the filling recipes for timing.

One 10- or 12-inch double crust

Spinach and Onion Quiche

Quiche is essentially a custard flavored with cheese. But traditional quiche is very rich, calling for cream, butter, and eggs. So instead of cream I use a combination of milk and spray-dried milk. The "enriched milk" makes a considerable difference in the calorie count at virtually no expense to flavor or texture.

Because the crust can be made far in advance and the filling only takes about 5 minutes to put together, quiche is an excellent dish to make when you are short on time. You needn't use spinach and onions—any blanched vegetable will do. Sautéed mushrooms work well, too. Combining sautéed onions with any vegetable you use will add a distinctive flavor and an appealing texture. The important ingredient here is the cheese, which is always Swiss or French Gruyère, or a combination of Gruyère and Emmenthaler; I sharpen it with a little Parmesan.

Since the use of enriched milk makes this a relatively light dish, a hearty soup such as Soupe au Pistou (page 56) or a rich Ratatouille (page 52) would be a suitable accompaniment, along with a green salad or marinated vegetables. For dessert, I would choose fruit, either fresh or poached in wine; certainly avoid anything made with eggs.

Quiches will keep for 3 or 4 days in the refrigerator and can be frozen for a couple of months.

½ recipe Whole-Wheat Pie Crust (page 102)
10 ounces fresh spinach, stemmed and washed carefully
½ cup minced onion
1 tablespoon butter or olive oil
3 large eggs, at room temperature
1 cup milk enriched with 2 tablespoons spray-dried milk (do this in a blender)
¼ teaspoon salt, preferably sea salt
Freshly ground pepper, to taste
Dash of Worcestershire sauce
Pinch of freshly grated nutmeg
1 cup grated Gruyère cheese or half Gruyère and half Emmenthaler
¼ cup freshly grated Parmesan cheese

Prepare a 9-inch pie shell as directed in the pie crust recipe; after you prebake it for 7 minutes, set it aside and let it cool.

Blanch the spinach by plunging it into boiling water for 10 to 15 seconds, then drain it and run it under cold water. Squeeze out the liquid by twisting the spinach in a towel; then chop it into fine pieces.

Sauté the onion in the butter or oil until crisp-tender; set aside.

Beat the eggs and blend with the milk, then beat in the salt, pepper, Worcestershire, and nutmeg.

continued

In a large bowl, toss together the onion, spinach, and the cheeses. Spread half the mixture over the bottom of the prepared pie shell. Pour the egg-milk mixture over, and top with the remaining cheese mixture.

Bake at 350 degrees for 30 to 40 minutes, or until firm to the touch. Let cool for 10 minutes before serving.

Serves 6

MENU SUGGESTIONS
See the suggestions at the beginning of this recipe; other good soups for accompaniment would be Leek Soup (page 69) or Blender Gazpacho (page 89).

Asparagus Quiche

For the spinach, substitute 1 cup 1-inch pieces of asparagus steamed briefly.

Mushroom Quiche

Substitute 1 cup sliced mushrooms for the spinach. Sauté the mushrooms, and a clove of minced garlic if you wish, with the minced onion in the butter or olive oil until tender. Toss together with the cheeses and proceed with the recipe.

Fresh Herb Quiche

For the spinach, substitute 1 cup minced fresh herbs, such as parsley, fennel, chives, and thyme.

Tomato Quiche

This satisfying dish is also good cold. The crust and the tomato part of the filling can be done in advance. Cook the tomato mixture until it is dry and thick or your quiche will be runny.

Chop two of the peeled tomatoes; you should have 2 cups. (Add 1 more tomato if you fall short.) Slice the remaining tomatoes and set aside.

Heat the olive oil in a skillet over medium heat and add the onion. Sauté, stirring, until the onion is tender, about 5 minutes. Add the garlic and stir for about 30 seconds. Add the chopped tomatoes, thyme, and a little salt and pepper; cover and simmer for 10 minutes. Mash the tomatoes with the back of a spoon, and cook uncovered over low heat until the mixture thickens and begins to stick to the pan, about 20 to 30 minutes. Set aside to cool.

Preheat the oven to 350 degrees.

Beat together the eggs, milk, and ½ teaspoon salt. Stir in the grated cheeses and the cooled tomato mixture.

Line the prebaked pie crust with the sliced tomatoes, then pour in the cheese, milk, and egg mixture.

Bake for 30 to 45 minutes, until a knife inserted in the center comes out clean. Remove from the oven and allow to sit for 20 to 30 minutes before serving.

Serves 6

4 to 5 large ripe tomatoes, peeled
1 tablespoon olive oil
1 onion, finely chopped
2 large garlic cloves, minced or put through a press
1 teaspoon fresh thyme leaves, or ½ teaspoon dried thyme
Salt, preferably sea salt
Freshly ground pepper, to taste
4 eggs, beaten
1 cup milk, enriched with 3 tablespoons spray-dried milk
½ cup freshly grated Parmesan cheese
1 cup (4 ounces) grated Gruyère cheese
One 12- or 14-inch Whole-Wheat Pie Crust (page 102), prebaked for 5 minutes

MENU SUGGESTIONS
Soups: Vichyssoise (page 76), Purée of Asparagus (page 68)
Salads: Mixed Green (page 215), Spinach (page 216), Salade Niçoise (page 218), or Green Bean, Almond, and Mushroom (page 224)
Desserts: Fresh fruit (page 234), Bananas Poached in White Wine (page 255), Oranges Grand Marnier (page 238), or Peaches Marsala (page 240)

Deep-dish Vegetable Torte

1 recipe Yeasted Olive Oil Pastry
  (page 104)
½ cup diagonally sliced or matchstick-cut carrots, steamed until
  just tender, about 5 to 8 minutes
1 cup broccoli florets, steamed until
  just tender, about 5 minutes
1 cup cauliflower florets, steamed
  until just tender, about 5 minutes
½ cup fresh peas, steamed until
  just tender (about 5 minutes),
  or thawed frozen peas
1 cup shredded cabbage, steamed
  until just tender, about 3 minutes
1 recipe Béchamel (page 200)
1 tablespoon olive oil
1 onion, chopped
1 cup sliced fresh mushrooms
Salt, preferably sea salt, to taste
2 large garlic cloves, minced or
  put through a press
2 tablespoons dry white wine
1 teaspoon fresh thyme leaves, or
  ½ teaspoon dried thyme
1 teaspoon chopped fresh rosemary, or ½ teaspoon crumbled
  dried rosemary
1 cup cooked pinto or borlotti
  beans (may use canned),
  (optional)
1 tablespoon chopped fresh sage
¼ cup chopped fresh parsley
Freshly ground pepper, to taste

A perennially popular dish. You can use whatever vegetables you have on hand for this, and it's good hot or at room temperature. As always, the crust can be made well in advance.

Prepare the crust, and while it is rising, prepare the filling. Steam the vegetables and transfer to a large bowl. Make the béchamel.

Preheat the oven to 400 degrees. Oil a 10- or 12-inch tart pan.

Heat the oil over medium heat in a large, heavy-bottomed nonstick skillet and add the onion. Sauté the onion until just about tender, about 5 minutes, and add the mushrooms and a little salt. Cook, stirring, until the mushrooms begin to release liquid, and add the garlic, white wine, thyme, and rosemary. Cook, stirring, for another 5 minutes, until the mushrooms are tender and aromatic. Remove from the heat.

Toss all the steamed and sautéed vegetables with the beans, sage, parsley, and béchamel. Salt and pepper lightly.

Roll out ⅔ of the pie crust and line your tart pan. Fill with the vegetable mixture. Roll out the remaining crust and lay over the top. Crimp the edges of the top and bottom crusts together, and pierce the top in several places with a knife.

Bake 40 minutes in the preheated oven. Remove from the heat and serve hot, warm, or at room temperature.

Serves 6

Asparagus or Broccoli Deep-dish Pie

Instead of the mixed vegetables used in the previous recipe, use 4 cups chopped, steamed asparagus or broccoli. Make the béchamel and stir in ½ cup Gruyère cheese as a last step before mixing with the vegetables.

MENU SUGGESTIONS
Soups: Vichyssoise (page 76), Potato–Cheese (page 71), or
    Curried Eggplant (page 88)
Salads: Mixed Green (page 215), Salade Niçoise (page 218),
    Marinated Vegetables Vinaigrette (page 35), or Avocado
    and Citrus (page 217)
Desserts: Fresh fruit (page 234), Bavarian Crème au Café
    (page 244), or Apricot Soufflé (page 247)

Cheese Soufflé

The prospect of making a soufflé always intimidated me until I gathered my courage and found out how simple it is. You start off with a classic sauce base enriched with egg yolks. Then all you do is beat the egg whites and fold them into the sauce with the cheese, or cheese and vegetables, or fruit (in the case of a dessert soufflé).

This cheese soufflé is a delightful main course. It makes a perfect luncheon or brunch dish, too. Avoid (obviously) soups and desserts that call for eggs.

A soufflé looks spectacular when it comes out of the oven. You must have a clear idea of when you are going to eat it, so you can start baking it 35 to 40 minutes beforehand. However, you can do the sauce base as far ahead as one or two days, and if you like you can even have the complete soufflé mixture made up to two hours before baking. Try to remember to take the eggs out of the refrigerator a few hours before you make the soufflé, because they need to be at room temperature for the whites to set right; if you forget, place them in a bowl of warm water for a few minutes. If the soufflé is done

continued

3 tablespoons butter

3 tablespoons unbleached white
   flour

1½ cups hot milk

Salt, preferably sea salt

⅛ teaspoon freshly ground pepper

Pinch of freshly grated nutmeg

6 eggs, at room temperature, plus
   2 egg whites

¼ teaspoon cream of tartar

1½ cups grated Gruyère cheese

¼ cup freshly grated Parmesan
   cheese, plus 2 tablespoons for
   soufflé dish

and your guests are not yet ready for it, turn off the oven and leave the door shut. This will delay the falling; your soufflé should still be dramatically puffed up when you serve it.

You will need a medium-sized, heavy-bottomed saucepan, a whisk, and a wooden spoon for the sauce, and another saucepan to heat the milk in. Have ready a 3-quart bowl and a clean dry whisk or egg beater for the egg whites, and a buttered 2-quart soufflé dish with a collar (see directions).

In a medium saucepan, heat the butter and stir in the flour to make a roux. Cook for a few minutes over low heat, stirring with a wooden spoon; allow the roux to bubble but not to brown. Meanwhile, heat the milk, and when it is hot slowly stir it into the roux, using a whisk. Stir quickly and thoroughly to mix well, then continue to stir over moderate heat until the very thick sauce comes to a boil; cook for 1 minute, stirring and bringing the sauce up from the bottom and sides of the pan. (Don't be alarmed by the thickness of the sauce; you're about to thin it out with egg yolks.) Remove the saucepan from the heat and stir in 1 teaspoon salt, the pepper, and the nutmeg.

Now separate the eggs, one by one, stirring each egg yolk into the sauce and adding each white to a mixing bowl containing the 2 extra whites; set the sauce aside. (At this point the sauce may be refrigerated for 1 or 2 days, tightly covered. If you do refrigerate the sauce base beforehand, reheat it gently in a double boiler before folding in the egg whites.)

Beat the egg whites, which should be at room temperature, until they begin to foam. Add the cream of tartar and a pinch of salt and continue beating until the egg whites are satiny and form peaks when lifted with the spatula or beater. Do not overbeat; the whites should remain smooth. Now stir ¼ of the egg whites into the sauce base with a spatula; this will lighten up the sauce so the folding procedure will be easier. Pour the sauce base into the middle of the bowl of egg whites. Fold the egg whites into the sauce with your spatula by gently scooping the sauce from the middle of the bowl, under the egg whites to the side of the bowl, and up over the egg whites back to the middle of the bowl. With each fold, sprinkle in a handful of the Gruyère and Parmesan cheeses and give the bowl a quarter turn, making sure you reserve 2 tablespoons of the Parmesan; continue this folding process until the mixture is homogenous. You should work rapidly yet lightly, and the process should take no more than a minute.

Prepare your soufflé dish. Butter it and dust it with 2 tablespoons Parmesan. Using waxed paper or aluminum foil, make a collar by wrapping a cylinder of the paper around the dish and taping or tying it; the cylinder should extend 2 to 3 inches above the edge of the soufflé dish. Now gently spoon in the soufflé mixture. At this point you may set the mixture aside for up to 2 hours, inverting a large bowl over it or placing a piece of waxed paper or foil over the top of the collar, or you may bake it.

Preheat the oven to 375 degrees.

Bake the soufflé for 35 to 40 minutes. If you wish—or dare—stick a thin skewer in to see if it's done. If the skewer comes out nearly clear, and the top of the soufflé is golden, the soufflé is done. If it comes out very wet, bake for another 5 to 7 minutes. Remove from the oven, detach the collar, and serve immediately.

Serves 6

Cheese Soufflé with Vegetables

Fold in 1 or 2 cups of blanched chopped vegetables—asparagus, spinach, broccoli, green beans—along with the cheese.

MENU SUGGESTIONS
Soups: Cream of Raw and Cooked Mushroom (page 62), Leek (page 69), or Stracciatella (page 54)
Salads: Mixed Green (page 215), Spinach (page 216), or Watercress and Mushroom (page 226)
Desserts: Mediterranean Fruit Compote (page 237) or Bananas Poached in White Wine (page 235)

Poached Eggs en Soufflé

This is a dramatic dish for a brunch, luncheon, or dinner. Like a surprise ball, it reveals one delight after another on the inside. Most of the steps can be done a day or two ahead of time. The eggs can be poached in advance—in fact, they must be—and kept refrigerated in a bowl of cold water; the sauce base for the soufflé and the creamed spinach can be made a day or two in advance and refrigerated, covered (warm the sauce through before folding in the beaten egg whites). If you do all these things ahead of time, all you will have to do before the final assembly is to whip the egg whites and fold them into the sauce base with the cheese. These conveniences are especially helpful if you are serving this for brunch; they will allow you a few more hours of sleep.

Once assembled, like other soufflés, this can sit up to two hours before being baked, but will fall if not served right away after being baked. The first time I made this dish, for a large brunch, the biggest challenge was poaching the eggs. I went through several dozen before I got the twenty or so that I needed. The biggest problem was that the eggs would stick to the pan and tear when I tried to remove them, a problem I solved by buttering the surface of my pan generously. I've tried to use an egg poacher in the preparation of this dish, but find it unsatisfactory because the top surface of the poached egg is so thin that it breaks easily and the yolk runs out. Here is what I've found to be the easiest method for poaching eggs:

Butter a large frying pan and fill it with water 2 to 3 inches deep. Bring to a boil and add 2 tablespoons vinegar (this helps to set the eggs), then reduce the heat so the water simmers very gently.

Break an egg into a tea cup. Lower the cup into the water and let it sit there for 15 seconds, then carefully tilt the cup, holding it right above the water, and let the egg slide into the simmering water.

For regular poached eggs you would cook the eggs for 4

minutes before removing from the water with a slotted spoon. Place immediately in cold water to stop the cooking and wash off the vinegar. For the poached eggs in this dish, though, cook only 3 to 3½ minutes, as they will heat through again when baked.

Note the order in which you put each egg in the water so you can take them out in order.

Don't worry if the cooked whites of your eggs are irregular and look messy. Trim them down with a sharp knife after they have cooled; remember that they will be hidden in a puffed, golden soufflé.

Prepare the spinach. If you are using fresh spinach, wash, remove the stems, and blanch the leaves in boiling salted water. Drain, squeeze out excess water, and chop. If you are using frozen spinach, allow to thaw, squeeze out excess water, and then chop. Heat the butter or olive oil over medium-low heat in a heavy saucepan or skillet and sauté the green onions or shallots until tender. Stir in the spinach and toss to mix; sprinkle in the flour and toss again. Cook for about 2 minutes, then add salt and pepper to taste and a little freshly grated nutmeg. Stir in the milk and cook, stirring, for about 2 minutes over low heat. The spinach should be creamy but should hold its shape in a spoon. If it begins to dry out, thin it out with a little more milk. Correct the seasonings and remove from the heat.

Make a soufflé mixture, using the same procedure as for Cheese Soufflé (page 109), beginning with the making of the roux and continuing through the folding of the cheese into the soufflé mixture—but this time set aside 3 tablespoons of the cheese.

Preheat the oven to 375 degrees; butter a flat 2-quart oblong baking or gratin dish.

Carefully remove the poached eggs from the cold water with a slotted spoon or your hands and drain on a kitchen towel. Arrange the toasted bread in rows in the baking dish. Place a mound of creamed spinach—approximately 1 heaped tablespoon—on each piece of bread. Make a depression with the back of a spoon in each mound of

continued

FOR THE EGGS AND CREAMED SPINACH:

2 pounds fresh or 2 packages (10 or 12 ounces each) thawed frozen spinach

2 teaspoons butter or olive oil

2 tablespoons minced green onions, both white part and green, or shallots

1 tablespoon unbleached white flour

Salt, preferably sea salt, to taste

Freshly ground pepper, to taste

Freshly grated nutmeg, to taste

½ cup low-fat milk (or more as needed)

6 eggs, poached as described in the instructions and chilled in cold water

Six 3-inch rounds or halved slices toasted whole-wheat bread (Mixed Grains Bread on page 3 is great)

FOR THE SOUFFLÉ:

2 tablespoons butter

2½ tablespoons unbleached white flour

1 cup hot milk

4 eggs, at room temperature, plus 1 egg white

Salt, preferably sea salt, to taste

Freshly ground pepper, to taste

Pinch of freshly grated nutmeg

¼ teaspoon cream of tartar

¾ cup grated Gruyère cheese

FOR THE GARNISH:

Chopped fresh parsley

spinach and carefully place a poached egg on top. Spoon the soufflé mixture over all, filling up the entire baking dish and mounding it over the poached eggs. Top each mound with a bit of the remaining 3 tablespoons cheese.

Bake for 25 to 30 minutes, until the soufflé is puffed and beginning to brown. Remove from the oven, garnish with chopped fresh parsley, and serve immediately, cutting square portions with a mound in the middle of each.

Serves 6

MENU SUGGESTIONS
Soups: Leek Soup (page 69), Purée of Asparagus (page 68)
Salads: Mixed Green (page 215), Tomatoes and Fresh Herbs (page 224), or Salade Niçoise (page 218)
Desserts: Fresh fruit (page 234), Grapefruit with Port (page 241), or Pears Poached in Red Wine with a Touch of Cassis (page 236)

Soufflé Omelets with Savory Mushroom Filling

FOR THE FILLING:

1 tablespoon olive oil
½ cup minced onion or shallots
1½ pounds fresh mushrooms, wild or cultivated or a mixture, cleaned, trimmed, and sliced
Salt, preferably sea salt, to taste
2 to 3 large garlic cloves, or to taste, minced or put through a press
1 teaspoon fresh thyme leaves, or ½ teaspoon dried thyme (or more to taste)

I've replaced the soufflé roll with mushroom filling in the original version of this book with this soufflé omelet. Why go through the trouble of preparing the soufflé roll, let alone introduce all of the fat that it requires, when you can produce something just as elegant in a quarter of the time? The omelet is puffy and ethereal, like a soufflé, but simple to make. Also, you can use fewer egg yolks if you want to keep the cholesterol down.

Prepare the filling:

Heat the oil over medium heat in a heavy-bottomed non-stick skillet and sauté the onion or shallots until tender, about 5 minutes. Add the mushrooms and a little salt and continue to cook, stirring, until the mushrooms release liquid, about 5 minutes. Add the garlic, thyme, white wine, soy sauce, additional salt, and pepper, and continue to cook, stirring, for about 15 minutes, until the mushrooms are tender and aromatic, and the liquid in the pan has just about evaporated. Taste and correct seasonings. Stir in the parsley and remove from the heat. At this point you may hold the filling, covered, in the refrigerator for 1 to 2 days (reheat to use), or simply set aside while you beat the eggs.

Now make the omelets:

It's easiest to make 2 large omelets in a large, nonstick frying pan. Beat 4 egg whites in a bowl until they begin to foam. Add salt and cream of tartar and beat until the whites form stiff peaks. Beat 3 egg yolks in another bowl and season with salt and pepper. Gently fold the yolks into the whites.

Heat 1½ teaspoons olive oil or butter in a 10- or 12-inch nonstick skillet over medium-high heat. Drizzle a tiny bit of the egg into the pan, and if it sizzles, gently pour in the omelet mixture. Cook for 2 minutes. Carefully spoon half the filling down the middle. Cook, shaking the pan very gently, for 1 more minute. Tilt the pan and turn the omelet onto a large plate or platter, using a spatula to fold the omelet in half as you turn it. Hold in a warm oven while you make the second omelet, using the remaining egg whites, yolks, and filling. Slice each omelet into 2 or 3 pieces and serve at once.

Serves 4 to 6

¼ cup dry white wine
2 to 3 teaspoons soy sauce
Freshly ground pepper, to taste
2 tablespoons chopped fresh
   parsley

FOR THE OMELETS:

6 eggs, separated and at room
   temperature
2 additional egg whites, at room
   temperature
Pinch of salt
Pinch of cream of tartar
Additional salt, preferably sea salt
Freshly ground pepper, to taste
1 tablespoon olive oil or butter

MENU SUGGESTIONS
Soups: Ratatouille (page 51), Blender Gazpacho (page 89),
   or Fruit (page 55)
Salads: Mixed Green (page 215), Tomatoes and Fresh Herbs
   (page 224), or Crudité (page 217)
Desserts: Pears Poached in Red Wine with a Touch of Cassis
   (page 236), Baked Apples (page 242)

Squash Soufflé

1½ pounds (4 or 5) yellow squash, or a mixture of yellow squash and zucchini

1 tablespoon salt, preferably sea salt, or more as necessary

½ onion, minced

1 tablespoon plus 2 teaspoons olive oil

4 eggs, beaten

¼ cup grated Cheddar or Gruyère cheese

½ cup cottage cheese

½ cup whole-wheat bread crumbs

2 tablespoons chopped fresh parsley

Freshly ground pepper, to taste

Squash soufflé has a delicate flavor and is wonderfully light and nutritious. It has the puffed-up quality of a traditional soufflé, but you won't have to bother with making a cream sauce or separating the eggs. You can assemble this dish a few hours before you bake it.

Preheat the oven to 350 degrees.

Grate the squash and toss it with the salt. Let sit for 20 minutes.

Meanwhile, sauté the onion in 2 teaspoons of the olive oil until tender. Combine with the beaten eggs, grated cheese, cottage cheese, bread crumbs, parsley, and salt and pepper to taste.

Squeeze out the excess water from the squash and rinse well. Squeeze in a towel to dry, then stir into the egg-cheese mixture. Turn into an oiled 2-quart casserole or soufflé dish. Drizzle the remaining 1 tablespoon olive oil over the top.

Bake for 45 minutes and serve immediately.

Serves 6

MENU SUGGESTIONS

Hors d'oeuvres: Vegetable Platter with Assorted Dips (page 40), Stuffed Mushrooms (page 28)

Soups: Fresh Pea (page 66), Tomato–Rice (page 78)

Salads: Mixed Green (page 215), Chick-pea (page 231), or Marinated Vegetables Vinaigrette (page 35)

Desserts: Pears Poached in Red Wine with a Touch of Cassis (page 236), Bananas Poached in White Wine (page 235), any fruit tart (pages 255, 263), or Peaches Marsala (page 240)

Piperade

This dish comes from the Basque regions of Spain and southern France. It's hardly more complicated than scrambled eggs, yet it can be as memorable as a soufflé. The authentic dish contains ham or bacon, but I think the peppers alone give it a rich, full-bodied flavor. It makes a nice Sunday evening dinner.

Heat the olive oil over medium-low heat in a heavy, nonstick frying pan and sauté the sliced onions with the garlic until tender. Add the peppers and cook a few more minutes, then add the tomatoes, salt, pepper, oregano, and marjoram or thyme. Stir this all together, then cook the mixture, covered, for about 15 to 20 minutes, stirring often, until the tomatoes have cooked down and the mixture is saucy and fragrant.

Pour in the beaten eggs and stir as for scrambled eggs. Remove from the heat as soon as the eggs have set, and serve at once.

Serves 6

MENU SUGGESTIONS

Hors d'oeuvres: Tiropites (page 32), Marinated Vegetables Vinaigrette (page 35)

Soups: Vichyssoise (page 76), Soupe au Pistou (page 56), or Fresh Pea (page 66)

Salads: Mixed Green (page 215), Watercress and Mushroom (page 226)

Desserts: Pineapple with Kirsch (page 241), Mediterranean Fruit Compote (page 237), or Raspberries in Red Wine (page 240)

2 tablespoons olive oil

1 pound onions, sliced

2 to 3 garlic cloves, to taste, minced or put through a press

4 green peppers, seeded and sliced in thin strips

2 red peppers, seeded and sliced in thin strips

1 pound (4 medium) tomatoes, peeled, seeded, and chopped

Salt, preferably sea salt

Freshly ground pepper

½ teaspoon oregano

½ teaspoon dried marjoram or thyme

6 to 8 eggs, beaten

Spanokopita (Greek Spinach Pie)

2 pounds fresh spinach or 2 packages (10 or 12 ounces each)
 frozen spinach
¼ cup olive oil
1 onion, chopped
½ pound fresh mushrooms, sliced
2 to 3 garlic cloves, to taste,
 minced or put through a press
Salt, preferably sea salt, to taste
Freshly ground pepper, to taste
5 eggs
½ pound feta cheese
½ cup freshly grated Parmesan
 cheese
¼ cup chopped fresh parsley
1 teaspoon oregano
¼ teaspoon dried rosemary
 (optional)
¼ cup (½ stick) butter
10 sheets filo dough

This is a spectacular dish for company—a golden, puffy spinach pie with a savory filling and a rich, crisp crust—and it also makes a wonderful hors d'oeuvre. It's most impressive when baked just before serving, but you can assemble it a day in advance and keep it in the refrigerator, or freeze it for a week or more and transfer it directly from the freezer to the oven to bake. It takes about an hour to put together.

Sometimes the sheets of packaged filo dough stick together and tear as you try to pull them apart. Don't be too discouraged if this happens. If some of the filo in your spanokopita is in shreds, nobody will really see it. It just slows you down (and tries your patience) when you're putting the dish together.

If you are using fresh spinach, wash the spinach and remove the tough stems. Quickly blanch in a large pot of salted boiling water, or wilt in a large, dry, nonstick skillet in the water left on the leaves after washing. Rinse with cold water, squeeze dry in a kitchen towel, and chop coarsely. (If you are using frozen spinach, just let it thaw, squeeze out excess moisture, and chop coarsely).

Heat 2 tablespoons of the olive oil in a heavy-bottomed nonstick skillet over medium heat and add the onion. Cook, stirring, until the onion is tender, about 5 minutes, and add the mushrooms. Cook, stirring, until the mushrooms begin to release their liquid, and add the garlic, salt, and pepper. Continue to cook, stirring often, for about 5 to 10 minutes, until the mushrooms are tender and aromatic. Remove from the heat.

Beat the eggs in a large bowl and crumble in the feta cheese; add the Parmesan, then the spinach mixture. Stir in the parsley, oregano, rosemary, some freshly ground pepper, and a little salt (remembering that the feta is very salty).

Preheat the oven to 375 degrees.

Combine the remaining 2 tablespoons of olive oil and the butter in a small, heavy-bottomed saucepan and heat over low heat until the butter melts. Brush a 10- or 12-inch pie plate or a 2- or 3-quart oblong baking dish with this mixture, and cover with a sheet of filo dough, letting the edges extend over the dish. Take another sheet and lay it on top of the first, not directly but in such a way that its edges extend over different parts of the dish. Brush with the butter/oil mixture. Layer 4 more sheets of dough, brushing every other one and turning each one slightly so that the edges fan out over the sides of the pan.

Now spread the spinach mixture evenly over the filo dough in the pan, pushing it into the corners. Take the edges of the filo and fold them in over the spinach mixture.

Take the remaining 4 sheets of filo and layer them one by one over the spinach mixture, again brushing every other sheet, but this time pushing the edges down into the sides of the pan. It is difficult to do this neatly; just crimp the edges down into the sides of the pan (they will form a nice crisp edge after baking). Brush the top of the spanokopita with oil and butter and make a few ½-inch-deep diagonal slashes across it with a sharp knife.

Bake for 40 to 50 minutes, until the crust is puffed up and golden; it will shrink from the sides of the pan. Cut into wedges, squares, or diamond shapes and serve immediately.

Serves 6

MENU SUGGESTIONS

Hors d'oeuvres: Vegetable Platter with Assorted Dips (page 40), Marinated Vegetables à la Grecque (page 39)

Soups: Egg–Lemon (page 70), Curried Eggplant, chilled (page 88), or Leek (page 69)

Salads: Cucumber (page 222), Mixed Green (page 215), Tomatoes and Fresh Herbs (page 224), or Tabouli (page 220)

Desserts: Fresh fruit (page 234), Bananas Poached in White Wine (page 255), or Oranges Grand Marnier (page 238)

Omelets

1½ teaspoons butter (or olive oil), or more as necessary

2 eggs

Salt, preferably sea salt

Freshly ground pepper

1 teaspoon milk

¼ cup of the filling of your choice (pages 122–124), prepared and heated if necessary

Omelets are an essential part of a vegetarian cook's repertoire. They're fast, versatile, and nutritious, and they can be filled with almost anything. In fact, the best omelets are often made from the leftovers in your refrigerator. Savory tomato-based leftovers from such dishes as eggplant Parmesan or ratatouille make excellent fillings.

There are two kinds of omelets. One is the folded omelet, which is wrapped around its filling. The other—from Spain, Italy, and the south of France—is flat, like a pancake. Eggs and filling are beaten together and cooked at the same time. The flat omelet has an advantage: You can cook it in advance and reheat it, or even eat it cold.

Use about ¼ cup filling per person. If you try to put too much inside a folded omelet, it may break apart as you turn it onto the plate. For a two-egg omelet, either folded or flat, to serve one person, proceed as follows:

Method 1 (for a folded omelet):

Be sure you have everything you need ready beforehand, including the serving plate. The folded omelet happens fast.

Use a heavy-bottomed nonstick omelet pan, and heat it slowly. Start to melt the butter or heat the oil in the pan over medium-high heat. Break the eggs into a bowl, add a little salt and pepper and the milk, and beat 30 times with a fork or whisk.

Meanwhile, the butter will have melted and begun to sizzle. Tip the pan from side to side to coat the bottom of the pan evenly, then turn up the heat to medium. As soon as the sizzling stops—and not a moment later—pour in the egg mixture. Tilt the pan with a rotating wrist motion so the bottom is coated with egg. As soon as you see that a thin layer of egg is cooked, shake the pan vigorously by pushing it away from you and then jerking it toward you. (It is this motion of the pan that assures a fluffy omelet and prevents it from browning.) If the jerking motion is not moving the egg mixture enough for the runny egg on top to flow underneath the cooked layer, lift the edge of the cooked layer with a spatula as you shake the pan so the egg can run underneath.

After a few shakes of the pan, place your filling in the center of the omelet, making a line of filling going across the diameter of the omelet.

Continue to jerk the pan so the omelet folds over on itself. If you are afraid of spilling the eggs out over the side of the pan, shake the pan with one hand while lifting the sides of the omelet with a spatula, allowing the uncooked egg to run underneath. Then, still shaking the pan, fold the omelet over with the spatula. Tilt the pan and roll the omelet out onto the serving plate, helping it along if necessary with the spatula. This entire operation should take about 1 minute.

Keep in mind that the center of the omelet should be undercooked, because once it's closed up it continues to cook in its own heat for a minute or so.

Method 2 (for a flat omelet):

The procedure for the flat omelet is not as fast. Melt the butter or heat the olive oil in an omelet or frying pan. Mix together your eggs, salt, pepper, and milk and beat 30 times with a fork or whisk. Stir in your filling and mix well. Pour the mixture into the pan and lower the flame. When a thin layer of egg has set, begin to gently shake the pan and continue cooking for 4 to 5 minutes. When the omelet has just about set, place the pan under the broiler for 2 to 4 minutes to finish it off. It should puff up. Serve immediately, or cool and chill. You can also make 1 large flat omelet in a 10- or 12-inch pan, and serve cut in wedges.

Note: Be careful not to let the butter burn.

For lower-cholesterol omelets, substitute 2 egg whites for one of the eggs.

Serves 1

continued

LEFTOVER RATATOUILLE, EGGPLANT PARMESAN, OR SPAGHETTI SAUCE FILLING

For this recipe, use leftovers from Ratatouille (page 52), or Eggplant Parmesan (page 132).

Have your filling heating in a separate pan; spoon on (or in) ¼ cup per person. For a folded omelet, sprinkle 1 teaspoon of grated Parmesan over the filling before you fold the omelet, and top the omelet with grated Parmesan and chopped fresh parsley. For a flat omelet, add the extra Parmesan and parsley to the egg and filling mixture and top with Parmesan and chopped fresh parsley.

FINES HERBES FILLING

Use whatever herbs you happen to have on hand for this. My favorites are parsley, tarragon, chives, basil, fennel, and dill. Though they are strong herbs, I like fresh rosemary and thyme as well. Chop up a cupful and add a little minced garlic and, if you wish, some grated Parmesan. Use 1 tablespoon for each 2-egg omelet. Top with a sprinkling of herbs and more Parmesan.

CHEESE FILLING

Use 2 to 3 tablespoons grated cheese per 2-egg omelet. I suggest Cheddar, Gruyère, Jarlsberg, or Emmenthaler, and the addition of a little Parmesan will give it zip. Garnish with parsley, which you may also combine with the cheese.

VEGETABLE FILLING

Anything you have on hand will do. Asparagus and broccoli are my favorites, and mushrooms. Blanch green vegetables and chop in small pieces. If you are using mushrooms, sauté first in butter or olive oil with a little onion and garlic, salt, and pepper. Use ¼ cup per person, and combine if you wish with a tablespoon of grated Parmesan or Gruyère.

SPINACH AND MUSHROOM FILLING

Combine the spinach and mushrooms, then stir in the salt, pepper, and herbs. Use ¼ cup per omelet.

Enough for six 2-egg omelets

1½ cups blanched, chopped spinach
¼ pound fresh mushrooms, sliced and sautéed until tender in 1 tablespoon olive oil
Salt, preferably sea salt, to taste
Freshly ground pepper, to taste
1 teaspoon each chopped fresh rosemary and thyme, or ½ teaspoon each dried rosemary and thyme

SPICED APPLE FILLING

Sauté the apples with the raisins and spices in butter until they begin to soften; remove from the heat before they get mushy. Add a little honey, if you wish, then divide the mixture evenly among your omelets, folded or flat.

Enough for six 2-egg omelets

2 apples, peeled, if desired, then cored and thinly sliced
¼ cup raisins
½ to 1 teaspoon ground cinnamon, to taste
½ teaspoon freshly grated nutmeg
½ teaspoon ground allspice
1 tablespoon butter
Mild honey, to taste (optional)

4 green onions, both white part
  and green, chopped
1 tablespoon canola oil or vegetable oil
Dash of tamari
1½ cups mung bean sprouts or
  alfalfa sprouts

1 tablespoon butter
1 teaspoon curry powder
2 to 3 seedless oranges, peeled and
  sectioned
½ cup plain nonfat yogurt, homemade (page 202) or commercial, or buttermilk
1 teaspoon chopped fresh mint

BEAN SPROUT FILLING

Sauté the green onions in the oil for a few minutes. Add the tamari and sprouts, then stir together and remove from the heat. Divide equally among your omelets, folded or flat.

Enough for six 2-egg omelets

CURRIED ORANGE FILLING

Heat the butter and sauté the curry powder for 1 minute. Add the orange sections and sauté, stirring, for 3 minutes. Remove from the heat, place in a bowl, and stir in the yogurt and mint. Divide among your omelets, folded or flat, and serve the omelets with Chutney (page 172).

Enough for six to eight 2-egg omelets

MENU SUGGESTIONS

Omelets make a simple main course with just about any eggless hors d'oeuvre, soup, salad, or dessert.

Crêpes

I love the concept of the crêpe, a paper-thin pancake wrapped around the filling of your choice. Crêpes are so easy to make and to store that they almost rank as a convenience food. They may be stored in the refrigerator for a few days, or frozen (stack them between pieces of waxed paper to avoid sticking and seal well in plastic, or wrap in a clean, dry cloth). They thaw quickly, so if you have a supply in the freezer you can make wonderful meals in no time.

The three crêpe recipes that follow are just a few suggestions to start you off. Leftovers make good fillings, and a popular crêpe in France is one filled with a fried egg and cheese. You see, one needn't get very fancy. I use a traditional crêpe pan. If you have an inverted crêpe pan (see Method 2 below), omit the melted butter.

Put the eggs, milk, water, butter, and salt in a blender. Turn it on and slowly pour in the flour. Whirl it all at high speed for 1 minute. Alternatively, sift together the flour and salt and beat in the eggs. Gradually add the milk, water, and butter, beating vigorously with a whisk, and strain through a sieve.

Refrigerate the batter for 1 to 2 hours. This will allow the flour particles to swell and soften so the crêpes will be light.

Method 1 (using a standard crêpe pan):

For this method, use a seasoned 6- or 7-inch crêpe pan or a cast-iron or nonstick omelet pan. Have the batter ready in a bowl, with a whisk on hand for stirring, as the flour tends to settle and the batter will need to be stirred before making each crêpe. Also have on hand a ¼-cup measure (preferably a ¼-cup ladle, available in restaurant supply stores) and a plate to stack the finished crêpes on.

Place the pan over moderately high heat and brush the bottom with butter. When the pan just begins to smoke,

continued

---

3 large eggs
⅔ cup milk
⅔ cup water
2 tablespoons melted unsalted
   butter (for Method 1 only)
½ teaspoon salt, preferably sea salt
1 cup sifted flour, either whole-
   wheat pastry or half whole-
   wheat pastry flour and half
   unbleached white

remove from the heat and pour in slightly less than ¼ cup batter, then tilt the pan to distribute the batter evenly. (Don't get nervous and think you should look like a crêperie chef; just slowly and methodically tilt the pan from side to side and watch the batter distribute itself evenly. Eventually you will be able to do it faster.) Return the pan to the heat and cook for about 1 minute. Loosen the edges gently with a spatula, and if the crêpe comes up from the pan easily, turn and cook for about 30 seconds on the other side. (If the crêpe sticks, wait for another 30 seconds, then turn.) Turn the crêpe from the pan onto a plate, with the first (or "good") side down; this will make filling the crêpes easier, since you want this golden side to show.

Brush the pan again with butter and continue with the remainder of the batter, a scant ¼ cup at a time. After the first 3 or 4 crêpes, you will not have to brush the pan with butter every time.

You might have a problem with the crêpes sticking to the pan. There are a few things you can do to avoid this. First, make sure that your pan is well seasoned and your batter is well blended so the flour doesn't settle. Do not panic if the first few crêpes stick. It might take about that many to get the pan sufficiently saturated with butter. Also, don't try to turn the crêpes until they come away from the pan easily, or they will tear.

Proceed as directed in any of the crêpe recipes that follow.

Method 2 (using an inverted crêpe pan):

I haven't seen as many of these around lately as I saw in the seventies, when they were a new and popular gadget. The pans make a nice, even, thin crêpe, but there is always some crêpe batter that you can't use up because it is too far down in the pie pan. Place your batter in a pie pan and heat the crêpe pan, inverted, over a moderate flame. If a drop of batter sizzles when you drop it on the pan, the pan is ready. Dip it evenly into the pie pan. A surface of batter will adhere immediately and begin to cook. (If the crêpe pan is too hot, the batter will immediately fall off, back into the pie pan. If this happens, allow the pan to cool for a minute, then dip it into the pie pan again.) Place the pan, inverted again, over the flame and cook for about 30 seconds. Loosen gently around the edges with a spatula and let the crêpe fall off onto a plate. The "good" side, the side you want to show when you roll the crêpe up, will be up when the crêpe falls onto the plate; you will have to turn it over to fill it.

Proceed as directed in any of the crêpe recipes that follow.

Makes 20 to 30 crêpes

Almond–Cheese Crêpes

The almond-cheese filling for these crêpes is exceptionally delicious. The ricotta-egg mixture is fluffy, and the ground almonds provide a wonderful crunch. Nutmeg makes it really special.

Have your crêpes stacked and ready to fill. Preheat the oven to 325 degrees; butter a 2-quart baking dish. Blend the ricotta and eggs together in a blender or in a large bowl with a whisk. Stir in the almonds, Parmesan, and yogurt. Season with salt and nutmeg to taste.

Place 2 to 3 tablespoons filling on the less-cooked side of each crêpe, then roll up in either of two ways: To fold like an enchilada, simply roll up. To fold like a blintz, fold the sides over the filling first, then roll up. (For these crêpes I prefer the latter method, because the filling is runny and the crêpes folded at the sides will contain it better.) Place the crêpes side by side in the buttered baking dish.

Cover the baking dish with foil to keep the moisture in and bake for 30 minutes. Serve hot, with the white wine sauce.

Serves 6
continued

1 recipe Crêpes (page 125)

12 ounces low-fat ricotta

2 eggs

½ cup almonds, chopped very fine or ground in a blender

½ cup freshly grated Parmesan cheese

⅔ cup plain nonfat yogurt, home-made (see page 202) or commercial

¼ to ½ teaspoon salt, preferably sea salt, or to taste

Freshly grated nutmeg, to taste

White Wine Sauce (page 199)

MENU SUGGESTIONS

Hors d'oeuvres: French Bread (page 10) and Baba Ghanoush (page 24), or Marinated Vegetables Vinaigrette (page 35)

Soups: Leek (page 69), Blender Gazpacho (page 89), or Purée of Asparagus (page 68)

Salads: Mixed Green (page 215), Spinach (page 216), Watercress and Mushroom (page 226), or Tender Lettuce and Orange (page 219)

Desserts: Fresh fruit (page 234), Pears Poached in Red Wine with a Touch of Cassis (page 236), Strawberry and Cassis Sherbet (page 261), Peaches Marsala (page 240), or Raspberries in Red Wine (page 240)

Ratatouille–Cheese Crêpes

1 recipe Ratatouille (page 52)

1 recipe Crêpes (page 125)

½ cup freshly grated Parmesan cheese

1 large or 2 medium-size tomatoes, peeled, seeded, and quartered

2 tablespoons chopped or slivered fresh basil

Chopped fresh parsley or basil leaves for garnish

Here is a way to transfrom ratatouille into a heady, satisfying main course. The sauce is remarkably simple: It's just a purée. As for any crêpe dish, the crêpes may be made in advance and frozen or refrigerated. You can also make the ratatouille in advance; it gets better as it matures.

Place the ratatouille in a colander set over a bowl and let drain for 30 minutes. Have your crêpes stacked and ready to fill.

Preheat the oven to 325 degrees; brush a 2-quart baking dish with olive oil.

Set aside 2 cups of the ratatouille mixed with the drained-off liquid, and about 3 tablespoons of the Parmesan. Place 2 to 3 tablespoons of the remaining ratatouille on each crêpe, sprinkle with some of the remaining Parmesan, and roll up. Place side by side in the buttered baking dish, cover the dish with foil, and heat the crêpes through in the oven for 20 minutes.

Meanwhile, make a sauce by puréeing the 2 cups ratatouille with the drained-off liquid and the tomatoes in a blender or food processor. Place this purée in a saucepan and heat through. Adjust seasonings and stir in the chopped basil.

Remove the baking dish from the oven, pour the purée over the crêpes, and sprinkle them with the reserved Parmesan. Garnish with fresh parsley or basil and serve.

Serves 6

MENU SUGGESTIONS
Hors d'oeuvres: Fresh Fruit and Nuts (page 43), Hummus (page 21), or Soya Pâté (page 22)
Soups: Leek (page 69), Fresh Pea (page 66)
Salads: Salade Niçoise (page 218), Green Bean, Almond, and Mushroom (page 224), or Crudité (page 217)
Desserts: Indian Pudding (page 252), Light Cheesecake (page 250), or Pineapple with Kirsch (page 241)

Crêpes Florentine

1 recipe Crêpes (page 125)

2 pounds fresh spinach, stemmed and washed, or 2 packages (10 ounces each) frozen spinach, thawed

1 tablespoon olive oil

2 tablespoons minced green onion, shallot, or white onion

½ pound fresh mushrooms, cleaned, trimmed, and diced

3 large garlic cloves, minced or put through a press

Salt, preferably sea salt, to taste

Freshly ground pepper, to taste

2 tablespoons dry white wine

1 teaspoon fresh thyme leaves, or ½ teaspoon dried thyme

1 teaspoon chopped fresh rosemary, or ½ teaspoon crumbled dried rosemary

1 cup low-fat cottage cheese

2 eggs, beaten

⅔ cup grated Gruyère cheese

Pinch of freshly grated nutmeg, or to taste

½ recipe Béchamel (optional, page 200)

The spinach filling here can be made a day ahead of time and kept refrigerated, tightly covered. The spinach is mixed with fragrant mushrooms and further enriched with cottage cheese and eggs.

Have your crêpes stacked and ready to fill.

Prepare the spinach. Blanch fresh, stemmed spinach in salted boiling water; drain and squeeze out excess liquid, then chop. (Or thaw frozen spinach, squeeze out excess liquid, and chop.) Place in a 2- or 3-quart bowl.

Heat the olive oil in a large, heavy-bottomed nonstick skillet over medium-low heat and add the green onion. Cook, stirring, until the onion begins to soften, about 3 minutes, and add the diced mushrooms, garlic, salt, and pepper. Cook, stirring, until the mushrooms begin to release liquid, about 5 minutes, and stir in the wine, thyme, and rosemary. Continue to cook, stirring often, for another 5 minutes, until the mushrooms are tender and aromatic. Remove from the heat and set aside.

Blend together the cottage cheese and beaten eggs and add to the spinach. Stir in the mushrooms and ½ cup of the Gruyère; mix together. Add the nutmeg. Correct the seasoning.

Preheat the oven to 350 degrees; butter or oil a 2- or 3-quart baking dish.

Place 2 heaping tablespoons of filling on each crêpe, roll up, and place side by side in the buttered baking dish. Pour on the béchamel, if using. Sprinkle the remaining cheese over the top and bake for 20 to 30 minutes, until bubbly.

Serves 4 to 6 (fills 12 crêpes)

MENU SUGGESTIONS

Soups: Leek (page 69), Egg–Lemon (page 70)

Salads: Mixed Green (page 215), Tomatoes and Fresh Herbs (page 224)

Desserts: Fresh fruit (page 234), Raspberries in Red Wine (page 240), or Pears Poached in Red Wine with a Touch of Cassis (page 236)

Eggplant Parmesan

2 pounds eggplant (2 medium)

2 tablespoons olive oil, approximately

1 onion, chopped

3 or more garlic cloves (to taste), minced or put through a press

3 pounds ripe tomatoes, peeled, seeded, and chopped, or three 28-ounce cans, drained and chopped

1 teaspoon salt, preferably sea salt, or to taste

Freshly ground pepper, to taste

1 tablespoon fresh basil or 1 teaspoon dried, or to taste

1 teaspoon oregano, or to taste

Pinch of ground cinnamon

½ pound skim-milk mozzarella cheese, sliced or grated

1 cup freshly grated Parmesan cheese

¼ cup whole-wheat bread crumbs

Eggplant Parmesan is a savory, filling dish. To complete the menu, you'll want just a light soup and green salad, and a light dessert. Like black bean enchiladas, this is a dependable choice for my catered dinners, and most of it can be prepared ahead. The tomato sauce can be made a few days in advance, and the casserole can be assembled a day in advance and refrigerated before you bake it. But do not use aluminum foil to cover it. The aluminum reacts with the tomato sauce and sheds itself onto the casserole; you will be alarmed to find holes in the foil and bits of gray all over the top of your beautiful eggplant Parmesan. So use plastic wrap when you store it.

As with every casserole, every part of the whole should taste good.

Grate your own Parmesan if you have the time, for it makes all the difference in the world. And use good olive oil and bread crumbs. Avoid running out of sauce by being sparing with the ingredients when you start to assemble the casserole, and becoming more extravagant as you near the top.

Preheat the oven to 450 degrees. Cut the eggplants in half lengthwise and pierce the cut sides in a few places with the tip of a knife. Place cut sides down on an oiled baking sheet and bake 20 minutes, until the eggplant is soft and beginning to shrivel. Remove from the oven and allow to cool.

Meanwhile, make the tomato sauce. Heat 1 tablespoon of the oil over medium heat in a large, heavy-bottomed nonstick pan or casserole and add the onion. Sauté, stirring, until the onion begins to soften, about 3 minutes, and stir in one of the garlic cloves. Continue to cook another few minutes, until the onion is soft and beginning to color, and stir in the tomatoes, salt, pepper, herbs, cinnamon, and remaining garlic. Bring to a simmer and cook, uncovered, for 30 to 40 minutes, until the sauce has cooked down and is just beginning to stick to the pan. Taste and adjust seasonings. Remove from the heat and put through the medium blade of a food mill, or purée in a food processor fitted with the steel blade.

When the eggplant is cool enough for you to handle, slice crosswise about ¼ inch thick.

Preheat the oven to 425 degrees. Oil a 2- or 3-quart gratin or baking dish. Spread a spoonful of tomato sauce on the bottom of the baking dish, then add a layer of eggplant slices. Cover with some of the mozzarella, a thicker layer of sauce, and a sprinkling of Parmesan. Continue in this order—eggplant, mozzarella, sauce, and Parmesan—finishing up with a lavish layer of sauce, the bread crumbs, and Parmesan. Drizzle on the remaining oil.

Bake for 30 to 40 minutes, until bubbling and beginning to brown, and serve.

Serves 6

MENU SUGGESTIONS

Hors d'oeuvres: Vegetable Platter with Assorted Dips (page 40)

Soups: Stracciatella (page 54), Leek (page 69)

Salads: Mixed Green (page 215), Spinach (page 216)

Desserts: Mediterranean Fruit Compote (page 237), Bavarian Crème au Café (page 244)

Stuffed Eggplant

2 large or 3 to 4 smaller eggplants, prepared as directed on page xxxiii

2½ tablespoons olive oil

1 medium or large onion, sliced

2 garlic cloves, minced or put through a press (more to taste)

2 red bell peppers, seeded and diced

Salt, preferably sea salt, to taste

2 medium-size tomatoes, peeled, seeded, and sliced

Freshly ground pepper, to taste

3 tablespoons chopped or slivered fresh basil

1 tablespoon lime juice, or to taste

¼ cup freshly grated Parmesan cheese (or more to taste)

⅓ cup whole-wheat bread crumbs

This is a savory, colorful eggplant dish. The original version had a great many nuts, an ingredient (along with cheese) we tended to overemphasize in the seventies. In fact, it's the vegetables themselves that make this so wonderful, so I've taken out the nuts. You can assemble this dish a day in advance and keep it in the refrigerator.

When you remove the eggplant from the hot oven to cool, reduce the oven heat to 400 degrees; oil a large rectangular baking or gratin dish.

When the "steamed" eggplant halves are cool, carefully scoop out most of the pulp, leaving a small amount of it in the skins. Dice the eggplant pulp and set aside for a moment.

Heat 2 tablespoons of the oil in a large nonstick skillet or wok over medium heat and add the onion. Sauté, stirring, until it begins to soften, about 3 minutes, and add the garlic, peppers, and a little salt. Cook, stirring, for 5 minutes, until the vegetables are just about tender. Add the eggplant and continue to sauté for about 5 minutes longer, stirring often, until the vegetables begin to stick to the pan.

Add all the remaining ingredients except the Parmesan and bread crumbs, then cover and cook over a low flame for another 5 to 10 minutes, stirring often, until the vegetables are tender, aromatic, and beginning to stick to the pan. Remove from the heat and stir in lots of freshly ground pepper, half the Parmesan, and half the bread crumbs. Taste and adjust seasonings.

Fill the eggplant shells with the mixture, sprinkle with the remaining Parmesan and bread crumbs, and place in the oiled baking pan. Drizzle on the remaining ½ tablespoon olive oil.

Bake for 20 to 30 minutes, until sizzling.

Slice larger eggplants crosswise to serve.

Serves 6

MENU SUGGESTIONS

Hors d'oeuvres: Marinated Vegetables Vinaigrette (page 35)

Soups: Purée of Asparagus (page 68), Fresh Pea (page 66)

Salads: Mixed Green (page 215), Spinach (page 216), or Watercress and Mushroom (page 226)

Desserts: Fresh fruit (page 234), Peach Pie (page 255), or Soufflé Grand Marnier (page 249)

Chick-pea and Bulgur Gratin with Garlicky Tomato Sauce

2 tablespoons olive oil

1 medium onion, chopped

4 large garlic cloves, minced or put through a press

3 pounds (12 medium) tomatoes, peeled, seeded, and diced

Pinch of sugar

Salt and freshly ground pepper, to taste

2 teaspoons fresh chopped oregano or thyme leaves, or 1 teaspoon dried oregano or thyme

2 tablespoons chopped fresh basil (or more to taste)

1 pound (2 large or 3 small) zucchini, sliced about 1/4 inch thick

1 cup medium bulgur, cooked (2 heaped cups cooked; page xxxv)

2 cups cooked chick-peas (may use canned)

¼ cup freshly grated Parmesan or Gruyère cheese

2 tablespoons fresh or dry bread crumbs

In my original version of The Vegetarian Feast, *this dish was called Italian Soybean–Grains Casserole. I had served it to the food activist and writer Frances Moore Lappé, and 400 of her associates, at a conference on world hunger, for it represents the low-on-the-food-chain kind of eating that was such a new idea at the time (1974). Now I find that other beans are infinitely more tasty than soybeans, and they all have high-quality protein. Chick-peas are a favorite, and go very well with bulgur.*

This gratin is a model of protein complementarity, with grains, beans, and cheese all working together to provide a complete set of amino acids. The tomato sauce and zucchini make it a delicious, wholesome, one-dish meal. You can assemble it a day in advance and refrigerate it before baking. As for eggplant Parmesan, do not cover with aluminum foil; the aluminum will react with the tomato sauce. Use plastic wrap. You will have to remember to soak and cook the whole beans (unless you're using canned, which is perfectly acceptable) in advance. The tomato sauce can be made a couple of days ahead of time.

Preheat the oven to 375 degrees. Oil a 2- or 3-quart gratin or baking dish.

Heat 1 tablespoon of the oil in a large, heavy-bottomed nonstick skillet over medium heat and add the onion. Cook, stirring, until it is translucent and tender, about 5 minutes, and add half the garlic. Stir together for a minute, then add the tomatoes, the remaining garlic, the sugar, salt and pepper, and oregano or thyme. Stir together and cook uncovered, stirring often, for 20 to 30 minutes, until the tomatoes have cooked down and the sauce is thick and fragrant. Stir in the basil, remove from the heat, taste and adjust salt and pepper.

While the tomato sauce is cooking, steam the zucchini until crisp-tender, about 5 minutes. Remove from the heat.

Mix the cooked bulgur and chick-peas with ¾ cup of the tomato sauce and spread over the bottom of your baking dish. Top with the zucchini. Spread the remaining tomato sauce over the zucchini, and sprinkle on the cheese. Top with the bread crumbs, and drizzle on the remaining tablespoon of olive oil.

Bake 30 minutes, until the top is just beginning to brown. Serve hot.

Serves 6

MENU SUGGESTIONS
Soups: Cream of Raw and Cooked Mushroom (page 62), Leek (page 69), or Stracciatella (page 54)
Salads: Mixed Green (page 215), Spinach (page 216), Watercress and Mushroom (page 226)
Desserts: Bavarian Crème au Café (page 244), Mediterranean Fruit Compote (page 237), or Bananas Poached in White Wine (page 235)

Picante Zucchini Gratin

2 tablespoons olive oil

4 large garlic cloves, minced or put through a press

3 pounds (12 medium) tomatoes, peeled, seeded, and chopped

Pinch of sugar

Salt and freshly ground pepper, to taste

1 jalapeño or serrano pepper, seeded and minced (or more to taste)

1 teaspoon chopped fresh rosemary, or ½ teaspoon crumbled dried rosemary

3 tablespoons chopped fresh cilantro

1½ pounds (3 medium) zucchini, sliced about ¼ inch thick

2 ounces sharp Cheddar or Gruyère cheese, grated (½ cup grated)

This is a zucchini and tomato gratin with a zesty twist. The rosemary and cilantro add an unusual touch to the sauce. You can top this with either Cheddar or Gruyère cheese.

Preheat the oven to 400 degrees. Lightly oil a 2-quart gratin or baking dish.

Heat 1 tablespoon of the olive oil in a large, heavy-bottomed nonstick skillet over medium heat and add half the garlic. As soon as it begins to color, after about a minute, add the tomatoes, the remaining garlic, sugar, salt and pepper, the chile pepper, and rosemary. Stir together and cook uncovered, stirring often, for 20 to 30 minutes, until the tomatoes have cooked down to a thick, fragrant sauce. Stir in the cilantro, taste, and adjust seasonings. Remove from the heat.

While the tomato sauce is cooking, heat the remaining tablespoon of oil in another pan over medium-high heat and add the zucchini. Sprinkle lightly with salt and cook, stirring or shaking the pan often, until the zucchini begins turning transparent, about 8 to 10 minutes. It can also be slightly browned. Remove from the heat and drain on paper towels.

Line the prepared baking dish with the zucchini. Spread the tomato sauce over the zucchini in an even layer. Sprinkle on the cheese.

Bake 20 to 30 minutes in the preheated oven, until the top is just beginning to brown. Serve hot.

Note: If you want a more substantial dish, line the bottom of the baking dish with cooked brown rice or bulgur.

Serves 6

MENU SUGGESTIONS:
Soups: Dill (page 77), Sopa de Ajo (Garlic) (page 64)
Salads: Chick-pea Salad (page 231), Mixed Green (page 215), or Avocado and Citrus (page 217)
Desserts: Orange Dessert Crêpes (page 243), Strawberry and Cassis Sherbet (page 261)

The Best Pizza in Town

You'll never go back to your local pizza parlor after this one. You can make the crusts in advance and freeze them before prebaking. If you have room in your freezer, I recommend that you go ahead and roll the dough out, then place it on the pizza pans. You can transfer the dough directly from the freezer to a hot oven with the topping. Then the pizzas will take minutes to assemble and bake. They're great for a party. It will help to achieve a crisp crust if you have baking tiles or a baking stone in your oven.

Make the dough:

Dissolve the yeast in the lukewarm water in a large bowl and let sit 5 minutes, until the yeast begins to bubble slightly. Stir in the semolina.

Mix together the whole-wheat flour and salt, and stir into the yeast mixture. Fold in the unbleached white flour, ½ cup at a time, until the dough can be scraped out of the bowl in 1 piece. Put ½ cup of unbleached flour on your kneading surface and knead, adding unbleached white flour as necessary, for 10 minutes. The dough will be sticky at first but will become very elastic. Shape into a ball.

Rinse out the bowl, dry, and brush lightly with olive oil. Place the dough in the bowl, rounded side down first, then rounded side up. Cover with plastic wrap and a kitchen towel and set in a warm place to rise for 2½ hours, or until the dough has doubled in size.

Make the sauce:

While the dough is rising, heat the olive oil in a large, heavy-bottomed nonstick skillet over medium heat and add the garlic. As soon as it begins to color, after a minute or so, add the tomatoes, sugar, salt, pepper, and oregano or thyme. Stir together and cook, uncovered, over medium heat, for 20 to 30 minutes, until the tomatoes have cooked

continued

FOR THE CRUST:
1 teaspoon active dry yeast
1½ cups lukewarm water
½ cup fine semolina
1 cup whole-wheat flour
2 teaspoons salt, preferably sea salt
2 cups unbleached white flour, plus up to 3/4 cup, as necessary, for kneading

FOR THE SAUCE:
1 tablespoon olive oil
3 garlic cloves, minced or put through a press
3 pounds tomatoes, peeled, seeded, and chopped
Pinch of sugar
Salt, preferably sea salt, to taste
Freshly ground pepper, to taste
1 teaspoon dried oregano or thyme
2 tablespoons chopped fresh basil

FOR THE TOPPINGS, CHOICE OF THE FOLLOWING, ALONE OR IN COMBINATION:
½ pound mozzarella, thinly sliced
½ cup freshly grated Parmesan
1 large onion, sliced in rings
¼ pound mushrooms, trimmed and sliced
1 or 2 green peppers, sliced in rings

A handful of black olives
1 jar artichoke hearts, sliced
1 medium eggplant, baked
    according to the directions on
    pages 132–133 and sliced
Hot pepper flakes
1½ tablespoons olive oil

down and are beginning to stick to the pan. Stir in the basil and remove from the heat. Set aside until you are ready to roll out and top the crusts.

Preheat the oven, with the baking stone or tiles in it, to 500 degrees. Punch down the dough and divide it into 2 equal pieces. Cover the piece you aren't rolling with plastic wrap or a damp kitchen towel. Roll out each piece and line 2 lightly oiled 14- or 15-inch pizza pans. The dough should be no thicker than ¼ inch.

Assemble the pizzas:

If using the cheeses, distribute half the cheeses evenly over the crusts. Spread the tomato sauce over the cheeses in an even layer. Arrange the remaining cheeses and the toppings of your choice over the sauce. Drizzle on the olive oil.

Bake 15 minutes in the preheated oven, until the crust is brown and the cheeses bubbling. Remove from the heat and serve.

Serves 6 to 8

MENU SUGGESTIONS:
Hors d'oeuvres: Marinated Vegetables Vinaigrette (page 35), Marinated Vegetables à la Grecque (page 39)
Soups: Minestrone (page 74), Soupe au Pistou (page 56)
Salads: Niçoise (page 218), Mixed Green (page 215)
Desserts: Mediterranean Fruit Compote (page 237), Bavarian Crème au Café (page 244)

Marinated White Beans

FOR THE BEANS:
2 cups small dried white beans,
    washed
3 quarts water
1 tablespoon olive oil

This is one of my favorite dishes; it's always a big success at dinner parties, with pasta and a vegetable dish on the side, or on a bed of leaf lettuce. It makes an elegant starter, main course, or salad.

Prepare the beans:

Wash the beans and soak in 1½ quarts of the water overnight or at least for several hours. Drain.

In a heavy-bottomed flameproof bean pot or dutch oven, heat the olive oil and sauté the onion and garlic until the onion is tender. Add the beans, remaining water, and bay leaf. Bring to a boil, then cover, reduce the heat, and cook for 1 hour. Add the salt and continue to cook for another ½ hour or an hour, until the beans are tender but still firm. Remove from the heat, drain, reserving the liquid, and remove the bay leaf.

Mix the salad:

In a 2- or 3-quart bowl, toss the cooked beans together with the parsley, green onions, herbs, green and red peppers, and the freshly grated Parmesan.

For the marinade:

Combine the lemon juice, vinegar, garlic, mustard, herbs, salt, and pepper in a small bowl. Stir in the olive oil and the liquid from the beans, then toss with the bean mixture and refrigerate for several hours. Before serving, garnish with fresh cherry tomatoes, if desired.

Serves 6 to 8

MENU SUGGESTIONS

Soups: Tortilla (page 60), Tomato–Rice (page 78), or Blender Gazpacho (page 89)

Salads: Avocado and Citrus (page 217), Spinach and Citrus (with oranges) (page 227), Beet and Endive (page 227), or Tomatoes and Fresh Herbs (page 224)

Desserts: Strawberry and Cassis Sherbet (page 261), Oranges Grand Marnier (page 238), or any dessert soufflé (pages 247–249)

1 onion, chopped

3 garlic cloves, minced or put through a press

1 bay leaf

1 teaspoon salt, preferably sea salt, or to taste

FOR THE SALAD:

¼ to ½ cup chopped fresh parsley

4 green onions, both white part and green, sliced

2 tablespoons fresh herbs (basil, marjoram, thyme, fennel)

1 green pepper, seeded and chopped

1 red pepper, seeded and chopped

¼ cup freshly grated Parmesan cheese

Cherry tomatoes (optional)

FOR THE MARINADE:

Juice of 1 lemon

¼ cup red wine vinegar or sherry vinegar

1 to 2 garlic cloves, to taste, minced or put through a press

1 teaspoon Dijon mustard

1 teaspoon fresh oregano, or ½ teaspoon dried oregano

1 tablespoon chopped fresh basil, or ½ teaspoon dried basil

1 teaspoon chopped fresh tarragon, or ½ teaspoon dried tarragon

Salt, preferably sea salt, to taste

Freshly ground pepper, to taste

⅓ cup olive oil

¼ to ½ cup cooking liquid from the beans, to taste

Vegetable Paella

2 cups raw brown rice

6 cups Vegetable Stock (page 49) or water

2 onions, thinly sliced

4 garlic cloves, minced or put through a press

2 green peppers, seeded and thinly sliced

2 red peppers, seeded and thinly sliced

2 medium tomatoes, sliced

2 tablespoons olive oil

½ to 1 teaspoon salt, preferably sea salt, or to taste

1 teaspoon saffron threads

1 bay leaf

2 cups cooked chick-peas (¾ cup dried; see page xxxvi)

1 package (10 ounces) frozen peas, thawed, or 2 cups fresh peas, steamed briefly until bright green

½ cup sliced black olives (optional)

1 jar (6 ounces) artichoke hearts (optional)

There are few entrées that can match the dramatic impact of paella, a Spanish creation traditionally made with seafood, chicken, and sausages. This version is a bountiful array of exquisitely seasoned vegetables; the rice has a rich yellow color and is subtly flavored by that aristocrat of spices, saffron. For an absolutely beautiful company dinner, cook and serve it in a wok or paella pan.

Cook the rice in 3 cups of the stock or water until the liquid is absorbed. In a large, heavy-bottomed skillet, wok, or flameproof casserole, sauté the onions, garlic, peppers, and tomatoes in the olive oil until the onions are tender. Stir in the rice, the remaining 3 cups stock or water, salt, saffron, bay leaf, and chick-peas. Cover and cook over low heat until the water is nearly absorbed, about 30 minutes. Add the green peas and optional olives; do not stir. Continue cooking, uncovered, until all the liquid is absorbed.

Garnish with artichoke hearts if you like, and serve.

Serves 6 to 8

MENU SUGGESTIONS

Soups: Blender Gazpacho (page 89)

Salads: Mixed Green (page 215), Spinach (page 216)

Desserts: Bavarian Crème au Café (page 244), Light Cheesecake (page 250), or Oranges Grand Marnier (page 238)

Vegetable Shish Kebab

Vegetable shish kebab is a delight—and an utterly beautiful dish besides. Serve it over saffron brown rice, saffron millet with Indian spices, or Indonesian rice. These vegetables can be roasted, or grilled on top of the stove, if you don't want to bother with skewers and a barbecue.

Combine the ingredients for the marinade in a large bowl. Prepare the vegetables and marinate for several hours at room temperature. Stir the vegetables from time to time.

Either prepare a fire in your grill or barbecue, preheat the oven to 425 degrees, light the broiler, or heat a nonstick grill pan over medium-high heat. Soak bamboo skewers for 30 minutes in water to prevent them from burning.

Place the marinated vegetables on skewers, alternating them to make a colorful arrangement. Roast the kebabs over the open fire, under the broiler, or in the hot oven, basting with the leftover marinade; this should take about 30 minutes. If you are not using skewers, just place the vegetables in a baking dish or directly on the grill pan, and turn often. The vegetables are ready when they begin to char on the outside and are crisp-tender and hot. When they are done, toss with the olive oil and any leftover marinade, and serve with any of the dishes suggested above, or with couscous.

Serves 6 to 8

MENU SUGGESTIONS
Hors d'oeuvres: Spring Rolls (page 44), Hummus (page 21)
Soups: Fruit (page 55), Cabbage–Cheese (page 73)
Salads: Cucumber (page 222), Mixed Green (page 215)
Desserts: Bavarian Crème au Café (page 244), Soufflé Grand Marnier (page 249), or Light Cheesecake (page 250)

FOR THE MARINADE:

1 cup plain nonfat yogurt
½ cup fresh lime juice
Seeds from 10 cardamom pods
1 teaspoon ground cumin
½ teaspoon ground allspice
1 bay leaf
6 garlic cloves, mashed or put through a press
Salt, preferably sea salt, to taste
Freshly ground pepper, to taste
1 tablespoon olive oil

FOR THE VEGETABLES:

1 pint cherry tomatoes
2 green peppers, seeded and quartered or cut in eighths (if very large)
2 red peppers, seeded and quartered or cut in eighths (if very large)
4 medium onions, cut in eighths or quartered
½ to ¾ pound mushrooms, stems removed
2 zucchini, sliced about ½ inch thick
1½ pounds potatoes, unpeeled, cut in 1-inch slices or quarters, and steamed until just tender
2 sweet potatoes, peeled, cut in 1-inch slices or chunks, and steamed until just tender
1 tablespoon olive oil

Stir-fry Chinese Tofu and Vegetables

FOR THE SAUCE:

5 tablespoons Vegetable Stock
    (page 49) or water

¼ cup tamari

2 tablespoons dry sherry

1 to 2 teaspoons Pernod (anise-
    flavored liqueur) or anisette, or
    ½ teaspoon crushed aniseed
    plus 1 teaspoon mild honey

2 teaspoons cider vinegar or wine
    vinegar

½ teaspoon freshly grated ginger-
    root, or ¼ teaspoon ground
    ginger

1 tablespoon arrowroot, or more
    as necessary

FOR THE VEGETABLES:

½ pound snow peas, strings
    removed

½ pound asparagus, sliced on the
    diagonal in 2-inch pieces, or 1
    cup broccoli florets, or 1 zuc-
    chini, sliced on the diagonal in
    ¼-inch pieces

½ cup sliced fresh mushrooms

1 cup diced tender turnips

1 cup sliced yellow squash or cau-
    liflower florets

2 tablespoons canola or peanut
    oil, or more as necessary

1 onion, sliced

1 garlic clove, minced or put
    through a press

*This is most definitely not the notorious ascetic rice and veg-
etables associated with the old vegetarianism ("R and V," we
used to call them). The sauce is rich and satiny, and the flavors and aromas are subtle. You can use other vegetables,
though for this particular version I like to use green and white
ones.*

*After experimenting with techniques for this recipe, I'm
most satisfied with steaming some vegetables and stir-frying
others, and then mixing them together with the sauce at the
last minute. With this method you can use a minimum of oil,
and the vegetables will be quite delicate. A tiered Chinese
steamer will help here to eliminate space and utensil prob-
lems.*

*The dish is cooked quickly just before serving, so organi-
zation is essential. Have all your vegetables cut and in separate bowls, and mix your sauce well in advance.*

*Serve over the grain of your choice; my favorites are mil-
let, brown rice, and couscous.*

Prepare the sauce:

Before you start to cook the vegetables, combine all the
ingredients and stir well.

For the vegetables:

In a tiered bamboo or stainless-steel steamer, steam each
vegetable until just crisp-tender and fragrant. The green
vegetables should be bright green and beautiful, which
should only take 5 minutes; the squash, turnips, and cauliflower should steam for about 8 minutes. When the vegetables are done, remove them from the heat and set aside.

Heat the oil over medium-high heat in the wok and
stir-fry the onion and garlic with the ginger until the onion
starts to become translucent. Add the tofu and the sesame
seeds and stir-fry for a few minutes; then add about 3 table-

spoons water and 1 tablespoon tamari. Cover and let simmer for 3 minutes.

Add the raw peanuts or cashews to the wok and cook, stirring, about 3 minutes. Now add the steamed vegetables and the raw bean sprouts; toss together. Stir together for a minute, until the vegetables are heated through. Give the sauce one last stir and add to the wok; stir until the sauce thickens and the vegetables are glazed. Stir in the cilantro and serve over the hot, cooked grains.

Serves 6 to 8

MENU SUGGESTIONS

Hors d'oeuvres: Spring Rolls (page 44), Soya Pâté (page 22)

Soups: Cream of Raw and Cooked Mushroom (page 62), Egg Drop (page 51), or Thick Cabbage (page 82)

Salads: Cucumber (page 222), Watercress and Mushroom (page 226)

Desserts: Any dessert soufflé (pages 247–249), Bavarian Crème au Café (page 244), Pumpkin Pie (page 258), or any fruit pie (pages 255–256)

½ to 1 teaspoon freshly grated gingerroot, or ¼ to ½ teaspoon ground ginger
½ pound tofu, diced
1 tablespoon sesame seeds
3 tablespoons water, approximately
1 tablespoon tamari
¼ cup raw peanuts or cashews
Handful of soybean or mung sprouts
1 tablespoon chopped fresh cilantro

FOR THE BED OF GRAINS:

3 to 4 cups hot cooked millet, brown rice, couscous, or other grain of your choice (1½ cups raw; see pages xxxv–xxxvii)

Won Tons with Spinach and Tofu Filling in Ginger–Garlic Broth

FOR THE GINGER-GARLIC BROTH:

2 quarts water

1 vegetable bouillon cube

One 2-inch piece of fresh ginger-root, peeled and sliced

10 garlic cloves, minced or put through a press

2 teaspoons salt, preferably sea salt, or to taste

A few sprigs of cilantro

FOR THE WON TONS:

¾ pound fresh spinach, washed and stemmed, or 1 package (10 ounces) frozen spinach, thawed and excess moisture squeezed out

1 tablespoon canola or peanut oil

½ cup chopped green onion, both white part and green

1 large garlic clove, minced or put through a press

½ to 1 teaspoon freshly grated gingerroot

½ pound tofu, diced small

2 tablespoons sesame seeds

2 to 3 tablespoons tamari, or to taste

2 teaspoons dry sherry

¼ cup chopped cilantro

1 package won ton wrappers

1 egg, beaten

3 tablespoons chopped cilantro

This is a delightful, soothing main dish. The spinach can be washed and stemmed well in advance; once that task is done, making the spinach filling is a quick process. You can make the filling up to a day in advance and refrigerate it, covered, although it's best to make the won tons right after you finish the filling. The won tons should be frozen if you make them more than an hour ahead of time. They can be transferred directly from the freezer to the simmering broth.

This filling is so delicious that you could serve it without the won tons, as a side dish. The broth is sublime, too.

Make the broth:

Combine the ingredients in a soup pot or a large saucepan and bring to a boil. Reduce the heat, cover, and simmer 30 to 45 minutes, while you prepare the filling and fill the wontons. Taste and adjust seasonings. Remove from the heat, strain, and return to the pot. Set aside until you are ready to cook the wontons.

Prepare the won tons:

If using fresh spinach, blanch in a large pot of boiling water, transfer immediately to a bowl of cold water, drain, and squeeze dry in a kitchen towel.

Heat the oil in a wok or large nonstick skillet over medium-high heat and sauté the green onion with the garlic and fresh ginger for 3 minutes, until the onions begin to soften. Add the diced tofu and the sesame seeds and stir-fry for 3 to 5 minutes over a medium-high flame, adding more oil if necessary. Add the spinach and continue to stir for another minute. Add the tamari and sherry, and continue to stir-fry over a medium flame for 5 minutes, until the mixture is fragrant. Turn up the flame, and cook, stirring, until all the excess liquid evaporates. Remove from the heat, add the chopped cilantro, and correct the seasonings.

Now remove the entire mixture from the wok or skillet and chop fine, either by hand or with a food processor (with the processor, just a second or two of chopping will be sufficient).

Fill the won tons:

Place a level teaspoonful of the chopped mixture in the middle of each won ton skin. Fold the skin diagonally, to make a triangle, then take the 2 ends of the triangle and join them together at the tips. Seal with a little beaten egg. Transfer to a cutting board or baking sheet that you have dusted lightly with cornmeal or rice flour, and when all of the won tons are filled, put the board in the freezer, unless you are cooking the won tons right away.

Bring the broth back to a simmer and add the won tons. Simmer 5 to 7 minutes, turning the wontons once, or until they are cooked through but the skins are still firm to the bite. Stir in the additional cilantro, and serve in wide soup bowls with some of the broth ladled in.

Serves 6

MENU SUGGESTIONS
Salads: Avocado and Citrus (page 217), Potato–Egg with Chilled Broccoli (page 228), Chick-pea (page 231), or Mixed Green (page 215)
Desserts: Indian Pudding (page 252), Light Cheesecake (page 250), or Gingerbread Soufflé (page 248)

Curried Tofu and Vegetables
Over Millet or Bulgur

½ cup diagonally sliced or match-
    stick-cut carrots
1 cup cauliflower florets
1 cup broccoli florets
1 yellow squash, sliced
1 tablespoon canola or peanut oil
1 teaspoon mustard seed
1 teaspoon cuminseed, crushed in
    a mortar
½ teaspoon ground coriander
½ teaspoon ground cloves
½ teaspoon chili powder
1 teaspoon turmeric
2 to 3 teaspoons curry powder
½ teaspoon salt, preferably sea
    salt, or to taste
1 onion, sliced
1 garlic clove, minced or put
    through a press
1 teaspoon freshly grated ginger-
    root, or ½ teaspoon powdered
    ginger
1 cup diced tofu
¼ cup raw peanuts or cashews
¼ cup raisins
2 cups shredded red cabbage
½ cup Vegetable Stock (page 49)
½ cup green peas, steamed until
    bright green
1 cup buttermilk
1 tablespoon chopped cilantro
3 to 4 cups hot, cooked millet or
    bulgur (1½ cups raw; page
    xxxv)

For several years I had been trying to develop a really fine curry. Finally I tasted a marvelous one at a friend's restaurant. The secret, she revealed, is to sauté the seasonings with the onions for a long time. This brings out their aromas without overcooking any of the vegetables. I use creamy buttermilk to thicken the curry, so it's quite delicious but low in fat.

Steam the carrots, cauliflower, broccoli, and squash for 5 minutes, until crisp-tender, and set aside.

Heat the oil over low heat in a heavy-bottomed dutch oven, wok, or large nonstick skillet with a lid, and add all the spices, from the mustard seed through the salt. Cook, stirring, for 1 minute, and add the onion. Stir together and cook for 8 to 10 minutes, stirring often, until the onions are thoroughly tender and beginning to stick to the pan. Add the garlic, and ginger and cook, stirring, for a minute, until they begin to color. Add the tofu, peanuts or cashews, and raisins, and cook, stirring, for 5 minutes.

Add the steamed vegetables and toss together for 3 minutes. Add the cabbage and pour in the ½ cup stock. Bring to a simmer, cover, and simmer for 10 minutes, until the vegetables are cooked through but still have some body. Add the peas and stir everything together.

Remove from the heat and let cool for a minute, then stir in the buttermilk and cilantro. Adjust the seasoning— you may want to add a little curry powder or salt—and serve immediately over the hot, cooked millet or bulgur, accompanied by the side dishes listed opposite.

Serves 6 to 8

MENU SUGGESTIONS

Soups: Curry-flavored Lentil (page 87), Fruit (page 55)

Salad: Grated Carrot (page 230)

Side Dishes: Chutney (page 173), Banana Raita (page 171),
  Cucumber Raita (page 171), or Lentil Dal (page 165)

Desserts: Bavarian Crème au Café (page 244), Gingerbread
  Soufflé (page 248), Strawberry and Cassis Sherbet
  (page 261), or Indian Pudding (page 252)

Curry Salad

1 recipe Curry Dressing (page 208)

1½ to 2 cups broccoli florets, steamed briefly until bright green

3 tablespoons whole almonds

1½ to 2¼ cups cooked brown rice (¾ to 1 cup raw; page xxxv)

1 to 1½ cups cooked wheat berries (½ cup raw; page xxxv)

1¼ cups cooked chick-peas (½ cup dried; page xxxvi)

1 teaspoon salt, preferably sea salt

¼ cup freshly grated Parmesan or Romano cheese

2 ribs celery, chopped

1 cucumber, peeled (if bitter or waxed) and sliced

4 green onions, both white part and green, chopped

¼ cup raisins

¼ cup cut green beans, steamed briefly until bright green

1 green pepper, seeded and chopped

1 sweet red pepper, seeded and chopped

1 head leaf lettuce, separated into leaves and washed

Halved cherry tomatoes for garnish

I love it when we make this in my cooking class, or I make it for a catering job, because I get to eat leftovers for as long as they last (usually not too long). It's one of my favorites, and is included in this section because it's such a good main dish in itself, especially on a warm evening. At first the combination of ingredients may sound strange to you, but you'll see that they make a remarkable dish with a fresh, health-giving quality. The combination of the grains and chick-peas with the Parmesan, and the yogurt in the dressing, makes this a good example of a "complementary" protein dish.

Remember to cook the beans and grains in advance, and give the salad a little time to marinate.

Prepare the curry dressing.

Set aside some of the broccoli and almonds for garnish. Toss the remainder together with all the other ingredients (except for the lettuce and cherry tomatoes) and the dressing.

Line a salad bowl with the lettuce leaves and mound the salad on top. Decorate with the reserved broccoli florets and almonds, and the cherry tomatoes.

Serve immediately or chill and serve cold.

Serves 6 to 8

MENU SUGGESTIONS

Hors d'oeuvres: Vegetable Platter with Assorted Dips (page 40)

Soups: Bulgarian Cucumber (page 91), Turkish Cucumber (page 92), or Purée of Strawberry (page 93)

Desserts: Strawberry and Cassis Sherbet (page 261), Peaches Marsala (page 240)

Baked Beans with Fruit and Chutney

Here's another sweet and pungent dish, this time with the warming, familiar taste of Boston baked beans and the exotic touch of chutney. Serve topped with yogurt, on thick slices of whole-wheat toast.

Drain the beans and combine with the 2 quarts water in a stockpot or dutch oven. Bring to a boil, reduce the heat, cover, and simmer 1 hour. Add the salt and simmer another 30 minutes, until the beans are tender but not mushy. Drain, reserving 1½ cups of the cooking liquid.

In a small bowl, dissolve the mustard in the bean liquid and combine with the finely chopped onion, chutney, and salt and pepper to taste. Stir this into the beans.

Preheat the oven to 325 degrees; oil a 2- or 3-quart lidded casserole or baking dish. Pour half of the bean mixture into the prepared casserole. Top with half of the sliced apples, peaches, and apricots, then pour in the rest of the bean mixture and top with the rest of the fruit. Combine the honey and molasses and pour evenly over the top.

Cover and bake for 1 hour, then remove the cover and bake for another 30 minutes.

Serve steaming hot, topped with yogurt if you wish.

Serves 6 to 8

MENU SUGGESTIONS

Soups: Corn Chowder (page 81), Cream of Wheat Berry (page 67)

Salads: Mixed Green (page 215), Avocado and Citrus (page 217), or Brown Rice (page 225)

Desserts: Fresh fruit and cheese (page 234), Light Cheesecake (page 250), or Buckwheat Cake (page 260)

2 cups dried navy beans, washed and soaked overnight or for at least 6 hours in 1½ quarts water

2 quarts additional water

2 teaspoons salt, preferably sea salt, or to taste

1½ teaspoons dry mustard, or 1 tablespoon Dijon mustard

1 onion, chopped fine

½ cup chutney, homemade (page 173) or commercial

Freshly ground pepper, to taste

2 apples, sliced

3 peaches (in season), peeled and sliced

½ cup dried apricots

¼ cup mild honey

¼ cup molasses

1 cup plain nonfat yogurt, homemade (page 202) or commercial (optional)

Potatoes Gruyère

1 garlic clove, cut in half lengthwise

3 pounds (12 medium) new or
waxy potatoes, peeled,
scrubbed, and sliced about ¼
inch thick

3½ cups low-fat or skim milk

2 large eggs, lightly beaten

1 teaspoon salt, preferably sea salt,
or to taste

Freshly ground pepper, to taste

3 ounces Gruyère cheese, grated
(¾ cup grated)

1 tablespoon butter

*This is a rich, satisfying dish that goes well with a tomato-
based soup and a crisp green salad.*

Preheat the oven to 400 degrees; rub the inside of a 3-quart
baking dish or gratin dish with the cut clove of garlic.

Place the potatoes in the baking dish in an even layer.
Beat together the milk, eggs, salt, and pepper. Stir in half
the cheese. Pour this mixture over the potatoes.

Place in the preheated oven and bake for 1 hour, stirring the gratin every 15 minutes. Sprinkle on the remaining
cheese and dot with butter. Continue to bake another 15 to
30 minutes, until the gratin is crusty and brown on the top.
Remove from the oven and serve.

Serves 6 to 8

MENU SUGGESTIONS

Hors d'oeuvres: Tiropites (page 32), Crudité Salad (page
217)

Soups: Blender Gazpacho (page 89), Egg Drop (page 51)

Salads: Mixed Green (page 215), Beet and Endive (page
227)

Desserts: Peaches Marsala (page 240), Raspberries in Red
Wine (page 240)

Grated Potato Pie

This has many of the qualities I love in potato pancakes, with none of the fuss or fat. Serve it with applesauce and a full-bodied salad.

Preheat the oven to 400 degrees. Oil a 10-inch tart pan or a 2-quart gratin dish.

Heat 1 tablespoon of the oil in a heavy-bottomed non-stick skillet over medium heat and add the onion and a little salt. Sauté, stirring, for about 8 minutes, until the onion is tender and beginning to color. Stir in the thyme and remove from the heat.

Grate the potatoes and press out excess water.

In a large bowl, beat together the eggs, milk, flour, pepper, and nutmeg. Add about ½ teaspoon of salt. Stir in the onion, potatoes, and Parmesan. Turn into the baking dish and sprinkle on the bread crumbs. Drizzle on the remaining tablespoon of olive oil.

Bake in the preheated oven for 40 to 45 minutes, or until the top is golden. Remove from the heat and serve hot or at room temperature, with homemade applesauce on the side.

Serves 6 to 8

MENU SUGGESTIONS

Soups: Cream of Raw and Cooked Mushroom (page 62), Fresh Pea (page 66)

Salads: Mixed Green (page 215), Green Bean, Almond, and Mushroom (page 224)

Desserts: Pears Poached in Red Wine with a Touch of Cassis (page 236), Mediterranean Fruit Compote (page 237)

2 tablespoons olive oil, plus more to oil the pan
1 medium onion, thinly sliced
Salt, preferably sea salt, to taste
1 teaspoon fresh thyme leaves, or ½ teaspoon dried thyme
2 pounds potatoes, peeled and grated
3 large eggs, beaten
2 tablespoons low-fat milk
1 tablespoon unbleached white flour
Freshly ground pepper, to taste
Pinch of freshly grated nutmeg
¼ cup freshly grated Parmesan cheese
2 tablespoons whole-wheat bread crumbs

Couscous with Vegetables

⅔ cup dried chick-peas

2 quarts water

2 onions, sliced

2 large carrots, sliced

4 large garlic cloves, minced or
    put through a press

1 bay leaf

2 teaspoons salt, preferably sea
    salt, or to taste

1 teaspoon dried thyme

½ teaspoon dried rosemary

½ teaspoon ground cinnamon

¼ teaspoon freshly grated nutmeg

2 medium zucchini, sliced

2 medium yellow squash, sliced

2 cups fresh or frozen green peas

Freshly ground pepper, to taste

1½ cups couscous

¼ cup chopped cilantro

Harissa or Tabasco sauce
    (optional)

Couscous is a grainlike pasta made from semolina wheat. Incredibly delicate and tasty, it is precooked and requires only a quick soak followed by steaming to cook through. You can steam the couscous in a colander placed over a pot, or in a couscoussière, a steamer made specifically for couscous. I've been quite satisfied with the first method, in which the only special equipment one needs is a colander.

Sometimes the little grains of couscous tend to stick together (which is why it is steamed instead of boiled). If after cooking they become sticky or gummy, just separate the grains with forks or with your hands.

One can go through an elaborate series of steps to make couscous. The best and most complete treatment of couscous cookery is to be found in Paula Wolfert's Couscous and Other Good Food from Morocco. *The simple method I am giving you here comes right off the back of the package, and it works well for me. Couscous is usually served with a spicy hot sauce on the side called* harissa, *which can be found in imported food shops.*

Wash the chick-peas and soak in 2 cups of water for 6 hours or overnight.

Drain the chick-peas and combine with the 2 quarts of water, the onions, carrots, half the garlic, and the bay leaf in a stockpot or dutch oven, or in the bottom part of a couscoussière. Bring to a boil, reduce the heat, cover, and simmer 1 hour. Add 2 teaspoons salt, the remaining garlic, the thyme, rosemary, cinnamon, and nutmeg, and simmer another 30 minutes to 1 hour, until the chick-peas are tender. Taste and adjust the salt. Add the zucchini, yellow squash, and peas, and simmer another 10 minutes, until the vegetables are tender. Add a generous amount of pepper.

Place the couscous in a bowl. Strain off 2 cups of the cooking liquid from the vegetables and pour over the couscous. Let sit for 10 to 15 minutes, until the water is absorbed. Stir every 5 minutes with a wooden spoon, or rub the couscous between your thumbs and fingers, so that the couscous doesn't lump. The couscous will now be soft; fluff it with a fork or with your hands. Taste the couscous and add salt if necessary.

Place the couscous in a colander, sieve, or the top part of a couscoussière and set it over the vegetable mixture, making sure that the bottom of the colander does not touch the liquid (remove some of the liquid if it does). Wrap a towel or cheesecloth around the space between the sides of the colander and the pot so that the steam will come up only through the colander. Now cover the couscous with a towel or with the lid of the pot and bring the liquid to a simmer. Simmer 10 minutes. Transfer the couscous to a serving bowl. Stir the cilantro into the vegetable/broth mixture.

To serve, spoon the couscous into warmed wide soup bowls and ladle on a generous helping of the stock and vegetables. Pass harissa or Tabasco sauce for those who want to spice up their couscous. Alternatively, you can add a bit of harissa or Tabasco directly to the broth.

Serves 6 to 8

MENU SUGGESTIONS
Hors d'oeuvres: Soya Pâté (page 22), Mushroom Pâté
    (page 23)
Salads: Mixed Green (page 215), Grated Carrot (page 230),
    Beet and Endive (page 227), or Spinach (page 216)
Desserts: Fruit pie (pages 255–256), Oranges Grand
    Marnier (page 238), or Pumpkin Pie (page 258)

Peppers Stuffed with Curried Millet

6 to 8 medium green peppers,
tops cut off, seeds and white
membranes removed

2 tablespoons peanut or canola oil

1 onion, chopped

2 teaspoons curry powder, or
more to taste

1 teaspoon ground cumin

2 large garlic cloves, minced or
put through a press

2 medium carrots, cut in 1-inch
matchsticks

Salt, preferably sea salt, to taste

1½ cups raw millet, cooked (see
page xxxv) with ½ teaspoon
saffron

1½ cups fresh or frozen green
peas, steamed until bright
green

½ cup chopped cilantro

Freshly ground pepper, to taste

1 cup Curry Dressing (page 208),
plain yogurt, or buttermilk

Here is an unusual curry filling for peppers. It's a nice break from the traditional cheese or brown rice stuffing. I prefer nice light millet for this dish, but any grains (including leftover ones) will do. You can make the filling and stuff the peppers a day in advance.

Preheat the oven to 350 degrees.

Blanch the peppers for 5 minutes in a large pot of boiling salted water. Rinse in cold water. Drain upside down while you prepare the filling.

Heat the oil in a wok or large, heavy-bottomed nonstick skillet over medium heat and sauté the onion with the curry powder and cumin for 5 minutes, until the onion is tender. Add the garlic and carrots and a little salt, and cook for 5 minutes longer, stirring. Add a little water if the vegetables begin to stick to the pan or more oil, if necessary, then add the cooked millet and peas. Stir together and remove from the heat. Add the cilantro and pepper, and adjust salt.

Fill each pepper with this mixture. Set them in an oiled 3-quart baking dish, place in the preheated oven, and bake for 30 minutes.

Serve with the curry dressing, yogurt, or buttermilk on the side.

Serves 6 to 8

MENU SUGGESTIONS

Hors d'oeuvres: Fresh fruit (page 234), French Bread (page 10) and Soya Pâté (page 22), or Tiropites (page 32)

Soups: Curried Eggplant (page 88), Dill (page 77), or Turkish Cucumber (page 92)

Salads: Mixed Green (page 215), Cucumber (page 222)

Desserts: Bananas Poached in White Wine (page 235), Baked Apples (page 242), or Watermelon–Fruit Extravaganza (page 239)

Stuffed Zucchini

This provençal-inspired dish is especially good for those huge zucchinis that grow in your garden and appear in produce markets in summer and fall.

Preheat the oven to 400 degrees.

Steam the zucchini for 10 minutes, then scoop out the seeds and stringy pulp. Cut away the inside flesh, leaving a ¼-inch-thick shell, and chop the flesh. Set shells aside.

Blanch the spinach in boiling water, or wilt in the water left on the leaves after washing, in a skillet over high heat. Rinse with cold water, squeeze dry in a towel, and chop.

Heat 1 tablespoon oil in a large skillet over medium heat and add the onion. Cook, stirring, until the onion is tender, about 5 minutes; add the garlic. Cook, stirring, for about a minute, until the garlic begins to color, then stir in the chopped zucchini and salt to taste. Cook, stirring, for about 5 minutes, until the zucchini is tender. Add the spinach, bulgur, and herbs. Stir and remove from the heat. Season with salt and pepper. Stir in the egg.

Stuff the zucchini shells with the mixture. Place in an oiled baking dish, sprinkle on the bread crumbs and Parmesan, and drizzle on the remaining tablespoon of olive oil. Bake for 30 minutes, until the top is browned. Serve hot or at room temperature, with the tomato sauce.

Serves 6 to 8

MENU SUGGESTIONS
Hors d'oeuvres: Tiropites (page 32), Spring Rolls (page 44)
Soups: Leek (page 69), Purée of White Bean (page 58)
Salads: Mixed Green (page 215), Spinach (page 216), or
     Watercress and Mushroom (page 226)
Desserts: Fresh fruit (page 234), Apricot Soufflé (page
     247), or Orange Dessert Crêpes (page 243)

1 huge or 2 large zucchini, cut in
     half lengthwise
10 ounces fresh spinach, washed,
     stems removed
2 tablespoons olive oil
1 onion, chopped
2 garlic cloves, minced or put
     through a press
Salt, preferably sea salt, to taste
2 cups cooked bulgur or couscous
     (1 cup raw; pages xxxv, xxxvii)
½ cup chopped fresh herbs, such
     as parsley, thyme, oregano,
     basil, rosemary, mint
Freshly ground pepper, to taste
1 large egg, lightly beaten
¼ cup whole-wheat bread crumbs
¼ cup freshly grated Parmesan
     cheese
1 recipe Easy Tomato Sauce (page
     201), for serving

Some Grain, Legume, and Vegetable Side Dishes

A curry is quite wonderful on its own, but with chutney and raita on the side it becomes truly outstanding. Grains will enhance a delicate Chinese vegetable dish and soak up its sublime, gingery sauce.

There are several criteria for choosing a side dish. Some give body to a main course and boost the protein. Grains, for example, complete the amino acid patterns of legumes, turning a curry or bean dish into a substantial meal. And grains and legumes can be dressed up: Brown rice cooked with saffron takes on a beautiful yellow hue; wild rice, chestnuts, and mushrooms together make an unforgettable side dish. Lentils, refried and seasoned with cumin and curry, are transformed into mouthwatering lentil dal, a perfect complement to curried tofu and vegetables.

Very often the need for color will determine the choice of a side dish. Though beautiful in themselves, soufflés and dishes like baked beans with fruit and chutney each display only one color, so your plate calls for another; perhaps the green of gingered broccoli or asparagus or artichokes. Or you might prefer the juicy red of tomatoes and fresh herbs. Similarly, a main dish in which there is one predominating flavor or texture will go well with a "busy" side dish, like Chinese-style snow peas and water chestnuts or saffron millet with Indian spices.

Sometimes the "main attraction" of your meal is in the spirit of a particular country. In this case, you'll most likely want to serve a side dish that conveys the same atmosphere. Whenever black bean enchiladas are requested for a catering job, so is Spanish rice. Vegetable shish kebab goes well with saffron brown rice or with couscous.

When I go to a restaurant, I am as critical of the vegetables that are served on the side as I am of the entrée. If the vegetables are overcooked or drowned in butter, the restaurant gets a lower rating. I prefer my green vegetables steamed just until they display their brightest color; this way they'll have a lively texture. If you boil them, they will lose not only their firmness but also many of their nutrients.

I hope these recipes will set your imagination going. You can try different vegetables with the same sauces and techniques, and experiment with new grains and legumes. There are enough recipes for side dishes to fill a book, but I've restrained myself here and limited this chapter to some of my favorites.

Spanish Rice

This beautiful, savory brown rice dish—my version of a classic recipe—is a good accompaniment for any Mexican dish. It helps to use a nonstick pan for this. If you don't have one, watch the rice closely and add stock as necessary so that it won't stick.

Have the stock simmering in a saucepan.

Heat 1 tablespoon of the oil over medium heat in a large, heavy-bottomed nonstick skillet or lidded wok and add the onion. Sauté, stirring, for about 5 minutes, until the onion has softened. Add 1 of the garlic cloves and both of the green peppers. Continue to cook, stirring, for another 5 minutes, until the peppers begin to soften. Add the remaining 1 tablespoon of oil and the rice. Sauté, stirring, until the rice begins to smell toasty. Add the tomatoes, the remaining garlic, salt, pepper, saffron, and 3 cups of the stock and bring to a simmer. Cover and cook for 30 minutes, or until the water or stock is absorbed and the rice is tender, adding more stock as needed (if the rice sticks to the bottom of the pan it will burn).

Serves 6

About 4 cups Vegetable Stock (page 49), or Garlic Broth (page 50), as necessary
2 tablespoons olive oil
1 onion, sliced
3 garlic cloves, minced or put through a press
2 green peppers, seeded and sliced thin
1½ cups raw brown rice
2 cups peeled, chopped tomatoes
Salt, preferably sea salt, to taste
Freshly ground pepper, to taste
½ teaspoon saffron threads

Saffron Brown Rice

Any time you want to dress up brown rice, saffron is the miracle seasoning. This rice goes well with curries and the Vegetable Shish Kebab on page 143.

Combine the rice and water and bring to a boil. Add the remaining ingredients, stir once, cover, and reduce the heat. Simmer 35 to 45 minutes, until all the water is absorbed. Serve hot.

Serves 6

1½ cups raw brown rice
3 cups water
1 teaspoon saffron threads
½ teaspoon salt, preferably sea salt
2 tablespoons lemon juice
½ cup currants (optional)

Saffron Millet with Indian Spices

3½ cups Vegetable Stock (page 49)

Seeds from 6 green cardamom pods

½ teaspoon coriander seeds

6 whole cloves

1 tablespoon canola oil

1½ cups millet

½ teaspoon saffron threads

¼ to ½ teaspoon salt, preferably sea salt (depending on how salty your stock is)

This fragrant dish can accompany vegetables or serve as a stuffing for peppers or squash.

Simmer the stock in a saucepan.

Pound the spices together in a mortar and pestle, or grind in an electric spice mill.

Heat the oil in a large, heavy-bottomed saucepan over medium heat and add the spices. Cook for 1 minute, until the spices begin to smell toasty, and stir in the millet. Cook, stirring, for another minute or two, until the millet begins to smell toasty, and stir in the hot stock. Bring back to a simmer, add the saffron and salt, reduce the heat, cover, and simmer 30 to 40 minutes, until the liquid is absorbed. Serve hot.

Serves 6

Wild Rice with Chestnuts and Mushrooms

I love the way the earthy flavor of the rice contrasts with the sweetness of the chestnuts in this delightful winter pilaf.

Preheat the oven to 425 degrees. Using a sharp knife, cut an "X" on the flat side of each chestnut. Place the chestnuts on a baking sheet and bake 10 to 15 minutes, until the shells are beginning to curl at the cuts, and the nuts smell toasty. Remove from the heat and transfer to a bowl. As soon as you can handle them, peel the chestnuts, making sure to remove the inner paper shell inside the hard shell. Cut the chestnuts in half and set aside.

Meanwhile, bring the stock to a boil in a large saucepan and add the wild rice. Bring back to a boil, reduce the heat, cover, and simmer 40 minutes, until the rice is tender. Remove from the heat and pour off any stock that remains in the pot.

Heat 1 tablespoon of the oil in a large, heavy-bottomed nonstick skillet over medium heat and add the onion or shallots. Cook, stirring, until tender, 3 to 5 minutes, and add the mushrooms. Cook, stirring, until they begin to release liquid, about 5 minutes, and add the sherry or wine, the garlic, thyme, and salt and pepper. Continue to cook, stirring, until the liquid has just about evaporated.

Add the remaining ½ tablespoon of oil and stir in the wild rice, the chestnuts, and the parsley. Stir together until the rice is heated through. Taste and adjust seasonings, and serve.

Serves 6

12 chestnuts in their shells
1 quart Vegetable Stock (page 49)
1½ cups wild rice
1½ tablespoons olive oil
1 medium onion or 3 shallots, chopped
½ pound mushrooms, trimmed and sliced
1 tablespoon dry sherry or dry white wine
2 garlic cloves, minced or put through a press
1 teaspoon fresh thyme leaves, or ½ teaspoon dried thyme
Salt, preferably sea salt, to taste
Freshly ground pepper, to taste
¼ cup chopped fresh parsley

Whole-Grain Pasta
with Olive Oil and Herbs

3 tablespoons olive oil, plus a
    tablespoon either olive oil or
    canola oil for the water
2 garlic cloves, minced or put
    through a press
¾ pound whole-grain pasta of
    your choice
¼ cup chopped fresh parsley
¼ cup chopped fresh basil, or use
    ½ cup chopped parsley in all
Freshly ground pepper, to taste
¼ cup freshly grated Parmesan
    cheese

Whole-grain pasta is readily available in natural foods stores. There are several combinations—whole wheat, soya, soy–whole wheat, whole wheat–sesame, on and on.

Heat the 3 tablespoons of olive oil in a saucepan with the garlic over medium-low heat, just until the garlic begins to sizzle. Remove from the heat at once and set aside.

    Bring a large pot of water to a boil, and add about a tablespoon of salt, a tablespoon of oil (canola or olive), and the pasta. Cook the pasta al dente. Drain and turn into a warmed serving dish. Toss at once with the olive oil and garlic, the herbs, and the pepper. Sprinkle on the Parmesan and serve.

Serves 6 to 8 as a side dish

Soba (Buckwheat Noodles)

¾ pound buckwheat noodles
2 tablespoons sesame oil
1 tablespoon tamari (optional)
3 tablespoons chopped cilantro
    (optional)

Buckwheat noodles, which are easy to find in Asian markets, have a marvelous nutty/earthy flavor.

Cook the buckwheat noodles al dente (they cook quickly, in about 4 minutes). Drain and toss with the sesame oil, tamari, and cilantro. Serve hot.

Serves 6 to 8 as a side dish

Lentil Dal

Lentil dal can be soupy, or it can be like Indian refried beans, as in this version. You can make it with split peas or chick-peas, but lentils, with their distinctive flavor, have always been a favorite of mine. This is always a good side dish for curries. The lentils will complement grains.

Heat 1 tablespoon of the oil in a heavy-bottomed saucepan or dutch oven over medium-low heat and add the onion. Cook, stirring, until it begins to soften, and add the garlic, ¼ teaspoon of the chili powder, the turmeric, cuminseed, and 1 teaspoon of the curry powder. Stir together for about 30 seconds, and add the lentils, bay leaf, and water, and bring to a boil. Reduce the heat, cover, and simmer 30 minutes. Add the salt and continue to simmer another 30 minutes, until the lentils are tender.

Heat the remaining tablespoon of oil in a heavy-bottomed nonstick skillet and add the ground cumin, the remaining ¼ teaspoon of chili powder, and the remaining teaspoon of curry powder. Fry the lentils in the same way that you refry beans (see page 98), mashing with a potato masher or the back of a spoon. The mixture should be like a moist, textured purée and should hold its shape in a spoon; don't allow it to become too dry. Turn into a warmed serving dish and serve with curries.

Serves 6

2 tablespoons canola or peanut oil
1 onion, chopped
1 garlic clove, minced or put
    through a press
½ teaspoon chili powder
½ teaspoon turmeric
½ teaspoon cuminseed
2 teaspoons curry powder
1 cup dried lentils, washed
1 bay leaf
3 cups water, or more if necessary
½ to 1 teaspoon salt, preferably
    sea salt, or more as desired
½ teaspoon ground cumin

Chinese-style Snow Peas and Water Chestnuts

5 tablespoons water

2 tablespoons tamari

1 tablespoon dry sherry

1 teaspoon Pernod or other anise-
flavored liqueur

1 tablespoon arrowroot, or more
if necessary

1 pound fresh snow peas, strings
removed

1 tablespoon canola or peanut oil

4 green onions, both white part
and green, chopped

1 garlic clove, minced or put
through a press

1 teaspoon freshly grated gingerroot

1 small can (4 ounces) water
chestnuts, drained, then sliced
or quartered

This is one of many satisfying Asian stir-fries. You can turn it into a main dish if you wish, by adding tofu to the mixture and sautéing it with the green onions and garlic.

In a small bowl, combine the water, tamari, sherry, Pernod, and arrowroot, stirring well; set aside.

Steam the snow peas briefly—about 5 minutes—just until they are bright green. Heat the oil in a large skillet or wok over medium-high heat, and sauté the green onions until tender, about 3 to 5 minutes. Add the garlic and ginger, and cook for another 30 seconds to a minute, until the garlic begins to color. Add the snow peas and water chestnuts and stir together. Add the sauce and stir until the vegetables are glazed, adding more arrowroot dissolved in a little water, if necessary.

Correct the seasoning and serve.

Serves 6

Gingered Broccoli

You can, of course, use other vegetables here. Whenever your menu calls for a crisp green side dish, this Asian-style glazed broccoli will fit in beautifully.

Steam the broccoli for 5 minutes, until crisp-tender.

Heat the oil over medium heat in a wok or heavy-bottomed skillet and sauté the ginger for 1 minute. Add the broccoli and stir together for about 1 minute, until the broccoli is coated with the ginger.

Dilute the honey in the soy sauce and water. Pour over the broccoli and continue to cook, stirring, for another 5 minutes. Stir in the arrowroot or cornstarch mixture and cook, stirring, until the sauce thickens and the broccoli is glazed.

Serve immediately.

Serves 6

1 bunch broccoli, broken into florets (large ones cut in half lengthwise)
1 tablespoon peanut or canola oil
2 to 3 teaspoons freshly grated gingerroot, to taste
1 tablespoon mild honey
1 tablespoon soy sauce
¼ cup water
1 tablespoon arrowroot or 2 teaspoons cornstarch, dissolved in a little water

Minted Fresh Peas

This sweet combination makes a delicate springtime dish.

Shell the peas and steam them until bright green and tender, about 5 to 10 minutes (depending on the size of the peas). Add salt and pepper, then toss with the mint and optional butter. Serve hot.

Serves 6

4 pounds (unshelled) tender, fresh green peas (4 cups shelled)
Salt, preferably sea salt, to taste
Freshly ground pepper, to taste
1 to 2 tablespoons chopped fresh mint
1 tablespoon butter (optional)

Grated Zucchini Sauté

2 pounds zucchini

Salt, preferably sea salt

1 tablespoon olive oil

½ onion, minced

1 red bell pepper, seeded and
minced

3 garlic cloves, minced or put
through a press

1 teaspoon fresh thyme leaves, or
½ teaspoon dried thyme

2 tablespoons freshly grated
Parmesan cheese (optional)

Freshly ground pepper, to taste

This is a beautiful dish with zesty Mediterranean flavors.

Grate the zucchini and sprinkle generously with salt. Let sit for 20 minutes. Squeeze out the moisture by twisting the grated zucchini in a kitchen towel. Rinse and squeeze out the moisture again.

Heat the oil over medium heat in a large, nonstick skillet or wok and sauté the onion until just about tender, about 3 minutes. Add the red pepper and a little salt, and sauté for 3 minutes, stirring or shaking the pan. Add the garlic and thyme, stir for about 30 seconds, and add the zucchini. Cook, stirring often, until the zucchini is tender and aromatic, about 5 minutes. Add the Parmesan if desired, stir everything together off the heat, taste, and add salt and pepper to taste. Serve at once, or transfer to an ovenproof serving dish and reheat for 20 minutes in a 350-degree oven before serving.

Serves 6

Baked Acorn Squash

Acorn squash has always been a favorite of mine. Here it is simply baked, enhanced with butter, honey, and a little cinnamon.

Preheat the oven to 375 degrees.

Cut the acorn squash in half with a sharp knife and remove the seeds. Place a teaspoon each of butter and honey in the hollow of each half, and sprinkle on some salt, pepper, and cinnamon.

Place the squash halves in 1 layer in an oiled baking dish, cover with foil, and bake for 1 to 1½ hours, basting every 15 minutes by brushing with the butter and honey that have melted together in the hollow. Remove from the oven when a toothpick can pierce through to the skin easily.

Serve hot.

Serves 6

3 acorn squash
2 tablespoons butter
2 tablespoons mild honey
Salt, preferably sea salt, to taste
Freshly ground pepper, to taste
Ground cinnamon, to taste

Spinach and Kale Gratin

2 pounds spinach, stems removed
  and leaves washed
1 pound kale, stems removed and
  leaves washed
1 tablespoon olive oil
4 large garlic cloves, minced or
  put through a press
2 teaspoons chopped fresh rosemary, or 1 teaspoon crumbled
  dried rosemary
1 teaspoon fresh thyme leaves, or
  ½ teaspoon dried thyme
1 recipe Béchamel, made with
  olive oil (page 200)
Salt, preferably sea salt, to taste
Freshly ground pepper, to taste
3 tablespoons freshly grated
  Parmesan or Gruyère cheese

This is a robust gratin, full of healthful greens and garlicky Mediterranean flavors. You may substitute other greens, such as turnip greens, beet greens, or Swiss chard, for the kale.

Preheat the oven to 400 degrees. Oil a 2-quart gratin dish.

Wash the spinach and kale and wilt in a large, nonstick skillet over high heat in the water left on the leaves (this should take no more than 3 minutes, once the water begins to boil). Remove from the heat, rinse with cold water, squeeze dry in a kitchen towel, and chop.

Heat the oil over medium-low heat in a large, heavy-bottomed nonstick skillet and add the garlic. As soon as the garlic begins to color, after about 1 minute, stir in the chopped greens, the rosemary, and the thyme. Stir together for about 1 minute and remove from the heat.

Stir the béchamel into the greens. Add salt and pepper, and turn into the prepared gratin. Sprinkle the cheese over the top.

Bake in the preheated oven for 20 to 30 minutes, until the top is just beginning to brown and the gratin is sizzling. Serve hot.

Serves 6

Winter Squash Gratin

A comforting gratin like this is one of the best vehicles I can think of for winter squash.

Preheat the oven to 400 degrees. Butter or oil a 2- or 3-quart gratin dish.

Steam the squash for 10 minutes, until tender. Transfer to a bowl and toss with the sage or thyme, the garlic, nutmeg, salt, and pepper. Stir in the béchamel.

Turn the squash mixture into the prepared baking dish. Sprinkle the top with the cheese, then the bread crumbs. Drizzle on the olive oil.

Bake 30 to 40 minutes, until the top is beginning to brown and the mixture is bubbling. Serve hot.

Serves 6

3 pounds winter squash, such as butternut or acorn squash, peeled, seeds and strings removed, sliced about ¼ inch thick

2 tablespoons chopped fresh sage, or 2 teaspoons fresh thyme leaves, or 1 teaspoon dried sage or dried thyme

2 large garlic cloves, minced or put through a press

¼ teaspoon freshly grated nutmeg

Salt, preferably sea salt, to taste

Freshly ground pepper, to taste

1 recipe Béchamel, either butter-based or olive oil-based (page 200)

¼ cup grated Gruyère or Parmesan cheese

2 tablespoons fresh or dry bread crumbs

1 tablespoon olive oil

Banana Raita

1 teaspoon butter

1½ teaspoons cuminseed

¼ teaspoon cardamom seeds

¼ teaspoon ground coriander

⅛ teaspoon cayenne pepper

2 cups mashed ripe bananas
(about 3 medium bananas)

2 cups plain low-fat yogurt,
homemade (page 202) or
commercial

A raita is a cooling, yogurt-based accompaniment to curries. This banana raita is almost dessertlike, and a pleasure to have on hand.

Melt the butter in a skillet. Pound the spices together in a mortar; they should not be completely crushed. Add them to the butter and stir for a minute, then quickly add the mashed bananas. Stir together for 1 minute.

Remove from the heat and stir in the yogurt. Transfer to a serving dish and chill well.

Serve with curries.

Serves 6

Cucumber Raita

1 cucumber, peeled and minced

1 cup plain nonfat yogurt, homemade (page 202) or
commercial

Salt, preferably sea salt, to taste

¼ teaspoon ground coriander

¼ teaspoon ground cumin

Here is another cooling mixture to eat with spicy curries. Leftover cucumber raita can be served as a salad.

Combine all the ingredients; stir together and chill well.

Serve with curries.

Serves 6

Chutney

Make up a large batch of chutney once a year and you'll always have a welcome accompaniment to curries and other dishes. We usually see expensive jars of chutney on gourmet shelves; you'll be pleased when you see how easy it is to make your own. Your kitchen will be redolent with the fabulous smells as it simmers.

Combine in a large, heavy saucepan the vinegar, honey, molasses, garlic, salt, ginger, and remaining spices and cook over a medium flame, stirring constantly, for 10 minutes.

Add the tomatoes and the remaining ingredients and bring to a boil. Cover and reduce the heat; simmer for 2 hours, until you have a chutney with a thick consistency. Adjust the seasoning.

If you are storing the chutney, seal it in hot, sterilized, airtight jars and store in a cool, dark place. Refrigerate the amount you wish to use in an airtight container.

Serve with curries.

Makes 2 quarts

1 cup cider vinegar
¾ cup mild honey
¼ cup molasses
2 garlic cloves, minced or put through a press
1 tablespoon salt, preferably sea salt
2 teaspoons freshly grated ginger-root, or 1 teaspoon ground ginger
¼ teaspoon freshly ground pepper
½ teaspoon ground cinnamon
1 tablespoon mustard seed
½ teaspoon ground cloves
½ teaspoon ground coriander
2 medium tomatoes, peeled and diced
1 small onion, chopped fine
2 apples, peeled and diced
2 pears, peeled and diced
½ cup raisins
½ cup chopped dried figs

Mashed Potatoes with Olive Oil

2 pounds waxy potatoes, peeled if
    desired
1 cup low-fat milk
2 tablespoons olive oil
Salt, preferably sea salt, to taste
Freshly ground pepper, to taste

Mashed potatoes are usually incredibly rich with butter. But butter isn't really necessary. Milk will do the trick. Add a little olive oil for a Mediterranean twist.

Steam the potatoes until tender, about 30 minutes. Heat the milk in a saucepan.

When the potatoes are tender, drain and mash with a potato masher, a fork, or a ricer. Add the oil, and work in the milk. Season to taste with salt and pepper. Place in a warm serving dish and serve immediately; or, if you can't serve right away, keep warm by placing, covered, in a pan of hot water, or in a low oven.

Serves 6

Pasta

If there is one type of food that has allowed more people in this country to become vegetarians, or at least partial vegetarians, since I first wrote this book, it is pasta. Pasta hit the big time sometime during the eighties, and there's been no looking back. Pasta takes all the mystery and challenge out of vegetarian eating; it's easy to prepare, and hard not to like it. And what a perfect vehicle it is for colorful, healthy, fragrant vegetables and herbs. It probably doesn't even occur to many people who are happy to eat pasta most nights of the week that by doing so they are eating a vegetarian diet.

Pasta is certainly what I eat more than any other type of dish. I am never without it, and given the fact that I always have garlic and olive oil on hand, all I need is a can of tomatoes (which I also always have on hand), or peas in the freezer, or a red pepper in the refrigerator, a bit of Parmesan, and I've got dinner. So many foods can transform a box of pasta into a delicious, easy, healthy, filling meal—a can of chick-peas, a handful of fresh herbs, any vegetable, be it fresh or left over from last night's dinner.

Although freshly made pasta is luxurious indeed, and I'm including a recipe for it, I love dried semolina pasta. Often it's preferable to fresh egg pasta, because it's firmer (and certainly cheaper). Each shape lends itself to a different sort of accompaniment. I often use shapes with hollows—penne or rigatone, or the wheel-shaped pasta, rotelle—when I have a pasta sauce that includes peas, because I love the way the peas lodge in the hollows of the pasta. Spiral-shaped pasta (fusilli) is nice with thick, creamy sauces like my low-fat cottage cheese pesto, because of the way the sauce nestles into the folds. I try to keep several different kinds on hand.

Although Italy and the Mediterranean come to mind when we think of pasta, Asian noodle dishes are equally exciting. I usually use buckwheat noodles (soba) for these pungent, gingery dishes.

Let this chapter be a starting point for you. Experiment with different sauces and accompaniments. I've tried to show you, with these dozen or so recipes, how versatile pasta can be.

Delicate Homemade Pasta

To me, fresh pasta is the most sensuous of foods. Its texture is light and smooth, its flavor elusive. I learned to make pasta from Ann Clark, a marvelous cook who teaches French cooking in Austin, Texas. This recipe is my partially whole-wheat version of her excellent pasta. It has a slightly nutty flavor.

Unless you're using a food processor, you'll find that as you make the dough little bits of flour will crumble off. Resist the temptation to incorporate these tiny pieces; the dough must be uniform in order to roll out well, and any little bits you try to attach will flake off when you roll it out or when you cook it.

You can make up the dough a day in advance, wrap it in plastic and a damp kitchen towel, and keep it refrigerated until you're ready to roll it out.

Making the dough by hand:

Sift together the flours and salt and pour out on a clean, dry board. Shape into a mound, then make a well in the center with the "walls" of flour even all around. Crack the eggs into the well and add the olive oil. Using a fork, mix the flour together with the egg mixture, keeping the "well" intact by cupping one hand around the wall of flour while you brush flour from the top wall into the well, incorporating it into the egg mixture. The mixture of eggs and flour will get very sticky; keep incorporating flour with the fork while you continue to confine the flour with your other hand so it doesn't scatter all over your working surface. (You won't be able to get all the flour incorporated, and some flakes of the mixture won't be absorbed, but don't be concerned with this small amount—you'll have plenty of pasta.)

When you have incorporated all the flour you can into the egg mixture, sprinkle with 1 tablespoon of the water. This may make the mixture sticky. Sprinkle with a little

continued

1 scant cup whole-wheat pastry flour

1 cup unbleached white flour

½ teaspoon salt, preferably sea salt

2 large eggs, at room temperature

2 teaspoons olive oil

2 tablespoons water, or more as necessary

more flour—just a little—so you can handle the dough, and mix the dough vigorously with your hands. This is fun; you just squeeze the dough in your hands, from one end to another, back and forth and from hand to hand. If the dough seems very stiff, add the remaining tablespoon of water, a little at a time. When the dough is smooth and elastic, knead it for 5 minutes (you can do this on the board or by continuing to squeeze it). Shape the dough into a ball, wrap it in plastic wrap or a damp towel, and let rest for 30 minutes to 1 hour.

Using the food processor:

Put the flours and salt in the bowl of your food processor and mix together by turning on the machine for a few seconds. With the machine off, add the eggs and 1 tablespoon of the water. Now turn on the machine and in just a few seconds to a minute the dough should come together on the blades, or instead of coming together, form many little balls in the bowl, which you can gather together in a solid mass with your hands. If the mixture seems wet, it will dry a little as you knead it, and you can dust the pasta with flour before you roll it out. If it seems too dry, add 1 to 3 teaspoons water to the food processor and continue to process a few seconds longer.

Remove the dough from the food processor and knead for 5 to 10 minutes, until stiff. Shape the dough into a ball, wrap it in plastic wrap or a damp kitchen towel, and let rest for 30 minutes to 1 hour.

Rolling out the dough:

Use a hand pasta machine to roll out the dough. This is a simple, inexpensive gadget. Cut the dough into quarters. Take 1 piece (keep the other pieces wrapped in plastic or covered with a damp towel), flatten it down a little, and with the roller set on 1, roll it through. The edges will be very jagged. Fold these jagged edges in toward each other and fold the pasta like a letter, then roll it through the first setting twice more. Dust the pasta, and roll it through the second setting twice, folding the edges in after the first time if they become jagged. Repeat this process through the third and fourth settings. (You might want to cut the sheet of pasta in half before rolling it through the fourth setting, if it is too unwieldy for you.) Lay the sheets of pasta out on lightly dusted cutting boards and allow to dry for 10 minutes before cutting. Attach the noodle-cutting piece to your pasta roller and cut thin or wide noodles (wide are easier to handle). If you are using the pasta for lasagne, cut wide noodles with a sharp knife or a crimped ravioli cutter.

Let the pasta dry for 15 to 30 minutes before cooking it: Lay it out on dusted waxed paper or hang it over the back of a chair or on a dowel. You can wrap handfuls of partially dry pasta loosely around four fingers to make "nests." The pasta will continue to dry and is more easily stored than long strands. If you wish to dry the pasta completely, leave it for 24 to 48 hours, until brittle. You can also dust the pasta with semolina, transfer it to a plastic bag, and freeze.

Cooking the pasta:

Bring a large pot of water to a boil. Add 1 teaspoon salt per quart of water and 1 tablespoon olive oil. Drop in the pasta; it should float to the surface very quickly, and as soon as it does, drain and toss with the sauce of your choice.

Serves 4 to 6

Fettuccine with Pesto Genovese

FOR THE PESTO:

3 medium or large garlic cloves, peeled

3 tablespoons pine nuts

3 cups firmly packed fresh basil leaves, washed and dried

½ teaspoon salt, preferably sea salt

½ cup olive oil

⅔ cup freshly grated Parmesan cheese

3 tablespoons freshly grated Romano-pecorino cheese

Freshly ground pepper, to taste

FOR THE PASTA:

1 tablespoon salt

2 tablespoons olive oil or canola oil

1 pound fettuccine, homemade (page 177) or fresh or dried commercial

Additional grated Parmesan for the table

Pesto, the definitive statement about basil, is one of my favorite foods. I make lots of it in the summer and freeze it for marvelous impromptu dinner parties. If you do make it for the freezer, omit the garlic and cheese, and add these ingredients after you thaw the pesto.

In a food processor fitted with the steel blade, blend together the garlic and the pine nuts. Add the basil and salt and process until very finely chopped. Add the olive oil through the feed tube with the machine running, and process until the mixture is thick and smooth. Stir in the cheeses and pepper.

Bring a large pot of water to a rolling boil, add a tablespoon of salt, 1 tablespoon of the olive oil or canola oil, and the pasta. Add a small ladleful of the boiling water to the pesto. Cook the noodles al dente, firm to the bite (homemade pasta will float to the surface and be ready in seconds; commercial pasta will take from 7 to 10 minutes). Drain and toss at once with the pesto and the additional tablespoon of olive oil or canola oil. Serve at once, passing additional grated Parmesan if you wish.

Serves 6

Fettuccine with Wild Mushrooms

The topping for this pasta will fill your kitchen with the savory smell of simmering mushrooms seasoned with thyme, garlic, parsley, and wine. The dish has a luxurious abundance of mushrooms. The sauce can be made several hours ahead of time and held, covered, on top of the stove.

Rinse the mushrooms and gently squeeze or pat dry. Cut in quarters, or thick slices if large. Place in a large nonstick skillet, sprinkle with salt, and heat the pan over medium-high heat until the mushrooms begin to release liquid. Cook, stirring, for 4 minutes, or until the liquid has just about evaporated, and add the tamari, wine, thyme, and rosemary. Turn the heat down to medium and cook, stirring often, for about 10 minutes, until at least half the liquid has evaporated. Add the olive oil, garlic, and pepper. Cook, stirring, for another 3 to 5 minutes, until the garlic begins to color. Remove from the heat, taste, and adjust seasonings. Stir in the parsley.

Bring a large pot of water to a rolling boil. Add a tablespoon of salt and a teaspoon of olive or vegetable oil, and the pasta. Cook al dente, until firm to the bite. Drain and toss with the mushrooms and Parmesan. Serve at once, passing additional Parmesan at the table.

Serves 4 to 6

2 pounds wild mushrooms, such as oyster mushrooms, morels, chanterelles, shiitakes, stems trimmed
Salt, preferably sea salt, to taste
1 tablespoon tamari
¾ cup dry, fruity red wine, such as Côtes du Rhône
1 teaspoon dried thyme
1 teaspoon crumbled dried rosemary
2 tablespoons olive oil
4 large garlic cloves, minced or put through a press
Freshly ground pepper, to taste
3 tablespoons chopped fresh parsley
1 pound fettuccine, homemade (page 177) or fresh or dried commercial
¼ cup freshly grated Parmesan (plus additional for passing at the table)

Pasta with Cottage Cheese Pesto and Broccoli

2 to 3 large garlic cloves (to taste), peeled

½ cup fresh basil leaves, washed and dried

1 cup nonfat cottage cheese

Salt, preferably sea salt, to taste

Freshly ground pepper, to taste

¼ cup plain nonfat yogurt

1 tablespoon olive oil

¼ cup freshly grated Parmesan cheese

1 pound fusilli (spiral-shaped pasta)

1 head—about 1½ to 2 pounds—broccoli, broken into florets

This is one of my most frequent impromptu meals, as it's easy to have all of the ingredients on hand and takes minutes to prepare. The cottage cheese pesto is a perfect low-fat yet creamy, richly flavored sauce.

Turn on a food processor fitted with the steel blade and drop in the garlic. Process until finely chopped. Add the basil and chop fine. Add the cottage cheese, salt, pepper, yogurt, olive oil, and Parmesan and purée until the mixture is creamy and smooth.

Bring a large pot of water to a rolling boil. Add about 1 tablespoon of salt and the pasta. Boil 4 minutes and add the broccoli. Continue to boil until the pasta is cooked al dente, firm to the bite, and the broccoli is crisp-tender, about 4 more minutes. Drain, toss with the cottage cheese mixture, and serve at once.

Serves 4 to 6

Penne or Rotelle with Cottage Cheese Pesto and Peas

This is another impromptu dinner dish. I almost always have frozen peas on hand for just such occasions. You can use either basil or parsley, or a mixture, for the sauce. Penne (or rigatone) and rotelle, the little pasta wheels, are good for this, as the peas get lodged in the hollows of the penne, or in the spokes of the little wheels, making each bite extra-sweet.

Turn on a food processor fitted with the steel blade and drop in the garlic. Process until finely chopped. Add the basil and/or parsley and chop fine. Add the cottage cheese, salt, pepper, yogurt, olive oil, and Parmesan, and purée until the mixture is creamy and smooth.

Bring a large pot of water to a rolling boil. Add about a tablespoon of salt and the pasta. Boil 10 minutes for penne or rigatone, 8 minutes for the wheels. Add frozen peas 2 minutes before the end of the cooking time; add fresh peas 5 minutes before the end of the cooking time. Drain, toss with the cottage cheese mixture, and serve at once.

Serves 4 to 6

2 to 3 large garlic cloves (to taste), peeled

½ cup fresh basil or parsley leaves (or a combination), washed and dried

1 cup nonfat cottage cheese

Salt, preferably sea salt, to taste

Freshly ground pepper, to taste

¼ cup plain nonfat yogurt

1 tablespoon olive oil

¼ cup freshly grated Parmesan cheese

1 pound penne, rigatone, or rotelle

2 cups peas, fresh or frozen and thawed

Pasta with Uncooked Tomatoes and Basil

2½ pounds (about 10 medium) ripe tomatoes, peeled, seeded, and finely chopped

3 large garlic cloves, minced or put through a press

1 tablespoon balsamic vinegar, or more to taste

½ teaspoon coarse sea salt, or more to taste

Freshly ground pepper, to taste

2 to 4 tablespoons chopped or slivered fresh basil, to taste

1 pound dried fusilli, fettuccine, or linguine

⅓ cup freshly grated Parmesan cheese

A frequent summer and early fall meal in our house, this is one of the best ways I can think of to show off tomatoes when they're at their best. You can serve this pasta hot or at room temperature.

Toss together the tomatoes, garlic, vinegar, salt, and pepper. Add the basil and let sit for 15 to 30 minutes. Taste and adjust seasonings.

Bring a large pot of water to a boil; add a tablespoon of salt and the pasta. Cook al dente, 7 to 10 minutes, depending on the pasta (see the time on the package). Drain, toss with the tomato sauce, and serve, passing the Parmesan at the table. Or cool and serve at room temperature.

Serves 4 to 6

Variations:

Use a mixture of yellow and red tomatoes, for an even more beautiful dish.

Add a cup or two of cooked fresh or thawed frozen peas to the dish.

Add a handful of pitted imported black olives to the dish.

Pasta Primavera on a Bed of Arugula

Here is a wonderful spring dish. Start with a sweet, garlicky mixture of roasted red peppers and tomatoes tossed with balsamic vinegar, which is tossed with fusilli after marinating for a couple of hours. The remaining green vegetables should depend on season.

Preheat the oven to 400 degrees. Bake the peppers on a baking sheet for 30 to 45 minutes, turning every 10 minutes, until their skins are brown and puffed. Remove the peppers from the heat and transfer to a bowl. Cover the bowl tightly by putting a plate over the top, and let sit for 30 minutes or longer.

Remove the skins and seeds from the peppers, holding them above the bowl so that you don't lose any of their liquid. Cut the peppers into thin strips, cut the strips in half crosswise, and combine with their liquid in the bowl. Toss with 1 of the garlic cloves, 1 tablespoon of the balsamic vinegar, and salt to taste. Cover and let marinate for at least 30 minutes. Add the tomatoes, another 2 cloves of garlic, another tablespoon of balsamic vinegar, a tablespoon of slivered basil, and 1 tablespoon of olive oil. Cover and marinate for 1 hour, or refrigerate for up to a day.

Steam the shelled peas and asparagus until tender, about 5 minutes, and refresh in cold water. Set aside.

Bring a large pot of water to a boil; add a tablespoon of salt and the fusilli. Cook al dente, drain, and toss with the peppers and tomatoes and all of their accumulated juice, the peas, asparagus, parsley, the remaining basil, and salt and pepper. Taste and add more garlic if desired.

Mix together the remaining 3 tablespoons of olive oil and the remaining ½ tablespoon of vinegar. Add a little salt and pepper. Toss with the arugula just before serving.

Line plates or a platter with the arugula and top with the pasta. Garnish with basil leaves, and serve.

Serves 6

2 large sweet red peppers
3 to 4 large garlic cloves, quartered
2½ tablespoons balsamic vinegar
Salt, preferably coarse sea salt, to taste
Freshly ground pepper, to taste
1 pound fresh ripe tomatoes, peeled, seeded, and diced
1 cup slivered fresh basil leaves
1/4 cup olive oil, in all
1 pound fresh peas in the shell (1 cup shelled)
½ pound asparagus, trimmed and cut in ½-inch lengths
1 pound fusilli
½ cup chopped fresh parsley
½ pound arugula, washed and trimmed
Fresh basil leaves for garnish

Pasta with Tomato Sauce and Beans

2 teaspoons olive oil

4 to 5 large garlic cloves, minced or put through a press

3 pounds tomatoes, canned or fresh, peeled, seeded, and chopped

¼ teaspoon sugar

Salt, preferably sea salt, to taste

3 tablespoons slivered fresh basil, or 1 teaspoon dried oregano and/or thyme

2 cups cooked chick-peas or white beans (may use canned)

Freshly ground pepper, to taste

1 pound dried fettuccine or tagliatelle

¼ to ½ cup freshly grated Parmesan cheese, to taste

This is one of my all-time favorites. There are many versions of pasta e fagiole, *this classic Italian dish. The recipe here is quick and simple. Canned beans are fine, and either white beans or chick-peas will do.*

Heat the oil over medium heat in a large, heavy-bottomed nonstick skillet and add the garlic. When the garlic begins to color, add the tomatoes, sugar, salt, and dried herbs if using. Cook, stirring often, for 20 to 30 minutes, until the tomatoes have cooked down and are beginning to stick to the pan. Stir in the chick-peas or beans and the fresh basil if using, and cook together for a minute or two. Add pepper, taste, and adjust seasonings. Keep warm while you cook the pasta.

Bring a large pot of water to a boil; add a tablespoon of salt and the pasta. Cook al dente, firm to the bite, about 7 to 8 minutes (see instructions on the package). Drain, toss with the sauce and the cheese, and serve at once.

Serves 4 to 6

Pasta with Giant White Fava Beans, Fresh Sage, and Garlic

Sage is one of my favorite herbs. It goes wonderfully with beans, especially white beans (as well as with vegetables like potatoes and winter squash). Here the white bean I've chosen is a giant white fava.

Drain the soaked beans and combine with the 2 quarts fresh water and the onion in a large soup pot or dutch oven. Bring to a boil and skim off any gray foam that rises. Add 2 of the garlic cloves and the bay leaf, reduce the heat, cover, and simmer 1 hour. Add the salt and simmer another 30 minutes to 1 hour, until the beans are tender but not mushy or falling apart. Remove from the heat, discard the onion, and drain, reserving ½ cup of the cooking liquid. Toss the beans with the remaining 2 cloves of garlic, the pepper, sage, lemon juice, olive oil, and the stock that you reserved. Taste and adjust the salt.

Bring a large pot of water to a boil and add a tablespoon of salt and the pasta. Cook al dente, until the pasta is firm to the bite (8 to 10 minutes depending on the pasta), drain, and toss with the beans and Parmesan. Serve hot.

Serves 4 to 6

2 cups dried giant white fava beans, washed, picked over, and soaked for 6 hours or overnight in 6 cups water

2 quarts water

1 medium onion stuck with a couple of cloves

4 garlic cloves, in all, minced or put through a press

1 bay leaf

2 teaspoons salt, or more to taste

Freshly ground pepper, to taste

15 to 20 fresh sage leaves, cut in thin slivers

Juice of 1 lemon

3 tablespoons olive oil

1 pound dried pasta, fettuccine, fusilli, or penne

⅓ cup freshly grated Parmesan cheese

Pasta with Roasted Red and Yellow Peppers

3 medium or 2 large red peppers

3 medium or 2 large yellow peppers

Coarse sea salt, to taste

Freshly ground pepper, to taste

2 to 3 large garlic cloves (to taste), minced or put through a press

2 tablespoons olive oil

3 tablespoons slivered fresh basil leaves, or more to taste

1 pound dried fettuccine, linguine, or tagliatelle

⅓ cup freshly grated Parmesan cheese

This gorgeous, fragrant pasta tastes luxurious. The "sauce" is the sweet juice that results from roasting the peppers. You can prepare the peppers a day or two ahead of time, but don't add the basil until the day you serve. Allow the peppers to come to room temperature before you cook the pasta.

Preheat the oven to 400 degrees. Place the peppers on a baking sheet or in a baking dish and bake in the hot oven for 30 to 45 minutes, turning every 10 minutes. The peppers are ready when the skin is brown and puffed.

Remove the peppers from the oven and transfer to a bowl. Cover the bowl tightly by putting a plate over the top, and let sit for 30 minutes or longer.

Remove the skins and seeds from the peppers, holding them above the bowl so that you don't lose any of their liquid. Cut the peppers into thin strips and combine with their liquid in the bowl. Add coarse salt to taste, pepper, the garlic, olive oil, and basil. Set aside while you cook the pasta.

Bring a large pot of water to a boil. Add about a tablespoon of salt and the pasta. Cook 7 to 8 minutes, until the pasta is cooked al dente, firm to the bite. Drain, toss with the peppers, and serve, passing the Parmesan at the table.

Serves 4 to 6

Pasta with Zucchini and Red Peppers

I have served this green, red, and white pasta for Christmas dinner. Nobody misses the turkey.

Heat the olive oil in a large, heavy-bottomed nonstick skillet over medium heat and add the onion. Cook, stirring, until the onion begins to soften, about 3 minutes, and add the red pepper, 1 of the garlic cloves, and a bit of salt. Cook, stirring, for 3 minutes, until the pepper has begun to soften, and add the zucchini, the remaining 2 cloves of garlic, and more salt. Cook, stirring often, for 5 to 10 minutes, until the zucchini is tender, fragrant, and still bright green. Add lots of pepper and the thyme. Taste, adjust seasonings, and remove from the heat.

Bring a large pot of water to a boil; add a tablespoon of salt and the pasta. Cook 7 to 8 minutes, until the pasta is al dente, firm to the bite. Drain and toss with the zucchini and peppers, the parsley, and half the Parmesan. Serve at once, passing the remaining Parmesan at the table.

Serves 4 to 6

1 tablespoon olive oil
1 small onion, chopped
1 large red bell pepper, minced
3 large garlic cloves, minced or put through a press
Salt, preferably sea salt, to taste
1 pound zucchini, cut in julienne or grated
Freshly ground pepper, to taste
1 tablespoon thyme leaves, or 1 teaspoon dried thyme
1 pound dried fettuccine, tagliatelle, or linguine
¼ cup chopped fresh parsley
½ cup freshly grated Parmesan cheese

Asian-style Braised Greens and Mushrooms with Pasta

¼ pound shiitake mushrooms, oyster mushrooms, or regular mushrooms, thickly sliced (leave small shiitake mushrooms whole)

Salt, preferably coarse sea salt to taste

2 tablespoons dry white wine

1 tablespoon peanut or canola oil

4 garlic cloves, minced or put through a press

1 tablespoon chopped or grated fresh gingerroot

1 pound mixed peppery and/or sturdy greens, such as baby bok choy, red and/or green chard, spinach, tat-soi, Asian mustard, beet greens, and/or mizuna, cut in 2-inch pieces if mature, left whole if young

1 teaspoon dark sesame oil

¾ cup Vegetable Stock (page 49) or bouillon

1 tablespoon soy sauce

1 pound buckwheat pasta (soba)

This dish is especially delicious if you use buckwheat pasta (soba), which is available in Asian grocery stores.

Salt the mushrooms and heat over medium-high heat in a large, heavy-bottomed nonstick skillet. They should begin to release liquid after a few minutes. Add the white wine and cook, shaking the pan or stirring from time to time, until most of the liquid has evaporated. Add the peanut or canola oil, garlic, and ginger. Cook, stirring for a few minutes, until the garlic and ginger begin to color, and stir in the greens and the sesame oil. Stir together.

Mix together the stock or bouillon and soy sauce and stir into the greens and mushrooms. Bring to a boil, stir for half a minute, and remove from the heat. Taste and adjust seasonings.

Bring a large pot of water to a boil. Add about a tablespoon of salt and the pasta. Cook al dente, firm to the bite, which shouldn't take more than 4 minutes for buckwheat pasta, drain, and toss at once with the greens. Serve hot.

Serves 4 to 6

Buckwheat Pasta with Tofu, Peas or Snap Peas, and Cilantro

Here's another pasta dish I often throw together just because I have tofu in the refrigerator and peas in the freezer. Sugar snap peas are incredibly sweet and marvelous, if you can find them. This is an Asian-style dish with pungent, gingery flavors mingling with the sweet peas and earthy soba.

Heat the canola or peanut oil in a large, heavy-bottomed nonstick skillet over medium heat and add the ginger and one of the garlic cloves. Cook for 1 minute, until the ginger and garlic begin to color, and add the tofu, chile pepper, and the remaining garlic. Cook, stirring, for 5 minutes, and add the tamari or soy sauce, cayenne pepper, vegetable stock, bouillon, or garlic broth, and sesame oil. Simmer for a couple of minutes, taste, and adjust seasonings. Keep warm while you cook the pasta.

Bring a large pot of water to a boil and add a tablespoon of salt, the pasta, and the peas. Cook until the pasta is al dente, firm to the bite, about 4 to 5 minutes. Drain and toss with the tofu mixture and the cilantro. Serve hot.

Serves 4 to 6

1 tablespoon canola oil or peanut oil

2 teaspoons finely grated or chopped fresh gingerroot

2 garlic cloves, minced or put through a press

1 pound firm tofu, cut in ½- by 1-inch pieces

1 serrano pepper, seeded and minced

2 tablespoons tamari or soy sauce (or more to taste)

Pinch of cayenne pepper (optional)

1 cup Vegetable Stock (page 49), bouillon, or Garlic Broth (page 50)

1 tablespoon dark Chinese sesame oil

1 pound buckwheat pasta (soba)

¾ pound sugar snap peas, trimmed, or 2 cups fresh or frozen peas, or fresh snow peas, strings removed

½ cup chopped cilantro

Lasagne

FOR THE TOMATO SAUCE:

1 tablespoon olive oil

1 small onion, chopped

4 to 5 large garlic cloves, minced
or put through a press

4 pounds fresh or canned tomatoes, peeled, seeded, and
chopped

Pinch of sugar

2 tablespoons tomato paste
(optional)

1 teaspoon dried oregano

½ teaspoon dried thyme, or more
to taste

Salt, to taste

Freshly ground pepper, to taste

2 tablespoons chopped fresh basil

FOR THE LASAGNE:

12 to 16 lasagne noodles, homemade (page 177) or
commercial

Vegetable oil or olive oil

1 pound low-fat ricotta cheese

¾ pound part-skim mozzarella,
thinly sliced

1 cup freshly grated Parmesan
cheese

¼ cup whole-wheat bread crumbs

1 tablespoon butter or olive oil

This is always a popular dish for big dinner parties. It can be assembled in advance and held in the refrigerator, but don't use aluminum foil to cover it or the foil will react with the tomato sauce.

Make the tomato sauce. Heat the olive oil in a heavy-bottomed nonstick skillet over medium heat and add the onion. Sauté, stirring, for about 5 minutes, until the onion is beginning to soften, and add half the garlic. Sauté for another few minutes, until the garlic begins to color, and add the tomatoes, sugar, the optional tomato paste, the oregano, thyme, salt, and pepper. Stir together and simmer uncovered for 30 minutes, stirring often, until the tomatoes are cooked down and fragrant. Add the remaining garlic and the basil, turn the heat to medium-low, and continue to cook, stirring often, for another 10 to 15 minutes. Remove from the heat, taste, and adjust seasonings.

Assemble the lasagne. Oil a shallow 3-quart baking or gratin dish. Preheat the oven to 375 degrees. Have all of your ingredients lined up in this order: pasta, tomato sauce, ricotta, mozzarella, Parmesan, and bread crumbs.

Cook 3 or 4 strips of pasta at a time as follows: When the water reaches a boil, add a teaspoon of salt and a teaspoon of vegetable or olive oil. Add the pasta. If you are using fresh pasta it will float to the surface at once. If you use commerical pasta it will take several minutes (see the instructions on the package). As soon as the pasta is cooked al dente, firm to the bite, remove it with a slotted spoon or a deep-fry skimmer, transfer it to a bowl of cold water, then drain at once on kitchen towels.

Mix about ½ cup of the tomato sauce with the ricotta to moisten. Spoon a small amount of tomato sauce into the baking dish and spread over the bottom of the dish. Layer 3 or 4 lasagne noodles over the sauce. Dot the noodles with spoonfuls of ricotta. Top the ricotta with a thin layer of mozzarella, and top the mozzarella with a layer of sauce, then a layer of Parmesan. Repeat the layers—pasta, ricotta, mozzarella, sauce, Parmesan—2 or 3 more times, depending on the shape of your pan. Make sure you end up with a layer of tomato sauce topped with Parmesan. Sprinkle on the bread crumbs. Dot with the butter or drizzle on the olive oil.

Bake 40 minutes, until the lasagne is bubbling and the top is beginning to brown. Serve hot.

Serves 6 to 8

Pumpkin Lasagne

12 to 16 lasagne noodles, homemade (page 177) or
commercial

2½ pounds fresh pumpkin cut in
large pieces, seeds and membranes removed, skin left on

¾ cup fruity red wine, such as
Beaujolais or Gamay

½ cup toasted and ground
almonds

½ cup plus 2 tablespoons bread
crumbs, preferably whole
wheat

2 tablespoons chopped fresh sage,
or 1 teaspoon dried sage

2 teaspoons mild honey, such as
clover or acacia

¼ teaspoon freshly grated nutmeg,
or more to taste

½ teaspoon cinnamon

Salt, preferably sea salt, to taste

Freshly ground pepper, to taste

1½ cups freshly grated Parmesan
cheese

1 recipe Béchamel (page 200)

Up to ¾ cup juice from the baked
pumpkin

1 tablespoon butter or olive oil for
topping the lasagne, plus oil for
cooking the pasta

*This makes a spectacular main attraction for Thanksgiving or
any special dinner. The pumpkin filling is based on one that is
used traditionally in Northern Italian tortellini. Use homemade noodles for an incredibly sensuous dish.*

Mix the pasta dough (if making your own), wrap in plastic,
and let rest while you prepare the pumpkin and béchamel.

Preheat the oven to 400 degrees. Place the pumpkin in a
lightly oiled baking dish, cover, and bake 45 minutes, or
until tender. Remove from the oven, allow to cool, and cut
away the rinds. Pour off any juice that has accumulated in
the baking dish into a measuring cup and set aside. Purée
the pumpkin in a food processor fitted with the steel blade,
or through a food mill. You should have about 2½ cups.

Combine the wine, almonds, ½ cup of the bread
crumbs, the sage, and honey in a large saucepan and bring
to a simmer. Stir until the wine has been absorbed and no
more liquid remains in the pan. Stir in the pumpkin purée
and spices. Add salt and pepper to taste and heat through.
Remove from the heat and stir in ½ cup of the Parmesan.
Set aside.

Make the béchamel as directed, but substitute up to ¾
cup of the liquid from the pumpkin for the equivalent
amount of milk, and add to the milk before you heat it.
Season the béchamel with salt, pepper, and nutmeg. Stir in
2 tablespoons of Parmesan after you remove the sauce from
the heat.

Rolling out the pasta and assembling the lasagne:

Roll out the pasta to the number 4 setting. Cut in wide
strips that will fit a shallow 3- or 4-quart baking dish. Allow
the noodles to dry for 15 minutes on a lightly floured board
or kitchen towel. Meanwhile, heat a large pot of water on
the stove.

When assembling the lasagne you need to work fairly

quickly, so get everything organized before you begin. Oil or butter your lasagne pan generously, and have your béchamel, pumpkin mixture, and Parmesan within reach. Spoon a small amount of béchamel over the bottom of the dish.

When the water in the large pot comes to a boil, add a tablespoon of salt and a drop of oil. Cook the lasagne noodles a few at a time (enough for 1 layer), just until they float to the surface of the pot, which happens in about 10 to 20 seconds if they are homemade. Remove them from the water, plunge into a bowl of cold water, and drain on clean dish towels. (Don't let the noodles sit too long on the towels once drained, or they'll become sticky.) Line the baking dish with a layer of slightly overlapping noodles. Spread a thin layer of pumpkin filling over this, and top with a layer of the béchamel. Use the back of your spoon or a spatula to spread the béchamel evenly over the pumpkin mixture. Sprinkle on some Parmesan. Set aside ½ cup of béchamel and 2 tablespoons of Parmesan for the top layer of the lasagne, and repeat the layers 3 more times: pasta, pumpkin, béchamel, Parmesan. Add a fifth layer of pasta and top this with the béchamel you set aside, the reserved Parmesan, and the remaining 2 tablespoons of bread crumbs. Dot with butter or drizzle on the olive oil. Cover with plastic wrap until ready to bake.

Preheat the oven to 325 degrees. Bake uncovered in the preheated oven for 30 minutes, or until the top is just beginning to brown.

Serves 8

Sauces and Dressings

Some of the recipes here are basic dressings or sauces that are called for as ingredients in other recipes in this book—mayonnaise, for example—while others like homemade yogurt can also stand alone. Indeed, yogurt is one of the best, easiest breakfasts I can think of. Many recipes, like tofu mayonnaise and green dressing, serve not only as salad dressings but also make excellent dips for vegetables and spreads for sandwiches.

I don't use too many roux-thickened sauces. The one that I do relish is white wine sauce, so I'm including it here. It's irresistible. Also, I'm including a basic béchamel, or white sauce, which you can use with gratins, and an easy tomato sauce for pastas and pizzas.

Several of the salad dressings can be made in advance and stored in the refrigerator, allowing you to put together a tasty salad in minutes. That said, vinaigrettes are simple and take only minutes to throw together; and the fresher a dressing with lemon juice and fresh herbs is, the better.

White Wine Sauce

This savory sauce is excellent with egg and cheese dishes, as well as vegetable gratins. It can be made a day in advance and it freezes well.

Combine the broth or stock, wine, and dried mushrooms and simmer together in a saucepan for about 30 minutes. Strain the liquid through a cheesecloth- or paper towel-lined strainer and either discard the mushrooms or set them aside for another purpose, such as an omelet filling or pasta sauce. Return the broth to the heat and keep at a bare simmer.

Heat the butter over medium-low heat in a heavy-bottomed saucepan. When it is bubbly, add a pinch of flour, and if it sizzles, add the rest. Stir together with a wooden spoon or a whisk and cook over medium heat, stirring constantly, for a couple of minutes. The mixture should not brown.

Remove the pan from the heat and whisk in the simmering broth all at once. Return to the heat and bring the sauce to a simmer, stirring constantly with a whisk. When the sauce begins to thicken, reduce the heat to low and simmer, stirring often and being careful not to let the sauce stick to the bottom of the pan and burn, for 15 to 20 minutes, until the sauce is smooth and creamy, and there is no trace of a floury taste. Add the salt and pepper, then remove from the heat.

Makes 2 to 2½ cups

1½ cups Garlic Broth (page 50) or Vegetable Stock (page 49)
1 cup dry white wine
5 to 6 dried dark Chinese mushrooms, or ½ cup dried porcini mushrooms
2 tablespoons butter
2 tablespoons unbleached flour
Salt and freshly ground pepper, to taste

Béchamel

3 cups skim or low-fat milk

2 tablespoons unsalted butter or
   olive oil

2 tablespoons sifted unbleached
   white flour

Salt, preferably sea salt, to taste

Freshly ground pepper, to taste

Pinch of freshly grated nutmeg
   (optional)

Classic béchamel, the French white sauce, is made with a butter roux; but in Provence olive oil often stands in for butter. Try both versions and see which you prefer. Béchamel can be kept in the refrigerator for up to a day. Cover with plastic and don't worry that a thin skin forms. Whisk the skin away when you gently reheat the sauce, stirring it over medium-low heat.

Bring the milk to a simmer in a saucepan. Meanwhile, melt the butter or heat the olive oil in a heavy-bottomed saucepan over medium heat. Add a pinch of flour, and if it sizzles, add the rest. Stir together with a wooden spoon or a whisk and cook over medium heat, stirring constantly, for a couple of minutes. The mixture should not brown.

Remove the pan from the heat and whisk in the simmering milk all at once. Return to the heat and bring the sauce to a simmer, stirring constantly with a whisk. When the sauce begins to thicken, reduce the heat to low and simmer, stirring often and being careful not to let the sauce stick to the bottom of the pan and burn, for 15 to 20 minutes, until the sauce is smooth and creamy, and there is no trace of a floury taste. Add the salt, pepper, and nutmeg if desired, then remove from the heat.

Makes 2½ cups

Fresh Tomato Salsa

When tomatoes are in season, there's nothing better or easier than fresh salsa. No Mexican meal should be without it.

Mix together all the ingredients. Chill until ready to serve.

Makes about 2½ cups

2 pounds (8 medium) fresh, ripe
   tomatoes, chopped
½ small red onion, minced
2 to 3 jalapeño or serrano peppers
   (to taste), seeded and minced
¼ cup chopped cilantro, or more
   to taste
1 tablespoon red wine vinegar or
   balsamic vinegar
Salt, preferably sea salt, to taste
Freshly ground pepper, to taste

Easy Tomato Sauce

You can make this fragrant sauce year-round, using canned tomatoes in winter, fresh in summer and early fall. (Keep canned tomatoes on hand at all times for easy pasta dinners.)

Heat the oil over medium heat in a large, heavy-bottomed nonstick skillet and add the garlic. When the garlic begins to color, add the tomatoes, sugar, salt, and dried herbs if using. Cook, stirring often, for 20 to 30 minutes, until the tomatoes are cooked down and beginning to stick to the pan. Stir in the fresh basil if using, and cook together for a minute or two. Add pepper and remove from the heat.

If you want your sauce to have a smooth, thick, uniform texture, transfer it to a food processor fitted with the steel blade and blend for about 30 seconds. Put it into a saucepan, taste and adjust seasonings, and heat through just before serving.

Makes 3 cups, serving 6

2 teaspoons olive oil
4 to 5 large garlic cloves, minced
   or put through a press
4 pounds (16 medium) tomatoes,
   canned or fresh, peeled, seeded,
   and chopped
¼ teaspoon sugar
Salt, preferably sea salt, to taste
3 tablespoons slivered fresh basil,
   or 1 teaspoon dried oregano
   and/or thyme
Freshly ground pepper, to taste

Sweet and Sour Sauce

One 8-ounce can tomato sauce
 (purée)
2 tablespoons soy sauce
2 to 3 tablespoons mild honey, to
 taste
3 tablespoons cider vinegar
1 tablespoon Dijon mustard, or 1
 teaspoon dried mustard (or
 more, to taste)
2 tablespoons dry sherry

This sauce is very easy to make. It's a perfect dipping sauce for spring rolls or egg rolls.

Combine all the ingredients in a small saucepan and heat through. Remove from the heat and allow to cool.

Makes about 1¾ cups

Homemade Yogurt

1½ quarts lukewarm water
3 to 4 tablespoons plain yogurt
 (see right)
1½ to 2 cups nonfat spray-dried
 milk (available in natural foods
 stores)
1 large can (13 ounces) evaporated
 skim milk

When you make this (it's from Adelle Davis), be sure you use either Dannon plain yogurt or a yogurt recommended by a natural foods store as a starter. The bacteria in most commercial brands aren't sufficient. If your yogurt does fail, it probably will be because you used the wrong kind of yogurt as a starter, or because your water bath was too hot or not warm enough. This will keep for five days in the refrigerator.

Blend 2 cups of the lukewarm water, the yogurt, and the spray-dried milk together in a blender until well combined. Pour into a large pitcher (one that holds at least 4 quarts) and add the remaining quart of lukewarm water. Stir in the evaporated milk.

Pour into sterilized jars, cover, and place in a pan of lukewarm water. Place the pan in a warm place where the temperature will remain constant (over a pilot light, on a heater, in a cooler full of warm water). Cover the pan and leave for 3 to 4 hours, checking the water from time to time to make sure it remains lukewarm. Refrigerate when thick (in summer, 3 to 4 hours; in winter, 5 to 6).

Makes about 2 quarts

Food Processor Mayonnaise

I bought my first food processor after watching mayonnaise being made in one: You can make it in minutes. Buy your fresh eggs from a reliable source. Free-range eggs are much safer than mass-produced commercial eggs.

Break the egg into the bowl of a food processor fitted with the steel blade. Add the vinegar, mustard, and salt. Turn on the food processor and add the oil in a very slow stream. The mayonnaise will bind quickly. Add the pepper and lemon juice.

Transfer the mayonnaise to a jar or a plastic container, cover tightly, and store in the refrigerator. It will keep for 3 to 5 days.

Makes about 1 cup

1 egg

2 teaspoons red wine vinegar or cider vinegar (optional)

½ to 1 teaspoon Dijon mustard, to taste (optional)

¼ to ½ teaspoon salt, preferably sea salt, to taste

⅔ cup canola oil, or ⅓ cup canola oil and ⅓ cup olive oil

Freshly ground pepper, to taste

1 to 2 tablespoons fresh lemon juice, or more to taste

Tofu Mayonnaise

2 tablespoons fresh lemon juice

2 tablespoons wine vinegar or
cider vinegar

1 garlic clove, minced or put
through a press (optional)

1 teaspoon Dijon mustard

¼ cup Food Processor
Mayonnaise (page 203) or
plain nonfat yogurt, homemade (page 202) or commercial

1 teaspoon miso paste or tamari

1 to 1½ cups cubed tofu

Salt and freshly ground pepper, to
taste

2 tablespoons olive oil

Additional plain nonfat yogurt (2
to 4 tablespoons) for thinning
out

*This is scrumptious as a dressing, mayonnaise, or dip. It's
essentially a low-calorie mayonnaise, and will be a blessing for
those who love mayonnaise but hate the fat. It keeps several
days in the refrigerator and is so easy to make that you can
have it on hand all the time.*

Combine all the ingredients in a blender and blend until
smooth. Use more yogurt to thin out the dressing, if desired.

Makes 1½ to 2 cups

Mary's Basic Salad Dressing

This lemony dressing is named after my stepmother, Mary Shulman, who taught me to cook. She started me off with salads, and this is the salad dressing she taught me to make when I was fifteen.

Method 1: Combine the lemon juice and vinegar in a small bowl or a 2-cup Pyrex measuring cup. Stir in the garlic and mustard with a fork or whisk. Add the salt, pepper, and herbs and blend well, then whisk in both types of oil. Refrigerate if not using right away and stir well before tossing the salad.

    Method 2: Do not stir the oil into the dressing. Toss your salad ingredients first with the lemon-vinegar-herb mixture, then with the oil.

Makes 1 cup

3 tablespoons fresh lemon juice

1 tablespoon wine vinegar, sherry vinegar, or cider vinegar

1 small garlic clove, minced or put through a press

½ teaspoon dry mustard, or 1 teaspoon Dijon mustard

Salt, preferably sea salt, to taste

Freshly ground pepper, to taste

½ teaspoon dried marjoram

½ teaspoon dried tarragon

1 tablespoon chopped fresh herbs such as basil, dill, or thyme (optional)

⅓ cup canola oil

⅓ cup olive oil

Vinaigrette

There are many variations on a vinaigrette, which is essentially an oil and vinegar dressing. I add a bit of lemon juice to mine, and tend to use more rather than less mustard. Experiment with this. You may find you prefer a less acidic dressing, in which case use the smaller amount of vinegar.

Method 1: Combine the lemon juice and vinegar, then stir in the garlic and mustard with a fork. Add the herbs, salt, and pepper; whisk in the olive oil. Stir well or shake vigorously in a covered jar before tossing your salad.

    Method 2: Do not blend the oil into the dressing. Toss your salad ingredients first with the lemon-vinegar-herb mixture, then with the oil.

Makes ⅔ to ¾ cup

1 tablespoon fresh lemon juice

2 to 3 tablespoons wine vinegar, sherry vinegar, or cider vinegar, to taste

1 small garlic clove, minced or put through a press

1 teaspoon Dijon mustard, or more to taste

¼ teaspoon dried tarragon, or 1 teaspoon chopped fresh herbs (basil, tarragon, dill, parsley, chervil)

Salt, preferably sea salt, to taste

Freshly ground pepper, to taste

½ cup olive oil

Low-Fat Yogurt Vinaigrette

2 tablespoons fresh lemon juice

1 to 2 tablespoons wine vinegar, sherry vinegar, or cider vinegar, to taste

1 small garlic clove, minced or put through a press (optional)

1 teaspoon Dijon mustard, or more to taste

Salt, preferably sea salt, to taste

Freshly ground pepper, to taste

½ to ⅔ cup plain nonfat yogurt, to taste

2 tablespoons olive oil

2 tablespoons chopped fresh herbs, such as tarragon, parsley, basil, chives, dill, chervil

With nonfat yogurt replacing all but 2 tablespoons of the olive oil, this creamy dressing has a fraction of the fat of a traditional vinaigrette. Use it for any of the salads that call for vinaigrette.

Combine the lemon juice, vinegar, garlic, mustard, salt, pepper, and yogurt in a measuring cup, jar, or small bowl and stir together well. Stir in the olive oil, and add the herbs. Taste and adjust seasonings. If the dressing tastes too tart, add an additional tablespoon or two of yogurt.

Makes 1 cup

Walnut Oil Dressing

This nutty dressing goes nicely with bitter lettuces like Belgian endive, radicchio, and curly endive.

Mix together the lemon juice, vinegar, garlic, mustard, tarragon, salt, and pepper. Whisk in the oils (or the oil and yogurt) and stir together well. Taste and adjust seasonings.

Makes about ¾ cup

1 tablespoon fresh lemon juice

2 tablespoons vinegar, either wine or sherry; or 1 tablespoon each balsamic vinegar and wine or sherry vinegar

1 small garlic clove, minced or put through a press

1 teaspoon Dijon mustard

¼ teaspoon dried tarragon, or 1 teaspoon minced fresh tarragon

Salt, preferably sea salt, to taste

Freshly ground pepper, to taste

3 tablespoons walnut oil

4 to 5 tablespoons olive oil, to taste, or for a lower-fat dressing, substitute plain nonfat yogurt

Poppy Seed Dressing

2 tablespoons fresh lemon juice

2 tablespoons wine vinegar or cider vinegar

2 tablespoons mild honey

1 teaspoon Dijon mustard

Salt, preferably sea salt, to taste

Freshly ground pepper, to taste

¼ cup canola oil

⅔ cup plain nonfat yogurt

3 tablespoons poppy seeds

This sweet and sour dressing is good with avocado and citrus salad, as well as with grated vegetable salads and slaws.

Mix together the lemon juice, vinegar, honey, mustard, salt, and pepper. Whisk in the oil, then the yogurt. Stir in the poppy seeds. Taste and adjust seasonings. Refrigerate until ready to use.

Makes about 1⅓ cups

Curry Dressing

½ cup Food Processor Mayonnaise (page 203) (use 2 tablespoons lemon juice, and include the vinegar and mustard)

1 cup plain nonfat yogurt, commercial or homemade (page 202)

1½ to 2 teaspoons curry powder, to taste

½ teaspoon turmeric

½ teaspoon chili powder

¼ teaspoon ground ginger

¼ teaspoon paprika

Salt, preferably sea salt, to taste

Freshly ground pepper, to taste

This luxurious dressing goes marvelously with grain salads.

Stir all the ingredients together. Taste and adjust seasonings, and chill in a covered container.

Makes 1½ cups

Green Dressing

This is a wonderfully creamy herbal dressing—a healthy "Green Goddess." Use it for vegetable and grain salads.

Combine all the ingredients in a food processor fitted with the steel blade or in a blender and blend until smooth. Add more herbs and spinach if you desire a darker, greener dressing, and add more lemon juice if you want it more tart.

Makes 1¼ cups

½ cup fresh spinach leaves, or more to taste

1 garlic clove

2 tablespoons chopped green onion, both white part and green, or fresh chives, or more to taste

1 tablespoon chopped fresh dill, or more to taste

1 teaspoon fresh tarragon, or more to taste

3 tablespoons chopped fresh parsley, or more to taste

¾ cup plain nonfat yogurt, homemade (page 202) or commercial

2 tablespoons fresh lemon juice, or more to taste

Salt, preferably sea salt, to taste

Freshly ground pepper, to taste

¼ cup olive oil

Sunflower Seed Dressing

¼ cup sunflower seeds
1 garlic clove
Salt, preferably sea salt, to taste
Freshly ground pepper, to taste
1 tablespoon chopped fresh herbs
   (parsley, tarragon, thyme, dill)
2 tablespoons lemon juice, or
   more to taste
1 cup plain nonfat yogurt, homemade (page 202) or
   commercial

This creamy, nutty dressing is one of my favorites. It goes beautifully with sprout salads, slaws, and green salads, and can also serve as a dip.

In a blender or food processor, grind the sunflower seeds fine, almost to a butter. Add the garlic, salt, pepper, and herbs, then blend in the lemon juice and the yogurt and mix until you have a smooth sauce. Adjust the seasoning and refrigerate until ready to use.

Makes about 1½ cups

Orange Juice Dressing

⅓ cup fresh orange juice
2 tablespoons fresh lemon juice
1 tablespoon balsamic vinegar
Salt, preferably sea salt, to taste
Freshly ground pepper, to taste
½ teaspoon dry mustard, or 1 teaspoon prepared Dijon-style
   mustard
½ cup plain nonfat yogurt
2 tablespoons vegetable oil or
   canola oil

This dressing is good with green salads, especially those with citrus, fruit salads, and especially good with avocado and citrus salad, beet and endive salad, and spinach and citrus salad.

Mix together the orange juice, lemon juice, balsamic vinegar, salt, pepper, and mustard; blend in the yogurt and the oil.

Makes about 1 cup

Mint Dressing

Mint is surprising and pleasing in a salad dressing. This goes especially well with cucumber and grain salads.

Combine all the ingredients in a blender or food processor fitted with the steel blade and pulse to mix, or finely chop the mint and stir it into the other ingredients.

Makes about 1 cup

¾ cup plain nonfat yogurt, home-made (page 202) or commercial
Juice of 1 large lemon (about ¼ cup juice)
1 tablespoon chopped fresh mint
Salt, preferably sea salt, to taste
1 small garlic clove, minced or put through a press (optional)
1 to 2 tablespoons olive oil, to taste (optional)

Tahini Dressing

Good on spinach salads, this thick, creamy dressing also makes a delightful dip.

Whisk together all of the ingredients, taste, and adjust seasonings. Refrigerate until ready to use.

Makes about 1 cup

⅓ cup sesame tahini, or to taste
Juice of 1 large lemon (about ¼ cup juice)
1 garlic clove, minced or put through a press
Salt, preferably sea salt, to taste
Freshly ground pepper, to taste
½ cup plain nonfat yogurt, home-made (page 202) or commercial
2 tablespoons water

Asian Sesame Dressing

1 tablespoon fresh lemon juice or
  lime juice

2 tablespoons rice wine vinegar or
  balsamic vinegar

1 small garlic clove, minced or put
  through a press

2 teaspoons finely minced fresh
  ginger

1 tablespoon tamari

¼ cup dark Chinese sesame oil

Pinch of cayenne (optional)

¼ cup canola oil, or for a lower-
  fat, creamier dressing, ¼ cup
  plain nonfat yogurt

Salt, preferably sea salt, to taste

Freshly ground pepper, to taste

1 to 2 tablespoons water, as
  needed

Try this pungent, nutty/gingery dressing on noodle and veg-etable salads.

Combine all the ingredients and blend well. Thin out with water as desired. Refrigerate until ready to use.

Makes about ¾ cup

Salads

A salad alone can make a delightful meal, especially with all the imaginative variations in the recipes that follow. It can consist of both cooked ingredients and raw ones, fruits as well as vegetables, cheeses, eggs, nuts, grains, and legumes.

The variety of textures and flavors in your salad will depend on how exotic or varied the rest of your meal is. To accompany rich meals, choose simple salads, using the tenderest lettuce you can find. Reserve the more complicated salads to go along with soups and main dishes that are lighter in nature. The salad is a good place to "sneak" protein into a meatless meal, in the form of roasted soybeans, perhaps, or tofu, sprouts, eggs, or cheese. Serve a rice salad ring around a lentil, garbanzo bean, or mixed bean salad for a perfect complementary meal. This principle also applies to dressings: If you think the meal you are serving needs a protein boost, use a yogurt- or tofu-based dressing.

Make sure you wash your lettuce and other greens well. There is nothing worse than a gritty salad, especially when you've chosen beautiful, tender lettuce. You can wash lettuce a day or two in advance if you drain it well, seal it in plastic bags, and refrigerate it. Make sure, too, that your lettuce is completely dry before you add it to the salad bowl.

If you like sprouts, try to have some on hand at all times. They keep well and are always a welcome, nutritious addition to a salad. (See the instructions for sprouting on page xxxviii.)

Mixed Green Salad

This salad consists of a lively mixture of lettuces and vegetables. You needn't stick to the suggestions here; vary the vegetables, using more or less depending on what you have on hand. The point is to have a beautiful contrast of textures and flavors.

Tear the lettuce in fairly large pieces and combine with the other ingredients, including any or all of the optional ones, in a large salad bowl. Toss just before serving with the dressing of your choice.

Serves 6

¾ pound mixed lettuces (leaf lettuce, red tip, romaine, Boston, or red or green oak leaf), leaves separated, thoroughly washed and dried (about 8 cups torn leaves)

1 cucumber, scored with a fork or peeled (if very waxy or bitter), seeded if desired, then sliced

1 green or red pepper, seeded, cored, and sliced in lengthwise strips

4 green onions, both white part and green, sliced

4 radishes, sliced

4 to 5 fresh mushrooms, trimmed, cleaned, and sliced

3 ripe tomatoes, cut in wedges, or 8 to 10 cherry tomatoes

¼ to ½ cup chopped fresh herbs, such as basil, chives, parsley, oregano, dill, sage, chervil, tarragon (use no more than 3 or 4 in any given salad)

½ to 1 cup sprouts (alfalfa, mung bean, lentil), optional

OPTIONAL:
½ cup Marinated Broccoli Stems (page 38)

2 hard-boiled eggs, sliced or diced

¼ cup grated or diced cheese

½ to 1 cup leftover grains or beans

2 to 4 medium-size potatoes, scrubbed, diced, and steamed until tender (about 15 minutes)

Pitted, sliced ripe olives

Vinaigrette (page 205), Low-Fat Yogurt Vinaigrette (page 206), or Mary's Basic Salad Dressing (page 205)

Spinach Salad

½ to ¾ pound fresh spinach,
    stemmed, washed thoroughly,
    and dried
6 large fresh mushrooms, cleaned,
    trimmed, and sliced
3 to 4 green onions, sliced
¼ cup Roasted Soybeans (page 45)

OPTIONAL:

½ cup cooked chick-peas
½ cup cooked brown rice
3 tomatoes, cut in wedges
½ cup sprouts (alfalfa, mung
    bean, lentil)
1 to 2 hard-boiled eggs, sliced

Vinaigrette (page 205), Low-Fat
    Yogurt Vinaigrette (page 206),
    Green Dressing (page 209), or
    Mary's Basic Salad Dressing
    (page 205)

This salad traditionally includes crumbled bacon. Soybeans have the salty, crispy quality of bacon and work just as well.

Combine the spinach, mushrooms, green onions, soybeans, and any other ingredients you wish to add in a large bowl. Just before serving add the dressing and toss together well.

Serves 6

Crudité Salad

This colorful salad makes an excellent starter.

Put each of the vegetables, and the rice salad, in separate bowls and toss each separately with portions of the dressing.

Line a platter with lettuce leaves and arrange the individual components in mounds on the lettuce, with tomatoes interspersed. (Alternatively, you can line individual salad plates with lettuce and place small amounts of each item on top.)

Serves 6 to 8

1 cup finely shredded green or red cabbage
1 cup finely grated carrot
1 cup finely grated beets
1 cup sliced fresh mushrooms
1 cup thinly sliced cucumber
2 tomatoes, thinly sliced
1½ cups Brown Rice Salad (page 225)
1 recipe Vinaigrette (page 205)
Leaf or Boston lettuce, leaves separated, washed, and dried

Avocado and Citrus Salad

This is a popular salad. You can't prepare it too far ahead of time or the avocado will discolor, but it's very easy to throw together. You can, however, prepare the dressing several hours in advance of serving.

Cut the avocados in half and remove the seeds; peel and slice according to the directions on page xxxi, then gently toss the slices with the lemon juice to avoid discoloration.

Arrange the avocado and citrus slices on a bed of watercress or leaf lettuce on a serving platter and sprinkle the minced green onion on top. Pour on the dressing and serve immediately.

Serves 6

3 avocados
Juice of 1 lemon
2 grapefruits or oranges (or one of each), peeled and white membranes removed, then sectioned
1 bunch watercress or leaf lettuce, leaves separated, then washed and dried
2 tablespoons minced green onion, both white part and green
1 recipe Poppy Seed Dressing (page 208)

Salade Niçoise

3 to 4 medium potatoes

¼ to ½ cup dry white wine

Salt and freshly ground black pepper, to taste

1 tablespoon minced green onion, both white part and green

1 tablespoon chopped fresh parsley

1 recipe Vinaigrette (page 205) or Low-Fat Yogurt Vinaigrette (page 206), with a hard-boiled egg yolk mashed into it, if desired

1 head Boston or red tip lettuce, or a combination of lettuces, leaves separated, then washed and dried

½ pound fresh string beans, trimmed, steamed briefly, and then chilled

4 ripe tomatoes, sliced in wedges, or ½ pint cherry tomatoes, halved

1 cucumber, scored with a fork or peeled (if very waxy or bitter), then sliced

¼ cup imported black olives

½ cup alfalfa sprouts (optional)

1 green or red pepper, or a combination, seeded and sliced crosswise

2 to 3 hard-boiled eggs, peeled and then halved or quartered

OPTIONAL:

2 celery ribs, sliced

1 yellow squash, very thinly sliced

1 ounce Parmesan cheese, cut in slivers using a vegetable peeler, or grated

This is not an authentic salade Niçoise, as the traditional salad contains tuna and/or anchovies. But my vegetarian version makes a beautiful, substantial dish.

There are many ways to present this dish. You can serve it as an hors d'oeuvre, with the vegetables arranged on a platter so that they can be handled easily with toothpicks or fingers. Or you can use a large bowl and toss everything together. If you want the salad to retain its composition in the bowl, toss each ingredient with the vinaigrette separately, then compose the salad bowl. Or put it all together in a beautiful salad bowl and toss it at the table. The salad can be served as a main dish.

The ingredients you use in the salad will depend on personal taste and what is in season. Provençal cooks insist that the salad contain no cooked vegetables, but my salade Niçoise almost always includes potatoes and at least one cooked vegetable.

Sometimes I add a hard-boiled egg yolk to the vinaigrette; it makes a creamier dressing and adds protein to the content of the meal.

Wash the potatoes, leaving on the peel, and steam about 20 minutes, until tender to the fork. Remove from the heat and slice immediately into a bowl, using a kitchen towel to steady the potatoes so that you don't burn your hand. Pour on the white wine and leave to cool for about 10 minutes, then toss gently with the salt and pepper, green onion, parsley, and ¼ cup of the vinaigrette.

For a platter:

Toss all the remaining components individually with portions of the dressing. Line the platter with the lettuce leaves. In the center, place the string beans. Around the string beans make a circle of potatoes interspersed with tomato wedges or cherry tomatoes. Circle the potatoes with cucumber, and celery and yellow squash, if using, alternating colors and scattering olives here and there. Surround this with clumps of sprouts and the remaining olives and tomatoes. Rounds of green or red pepper can be placed on top of the arrangement, and the egg segments placed here and there. Sprinkle the optional Parmesan over the top.

In a bowl:

You can design a similar arrangement in a large bowl. Either toss each ingredient separately before making the arrangement or toss the entire salad at the table (making sure everyone gets to see it beforehand).

Serves 6

Tender Lettuce and Orange Salad

This delicate salad is perfect with a rich meal; the oranges are especially refreshing. It's also nice as a starting salad.

Wash and dry the lettuce and tear into large pieces, then toss together with the oranges, herbs, and chives. Toss with the dressing just before serving.

Serves 6

1 head large or 2 small heads Boston lettuce or tender red tip lettuce
2 oranges, peeled and white membranes removed, then cut in sections
1 to 2 tablespoons chopped fresh fennel or tarragon
2 tablespoons chopped fresh chives
1 recipe Vinaigrette (page 205), or Orange Juice Dressing (page 210)

Tabouli

1 cup uncooked medium-grain
 bulgur

1 cup fresh lemon juice (from 3 to
 4 large lemons)

1 to 2 garlic cloves, to taste,
 crushed

Salt, preferably sea salt, to taste

Freshly ground pepper, to taste

½ teaspoon ground cumin

¼ cup olive oil

1 to 1½ cups cooked chick-peas (½
 cup dried; see page xxxvi, or
 use canned)

3 cups chopped fresh parsley
 (from 3 large bunches)

½ cup chopped fresh mint

1 cup minced green onions, both
 white part and green

1 small cucumber, peeled (if bitter
 or waxy) and diced (optional)

4 tomatoes, diced

1 head romaine lettuce, leaves
 separated, then washed and
 dried

Halved cherry tomatoes and
 cucumber slices for garnish

Tabouli is a splendid Middle Eastern salad combining bulgur and fresh herbs in a lemony dressing. Fresh mint is essential here. This version uses chick-peas (or garbanzos), which boost the protein.

Place the bulgur in a bowl and pour on water to cover. Let sit 20 minutes, until slightly soft. Squeeze out excess water.

Combine the lemon juice, garlic, salt, pepper, cumin, and olive oil and toss with the bulgur. Let sit 30 minutes, or until the bulgur is softened. Taste and correct seasonings.

Combine the bulgur mixture with the chick-peas, parsley, mint, green onions, cucumber, and diced tomatoes.

Line a bowl with the outer leaves of the romaine lettuce. Place the tabouli on top of the leaves, garnish with cherry tomatoes and sliced cucumbers, and serve, using the smaller inner lettuce leaves as dippers if you wish.

Serves 6

Guacamole

Guacamole can be served as an hors d'oeuvre as well as a salad, and is an essential ingredient in the recipe for extraordinary chalupas.

Place the avocado flesh in a bowl and mash with a fork or potato masher, or mash in a mortar and pestle. Add the tomato and continue to mash with the avocado. Work the mixture until fairly smooth, but allow the avocado and tomato to retain some texture. Add the garlic, onion, lemon or lime juice, and salt, cumin, and chili powder to taste. Stir together well and adjust seasonings.

If you are not serving the guacamole right away, place an avocado seed in the middle. (Some say this helps to keep the guacamole from turning brown.) Cover tightly with plastic wrap and refrigerate. When you are ready to serve it, remove the avocado seed and stir the guacamole. Even if the top has discolored, the rest of the guacamole will be fine.

Garnish with chopped cilantro and serve.

Serves 6

2 to 3 avocados, halved and peeled
1 large tomato, seeded and chopped
1 small garlic clove, minced or put through a press (optional)
¼ cup finely minced onion
Juice of ½ lemon or lime, or more to taste
Salt, preferably sea salt, to taste
Ground cumin and chili powder, to taste
Ground chili powder, to taste
Chopped fresh cilantro for garnish

Cucumber Salad

2 long English (seedless) cucumbers, scored with a fork or
peeled (if very waxy or bitter),
then sliced very thin
4 green onions, both white part
and green, sliced
2 to 4 tablespoons chopped fresh
dill
2 tablespoons fresh mint (omit if
you're using the mint dressing)
1 cup Low-Fat Yogurt Vinaigrette
(page 206), Mary's Basic Salad
Dressing (page 205), Vinaigrette (page 205), or Mint
Dressing (page 211)

This easy-to-assemble salad is wonderfully refreshing.

Toss together the cucumbers, green onions, dill, and mint
with the dressing and refrigerate for an hour or so before
serving.

Serves 6

Spicy Tofu Salad

FOR THE DRESSING:
1 large tomato, peeled
¼ cup cilantro leaves
¼ cup fresh mint leaves
1 small hot chile, fresh or canned
1 garlic clove
½ teaspoon freshly grated gingerroot
2 green onions, both white part
and green, sliced
¼ cup lemon juice
½ cup plain nonfat yogurt, homemade (page 202) or
commercial

*Tofu, walnuts, tomatoes, crunchy and succulent cucumbers,
and green peppers combine with juicy oranges and bananas in
a spicy sauce to make this chilled salad one of the most
refreshing I've ever eaten. An adaptation of an Indian chicken
salad (with tofu replacing the chicken), it's seasoned with
many of the raw ingredients of a curry. But if you don't like
cilantro or hot chiles, this one isn't for you.*

*The composition is perfect—there's just enough fruit to
temper the heat of the chile and spices, like a raita or chutney
alongside a hot curry. This picante salad is good as a first
course; serve a raita on the side, if you wish.*

222   *The Vegetarian Feast*

Make the dressing.

Combine the ingredients in a blender or food processor and purée until smooth. Adjust the seasoning to your taste and refrigerate the dressing while preparing the salad.

For the salad:

Heat the oil in a heavy-bottomed nonstick skillet over medium-high heat and sauté the tofu for 5 minutes. Add the garlic and stir for 30 seconds, or until the garlic begins to color. Add the tamari and water and continue to cook, stirring occasionally, until the liquid evaporates. Remove from the heat, then toss the tofu gently with the remaining salad ingredients. Pour on the dressing and toss again, gently. Refrigerate for 1 or 2 hours before serving.

To serve:

Place a piece of leaf lettuce on each plate and spoon the salad over; or line a salad bowl with lettuce leaves and fill with the tofu mixture. Garnish with the 2 tablespoons of walnuts and the optional sprouts and cilantro leaves.

Serves 6

½ teaspoon whole coriander seed
Salt, preferably sea salt, to taste
Freshly ground pepper, to taste

FOR THE SALAD:
2 tablespoons canola oil
3 cups diced tofu
1 garlic clove, minced or put
   through a press
2 tablespoons tamari
3 tablespoons water
1 cucumber, peeled and diced
1 large tomato, peeled and
   chopped
1 small green pepper, seeded and
   diced
½ cup sliced fresh mushrooms
   (optional)
3 green onions, both white part
   and green, chopped
1 orange, peeled and white mem-
   brane removed, then sectioned
1 banana, sliced and tossed with 1
   tablespoon lemon juice
¼ cup broken walnuts, plus 2
   tablespoons for garnish

FOR THE GARNISH:
Leaf lettuce
½ cup alfalfa sprouts (optional)
Cilantro leaves

Green Bean, Almond, and Mushroom Salad

1 pound green beans (4 cups trimmed), trimmed and cut into 2-inch lengths

½ pound fresh mushrooms (3 cups sliced), cleaned, trimmed, and sliced

¼ cup slivered almonds

2 tablespoons minced fresh chives

1 to 2 tablespoons minced fresh parsley or marjoram

1 cup Vinaigrette (page 205) or Low-Fat Yogurt Vinaigrette (page 206)

This elegant salad combines three foods with distinctive textures: crisp, fresh green beans; porous, subtle mushrooms; and crunchy almonds. The contrast is luscious.

Steam the beans until bright green and crisp-tender and rinse under cold water to stop the cooking. Toss with the remaining ingredients and serve.

Note: You can cook the beans an hour ahead of time and toss with half the dressing. Hold in or out of the refrigerator. Don't let the beans sit in the dressing for more than an hour or they'll lose their bright color.

Serves 6

Tomatoes and Fresh Herbs

2 pounds ripe, red tomatoes, peeled and thinly sliced

Coarse sea salt, to taste

2 tablespoons balsamic vinegar

1 to 2 garlic cloves, minced or put through a press

¼ cup fresh basil leaves, slivered with scissors

2 tablespoons chopped fresh parsley

1 tablespoon chopped fresh tarragon

Freshly ground pepper, to taste

¼ cup olive oil

2 tablespoons freshly grated Parmesan cheese (optional)

A summer salad, this isn't worth making unless you can find ripe, fresh tomatoes. I eat this salad all through the late summer and early fall, when tomatoes are at their best.

Toss the tomatoes gently with the salt, balsamic vinegar, and garlic. Let sit for 10 to 30 minutes. Just before serving, combine the tomatoes with all the remaining ingredients except the Parmesan. Sprinkle the Parmesan over the top, and serve.

Serves 6

Brown Rice Salad

This has always been one of my most popular salads; the combination of rice, vegetables, and nuts is pure ambrosia. It keeps well, refrigerated, for a day (but you will lose the bright green color of the vegetables, as the green fades when it mixes with the acid in the dressing) and can be presented in a bowl or, more elaborately, molded in the shape of a ring and filled with another salad. You can also make this salad with white rice.

Cook the rice with the water and salt as directed on page xxxv, adding the saffron, lemon juice, and olive oil when you reduce the heat before covering. Allow the rice to cool and combine with the remaining salad ingredients except the lettuce, dressing, and garnishes. Toss with the salad dressing and correct the seasoning.

In a bowl or on a platter:

Line a bowl or platter with lettuce leaves. Place the rice salad over the leaves in a mound. Garnish with tomato wedges or cherry tomatoes and sliced hard-boiled eggs, black olives, green onions, and fresh herbs.

Molded in a ring:

Pack the rice salad into a well-oiled 4-cup ring mold and chill for several hours. Line a platter with lettuce leaves. Dip the mold into warm water for a few minutes, then unmold onto the platter. For a protein-complementary meal, place a leguminous salad, such as marinated lentil salad, chickpea salad, or mixed bean salad, in the middle. Or fill the center with tomato wedges or cherry tomatoes, sprouts, herbs, and sliced hard-boiled eggs

Serves 6

1 cup raw brown rice
2 cups water
½ teaspoon salt
Pinch of saffron (optional)
Juice of ½ lemon
2 tablespoons olive oil
1 green pepper, seeded and diced
1 red pepper, seeded and diced
4 radishes, sliced
½ cucumber, peeled (if waxed or bitter) and diced
5 green onions, both white part and green, chopped
1 celery rib, minced
¼ cup pine nuts, sunflower seeds, or chopped walnuts
½ cup chopped fresh parsley
¼ cup other chopped fresh herbs (tarragon, marjoram, basil, thyme, fennel), if available
⅓ cup freshly grated Parmesan cheese (optional)
1 head leaf lettuce or romaine lettuce, leaves separated, then washed and dried
1 recipe Vinaigrette (page 205) or Low-Fat Yogurt Vinaigrette (page 206)

FOR THE GARNISH:

Tomato wedges or halved cherry tomatoes
Hard-boiled egg slices
Sliced or whole black olives
Chopped green onions
Fresh herbs

Watercress and Mushroom Salad

FOR THE DRESSING:

2 tablespoons fresh lemon juice

1 tablespoon wine vinegar or
   sherry vinegar

½ teaspoon dry mustard, or 1 teaspoon prepared Dijon-style
   mustard

1 small garlic clove, minced or put
   through a press

1 teaspoon chopped fresh
   tarragon, or ¼ teaspoon dried
   tarragon

Salt, preferably sea salt, to taste

Freshly ground pepper, to taste

⅓ cup olive oil

FOR THE SALAD:

1 large or 2 small bunches fresh
   watercress, stems trimmed,
   leaves washed and dried

½ pound fresh mushrooms, sliced

I love the peppery flavor of watercress. It contrasts nicely with the subtle, clean flavor of the mushrooms.

Make the dressing: Combine the lemon juice, vinegar, mustard, garlic, tarragon, salt, and pepper; stir in the olive oil.

Combine the watercress and mushrooms and toss with the dressing just before serving.

Serves 6

Beet and Endive Salad

The colors alone make this a divine salad. Beets are sweet and crunchy; they contrast with the slight bitterness of the endive.

Steam the beets until crisp-tender, about 30 minutes. Run them under cold water, then peel and cut into matchsticks or slice thin.

Combine the beets with the endive, green onions, and parsley. Toss with your choice of dressing.

Serves 4 to 6

1 pound beets, quartered
½ pound (2 medium) Belgian endive, leaves separated, then washed and dried
3 green onions, both white part and green, chopped, or 3 tablespoons chopped fresh chives
Chopped fresh parsley, to taste
1 recipe Orange Juice Dressing (page 210), Vinaigrette (page 205), or Walnut Oil Dressing (page 207)

Spinach and Citrus Salad

The sweet juice of oranges or tangerines bursts into every bite of this luscious combination.

Combine the spinach, mushrooms, and orange or tangerine sections in a salad bowl. Just before serving, add the sprouts and toss with the dressing of your choice.

Note: You can add other vegetables, such as red bell pepper, cucumber, or green onions, to this salad, if you wish.

Serves 6

¾ pound fresh spinach, stems removed, leaves washed thoroughly and dried
½ pound fresh mushrooms, trimmed, cleaned, and sliced
2 oranges, peeled and white membranes removed, then sectioned, or 2 seedless tangerines, peeled and sectioned
Handful of sprouts (alfalfa, mung bean, lentil), optional
1 recipe Mary's Basic Salad Dressing (page 205), Vinaigrette (page 205), Tahini Dressing (page 211), or Orange Juice Dressing (page 210)

Potato–Egg Salad
with Chilled Broccoli

1 pound broccoli, trimmed and
    cut into florets

4 hard-boiled eggs, peeled

2 pounds (8 medium) waxy pota-
    toes, unpeeled, steamed, and
    diced

4 celery ribs, chopped

1 green or red bell pepper, seeded
    and chopped

4 green onions, both white part
    and green, sliced, or ½ medium-
    size Bermuda onion, minced

½ cup chopped fresh parsley, or a
    mixture of parsley and other
    fresh herbs, such as tarragon,
    sage, dill, thyme

Salt, preferably sea salt, to taste

Freshly ground pepper, to taste

1 cup Mary's Basic Salad Dressing
    (page 205) or Vinaigrette (page
    205), made with an additional
    tablespoon Dijon-style mus-
    tard, or to taste

½ cup plain nonfat yogurt

½ head leaf lettuce or romaine,
    leaves separated, then washed
    and dried

2 tomatoes, cut in wedges, or ½
    pint cherry tomatoes

Fresh herb sprigs (parsley,
    tarragon, dill), for garnish

More yellow and "eggy" than the familiar potato salad, this also shines with the bright green broccoli and red tomatoes.

Steam the broccoli for about 5 minutes, until it is crisp-tender and bright green. Remove from the heat immediately and rinse in cold water, dry, and chill.

Chop or mash the hard-boiled eggs. Combine with the potatoes, celery, bell pepper, onions, and fresh herbs. Add salt and pepper to taste.

Mix together the salad dressing and the yogurt. Taste and add more mustard if you wish. Toss with the salad.

Line a large platter or salad bowl with the leaf lettuce or romaine leaves. Mound the potato salad in the center, then arrange the broccoli florets in a ring around the edge (the green color will look beautiful against the potato salad). Inside this ring, place a ring of tomato wedges or cherry tomatoes. Garnish the top of the salad with fresh herb sprigs.

Cover and chill before serving, or serve at room temperature.

Serves 6

Mixed Bean Salad

This lovely salad makes a substantial main dish as well as a delicious starter. You can make this with canned beans to save time.

Combine all the beans, the onion, garlic, and bell pepper in a salad bowl. Stir the cumin into the salad dressing, and add pepper. Pour the salad dressing over the bean mixture. Toss well, cover, and refrigerate for 1 hour, tossing every once in a while to bind the oil and vinegar and to make sure the salad marinates evenly. Stir in the cilantro, taste, and adjust seasonings. Serve cold, or heat through slightly and serve warm.

Serves 6

1 to 1½ cups each cooked chick-peas, kidney beans, and white navy beans (½ cup each dried; see page xxxvi)

1 to 1½ cups cooked black beans (½ cup dried; see page xxxvi), optional

1½ cups green beans, cut into 1-inch pieces and steamed briefly

1 cup yellow wax beans, cut into 1-inch pieces and steamed briefly

1 Bermuda onion, thinly sliced

1 garlic clove, minced or put through a press

1 green or red bell pepper, or a combination, seeded and chopped

½ teaspoon ground cumin

1 recipe Mary's Basic Salad Dressing (page 205) or Vinaigrette (page 205)

Freshly ground pepper, to taste

2 tablespoons chopped cilantro

Marinated Lentil Salad

1 tablespoon olive oil

1 onion, chopped

3 garlic cloves, minced or put
through a press

1 pound (2 cups) dried lentils,
washed

1½ quarts water

Pinch of cayenne pepper

2 bay leaves

1 teaspoon salt, preferably sea salt

Freshly ground pepper, to taste

1 cup Vinaigrette (page 205) or
Low-Fat Yogurt Vinaigrette
(page 206), made with extra
Dijon mustard

¼ cup chopped fresh parsley or
cilantro

FOR THE GARNISH:

Chopped fresh parsley or cilantro
Tomato wedges

This dish is always a hit. The usual comment I get from guests and cooking students is: "I never thought of doing this with lentils!" Then they go back for seconds.

Heat the oil in a large, heavy-bottomed saucepan or soup pot over medium heat and add the onion. Cook, stirring, until the onion begins to soften, about 3 to 5 minutes, and add 1 of the garlic cloves. Cook, stirring, for another minute, until the garlic begins to color, and add the remaining garlic, the lentils, water, cayenne, and bay leaves and bring to a boil. Reduce the heat, cover, and simmer 30 minutes. Add the salt and freshly ground pepper, and continue to simmer for another 20 to 30 minutes, until the lentils are soft but not mushy. Drain, retaining ½ cup liquid from the lentils. Discard the bay leaves.

Transfer the lentils to an attractive serving bowl and toss with the dressing. If you wish, add some or all of the cooking liquid to the lentils. Allow to cool, toss the lentils with the parsley or cilantro, and refrigerate for an hour or more. Serve, garnished with additional chopped fresh herbs and tomato wedges.

Serves 6

Grated Carrot Salad

1½ pounds (about 6 medium)
carrots, finely grated

½ cup chopped fresh parsley

1 recipe Mary's Basic Salad
Dressing (page 205)

1 head leaf lettuce, leaves separated, then washed and dried

There are many versions of this salad. My favorite is a simple mixture of carrots and parsley tossed with a lemony dressing.

Toss together the carrots, parsley, and salad dressing. Line a platter or salad bowl with the lettuce leaves, top with the salad, and serve.

Serves 6

Chick-pea Salad

I love the comforting taste of chick-peas, and I especially love the way their texture contrasts with the crunchy red peppers here. This gutsy salad makes a meal, but could also be served as a first course.

Drain the soaked chick-peas and transfer to a large soup pot or dutch oven. Add the 2 quarts of water, the thyme, garlic, carrot, onion, parsley sprigs, rosemary, and bay leaf, and bring to a boil. Cover, reduce the heat, and simmer for 1 hour. Add the salt and continue to simmer for another 30 minutes to an hour, until the chick-peas are tender but not mushy.

Drain the chick-peas and remove the bay leaf. Toss immediately with the vegetables, herbs, and the vinaigrette. Allow to cool and chill for an hour, stirring occasionally, or serve warm. Stir in the Parmesan shortly before serving. (If you are going to refrigerate the salad for more than an hour, add the herbs an hour before serving. They will lose their bright color if marinated for too long).

Line a platter or bowl with leaf lettuce. Place the salad over the lettuce on the platter or in the bowl; decorate with tomatoes and radishes, and serve.

Serves 6

FOR THE BEANS:

2 cups dried chick-peas, washed, picked over, and soaked overnight or for 6 hours in 6 cups of water
2 quarts additional water
1 teaspoon dried thyme
1 garlic clove, minced or put through a press
1 carrot, chopped
1 onion, chopped
2 sprigs fresh parsley
½ teaspoon dried rosemary
1 bay leaf
2 teaspoons salt, preferably sea salt

FOR THE SALAD:

1 bunch green onions, both white part and green, chopped
2 medium-size red peppers, seeded and chopped
½ cup chopped fresh parsley or a combination of parsley and other fresh herbs (basil, marjoram, sage, tarragon, thyme)
1 recipe Vinaigrette (page 205)
¼ cup freshly grated Parmesan cheese

FOR THE GARNISHES:

½ head leaf lettuce, leaves separated, then washed and drained
2 tomatoes, sliced or cut in wedges
4 radishes, sliced

Cole Slaw

FOR THE SALAD:

½ head green cabbage, finely shredded

2 carrots, grated

½ small onion, thinly sliced or grated (optional)

FOR THE DRESSING:

2 tablespoons wine vinegar

1 tablespoon Dijon mustard

½ to 1 teaspoon prepared horseradish, to taste

⅔ cup plain nonfat yogurt

½ teaspoon sugar

¼ cup low-fat milk

Salt, preferably sea salt, to taste

Freshly ground pepper, to taste

I've always had a terrible weakness for cole slaw. Horseradish gives this dressing a pleasing bite.

Toss the salad ingredients together. Mix together all the ingredients for the dressing. Blend well and toss with the vegetables. Chill and serve, or serve immediately.

Note: For a sweet cole slaw, use the Poppy Seed Dressing on page 208.

Serves 6

Desserts

Desserts are treats by definition, and can be the most extraordinary part of a meal. Most in this chapter are uncomplicated. You will find fruits and liqueurs used often; fresh fruit alone, or fruit and cheese, will often suffice after a meal, and you should feel free to omit the liqueurs called for in many of these recipes. You'll recognize some of these desserts as protein-rich, with an abundance of eggs and/or milk, perfect after a vegetable-oriented meal (don't forget that this course is often the easiest place to add protein). Others, such as the simple fruit desserts, are light and most welcome after a rich meal. In all cases, where dairy products are called for, I use low-fat or nonfat versions.

A dessert will lose its magic if you serve it while people are still full from the dinner. Allow a little time to elapse after the last course, then serve it. I also find that very sweet food should not follow too quickly upon the heels of a main dish. So sit back and digest for a while; make tea or coffee; then you and your guests will really appreciate the grand finale.

Though liqueurs are high in sugar, few of these desserts call for refined sugar as such. I use honey most often in my desserts, replacing sugar with it in many recipes. There are a few things one needs to know for honey cookery, rules that apply to all kinds of dishes. The first and most important is use mild honey. I think the reason so many "health food" desserts are so bad is that they're dominated by the taste of a strong honey. There are many, many kinds; their taste and scent comes from the flowers that are the source of the nectar from which the honey is made. Some are strong, some mild. As a rule of thumb, the darker the honey is, the stronger the flavor. Avoid orange blossom honey, wild flower, sage, chestnut, and buckwheat honeys. The mildest are clover, cotton, and acacia. Mild honey has a slightly waxy taste (or maybe it's that the taste of the wax isn't dominated by the other strong scents and flavors). Shop around, taste, and find one you like.

Honey often crystallizes, especially in cold weather. Keep it in a glass jar, and to melt it down place the jar in a heavy-bottomed saucepan. Fill the pan with water and place over a low flame. Let the water around the jar simmer until the honey is melted.

To convert any recipe using sugar to a honey recipe, use one-quarter less honey than the amount of sugar called for, and decrease the total liquid content by one-eighth.

Molasses is another important sweetener. Its flavor is so strong that it acts as a spice as well, and should only be used when called for. Like honey, molasses comes in different strengths, which are discernible by the color. Dark, thick molasses is very strong, and the lighter ones are milder, with a less spicy sweetness.

Choose your fruits according to the season. You will be hard-pressed to find good melons in the fall and winter, or good pears in the spring and summer. Choose carefully. Unripe pineapple is a disaster, as are unripe melons. I've heard of various methods for testing certain fruits for ripeness; mine are simple and straightforward. I smell, feel, and look. Bananas should be yellow, not green, and even a few brown spots are good to indicate that they are really ready. Pineapples, melons, peaches, pears, apricots, and nectarines should smell sweet and fragrant, as if you could almost taste them. Thump watermelons—they should have a hollow resonance. Look carefully at the color and choose the reddest strawberries, the pinkest peaches, the deepest purple plums. Feel the fruit carefully; it should be firm but not hard, as if it were about to burst with juice, and it should give you the feeling that if you squeezed it *would* burst. If it's soft and bruises at the lightest amount of pressure, it's not good. Search for local fruit stands, which are more apt to have ripe fruit than are supermarkets. The more locally grown fruit you can get, the better.

Bananas Poached in White Wine

This is my most frequent dessert choice for catered dinners. It can be made early on the day you wish to serve it, and kept either in or out of the refrigerator (warm it up before serving). It's easy and quick; I have often gone to a catering job with the ingredients and made poached fruit while the soup and main dish were being served. This is a sweet, enticing compote. My guests have always loved it.

In a bowl, combine the lemon juice and enough water to cover the bananas. Cut the bananas and drop into the water (the acidity of the lemon juice will prevent the bananas from discoloring).

Combine the wine, vanilla, cinnamon stick, honey, raisins or currants, and dried apples in a medium-sized saucepan and bring to a simmer. Simmer for 5 minutes, covered.

Meanwhile drain the bananas. Add them to the mixture in the saucepan, along with the nutmeg. (If the bananas are not completely covered, add a little water.) Simmer, covered, for 10 minutes and remove from the heat. Remove the cinnamon stick and add more nutmeg, if you wish.

Serve warm, topped with the vanilla-flavored whipped cream.

Serves 6

Juice of ½ lemon

3 to 4 ripe but firm bananas, cut in half lengthwise and then into 2-inch lengths

2 cups semidry white wine, such as a California Riesling

1 tablespoon vanilla extract

One 3-inch cinnamon stick

½ cup mild honey

½ cup raisins or currants

½ cup dried apples

½ teaspoon freshly grated nutmeg, or to taste

⅓ cup heavy cream, whipped and flavored with vanilla extract

Pears Poached in Red Wine with a Touch of Cassis

3 firm, ripe pears, peeled, cored, and sliced
Juice of ½ lemon
2 cups red wine
½ cup mild honey
½ cup raisins
¼ cup crème de cassis liqueur
One 3-inch cinnamon stick

These can be prepared hours in advance and reheated, or served at room temperature. The dish may be made a day in advance, but the pears will be firmer if they are cooked the same day you plan to serve them.

Prepare the pears and drop them into a bowl containing the lemon juice and enough water to cover.

Combine the wine, honey, raisins, cassis, and cinnamon stick in a medium-sized saucepan. Cover and simmer for 5 minutes, removing the cinnamon stick when the 5 minutes are up.

Drain the pears and drop them into the simmering liquid. Simmer, covered, for 10 to 20 minutes.

Serve warm or chilled.

Serves 6

Mediterranean Fruit Compote

This delightful compote can be made several hours before you wish to serve it.

Combine the currants, wine, banana, vanilla, cinnamon, and honey in a saucepan and bring to a simmer. Simmer 5 minutes and remove from the heat.

Meanwhile, peel and dice the apple and the pears and toss with the lemon juice.

In a large chilled bowl, preferably glass, toss all the ingredients together with the grapes, figs or dates, and the optional pomegranate seeds.

Chill until ready to serve, and top, if you wish, with a little vanilla-flavored yogurt.

Serves 6

½ cup currants

1¼ cups semidry or sweet white wine (a sweet Muscat wine, such as a Muscat de Beaumes de Venise, is very nice here)

1 banana, sliced

1 teaspoon vanilla extract

⅛ teaspoon ground cinnamon

3 tablespoons mild honey, or to taste

1 apple, peeled and diced

2 pears, peeled and diced

Juice of ½ lemon

1 small bunch red grapes, halved and seeds removed (if you want to take the time)

1 small bunch green seedless grapes, halved (about 1½ cups red and green grapes, in all)

4 figs or dates, dried or fresh, chopped

½ cup pomegranate seeds (optional)

Plain nonfat yogurt, flavored with a little vanilla if you wish, for garnish (optional)

Oranges Grand Marnier

4 oranges

2 to 3 tablespoons chopped fresh
  mint, plus additional for garnish, if desired

¼ to ½ cup Grand Marnier

2 to 3 tablespoons slivered
  almonds (optional)

This is the kind of dessert that goes with absolutely any meal, and that you can always throw together in a pinch. It always comes as a delightful surprise to my guests. What looks like plain sliced oranges turns out to be a perfect combination of sweet citrus and heady liqueur with the marvelous zip of fresh mint.

You can make this at any time prior to your dinner. I once made five gallons for a wedding and served it in a punch bowl. The oranges looked beautiful, and the leftover fruit lasted for several days.

Simultaneously peel the oranges and cut away the membranes by cutting the peel off in a spiral, using a very sharp knife and cutting all the way through to the pulp. Slice the oranges crosswise.

Place in a decorative bowl and toss gently with the mint and Grand Marnier. Cover and refrigerate for an hour or more. Before serving, toss again with the almonds and more fresh mint, if you wish.

Note: For dramatic impact, these can be flambéed. Heat a little Grand Marnier and brandy in a saucepan. When it is warm, light it and carefully pour it over the fruit. Or, you can warm the brandy and Grand Marnier, pour it over the fruit, and then light it.

Serves 6

Melon with Port

This is an easy, refreshing summer dessert.

Cut the melons in half and remove the seeds. Cut into large slices (one melon should yield 6 to 8 slices, depending on the size of the melon). Now make several crosswise slashes, about 1 inch apart, down to the rind but not through it, across each slice. Place the melon on a platter or on individual plates and spoon 1 to 2 tablespoons port over each.

Serve garnished with lime wedges.

Serves 6

1 or 2 cantaloupes, depending on the size, or 1 Crenshaw melon
1 to 2 tablespoons port per serving, to taste
Lime wedges for garnish

Watermelon–Fruit Extravaganza

In summer I always made these beautiful watermelon baskets for my supper club. Watermelon balls always please, especially when accented with fresh mint. This can be made up to four hours in advance and chilled, covered.

Remove the fruit from all the melons with a melon-ball spoon or regular spoon, being careful not to damage the watermelon shell, since you will be using it for your fruit bowl. Toss the melon balls with the grapes, berries, and mint in a very large bowl. Discard the cantaloupe and honeydew rinds.

Scallop the edge of the watermelon shell with a very sharp knife. Fill it with the melon ball and fruit mixture, top with peach slices, and garnish with mint leaves.

Place on a tray and surround with any extra fruit mixture.

Note: If you want a basket, start with a whole watermelon. Cut a handle across the top, then cut around the sides. Remove the 2 top pieces on either side of the handle and cut away the flesh under the handle. Proceed as above, and scallop only the sides.

Serves 12

½ watermelon (see Note)
1 cantaloupe, halved and seeded
1 honeydew melon, halved and seeded
½ pound seedless green grapes
½ pint berries in season
2 to 3 tablespoons fresh mint leaves, plus additional for garnish
3 peaches, sliced

Peaches Marsala

3 to 4 firm, ripe, sweet peaches
Marsala to cover
Fresh mint for garnish and sliced
   strawberries (optional)

Good, sweet ripe peaches have such a short season that it's tempting to serve them every night for dessert. Here they're dressed up by serving them in wine glasses and splashing them with marsala.

Drop the peaches into boiling water to cover for 1 minute, then drain and run under cold water. Peel off the skins; they will come off easily. Slice the peaches and place in individual wine glasses or dessert dishes. Cover the peaches with marsala and serve, garnished with fresh mint and, if you wish, sliced fresh strawberries.

Serves 6

Raspberries in Red Wine

2 pints raspberries
¾ cup fruity red wine, such as a
   Beaujolais

Rasberries are so delicate, you don't want to dress them too much. A little red wine is the only addition here.

Wash and drain the berries and place in wine glasses. Spoon 2 tablespoons wine over each portion, and serve.

Serves 6

Grapefruit with Port

These half-grapefruits dressed up with port make a great winter dessert.

Spoon about 1 tablespoon port over each grapefruit half. Garnish with strawberries and/or orange slices and mint, and serve.

Serves 6

⅓ cup port

3 pink grapefruit, cut in half, sectioned, and, if you wish, edges scalloped

Strawberries and/or orange slices and mint for garnish

Pineapple with Kirsch

Make sure your pineapple is sweet and ripe. The best way to choose one is to smell it. Pull out a leaf, too. It should come out easily.

Toss the pineapple and strawberries with the kirsch and serve garnished with fresh mint.

Serves 6

1 large, ripe pineapple, skinned, cored, and chunked

1 cup sliced strawberries

⅓ cup kirsch

Fresh mint for garnish

Baked Apples

6 large, tart apples, such as
    pippins or McIntosh
½ cup raisins or currants
⅓ cup mild honey, approximately
Ground cinnamon, freshly grated
    nutmeg, and ground allspice,
    to taste
Apple juice or cider
One 3-inch cinnamon stick
½ cup plain nonfat yogurt
    (optional)

Baked apples are such a homey dessert that I never tire of them. Don't forget about this recipe when you give an impromptu dinner party. Even though it is incredibly easy, you're guests will feel that you've gone to some trouble.

Preheat the oven to 350 degrees.

Core the apples from the top, not cutting all the way through the bottom but cutting out a cone shape, so that you have a large hole in the top that narrows as you reach the bottom.

Fill each cavity with raisins or currants and drizzle in some honey, not quite a tablespoon per apple. Sprinkle with cinnamon, nutmeg, and allspice.

Butter a baking dish and place the apples in it, with the open end of the cone up. Pour apple juice or cider into the pan so the pan is half full. Place a stick of cinnamon in the cider. Bake in the preheated oven for about 45 minutes, basting the apples every 15 minutes with the apple juice. Serve warm or at room temperature, garnished, if you wish, with a dollop of yogurt.

Serves 6

Grain-stuffed Baked Apples

Mix together the raisins or currants, honey, and spices with 1 cup cooked brown rice or other cooked grains. Moisten with a little milk and fill the apples with the mixture. Bake as above.

Serves 6

Dessert Crêpes

Use these crêpes for the dessert that follows. They can also be wrapped around any number of other sweet fillings.

Put all the ingredients except the flour in a blender and turn it on. Add the flour and blend at high speed for 2 to 3 minutes. Refrigerate for at least 2 hours and at the most a day. (If you do not have a blender, beat up the eggs, then beat in the liquids and the salt. Gradually beat in the flour with a wire whisk. Strain the batter and let rest for 2 hours.)

Make the crêpes according to the directions on pages 126–128.

Makes 15 to 20 crêpes

2 large eggs
¾ cup low-fat milk
¼ cup Grand Marnier or orange juice
2 tablespoons unsalted butter, melted
¼ teaspoon salt, preferably sea salt
1 scant cup (1 cup minus 2 tablespoons) unbleached white flour, whole-wheat pastry flour, or a combination of the two

Orange Dessert Crêpes

Although this impressive dessert looks very dramatic, flambéed as it is with Grand Marnier, it's actually a simple, easy-to-throw-together dish.

Have the crêpes stacked and ready to be filled. Preheat the oven to 350 degrees. Butter a baking dish large enough to accommodate all of the crêpes once they have been folded into quarters.

Combine the orange juice and honey and whisk together. Add the optional almond extract, the ground almonds, and the orange peel and whisk together until thoroughly blended.

Spoon a tablespoon of the orange-honey mixture over a crêpe. Lay a few orange slices on one quarter of the crêpe. Fold the crêpe in half, then in half again and place in the buttered baking dish.

Cover the baking dish with foil and heat the crêpes through for 20 minutes.

continued

12 Dessert Crêpes (above)
¼ cup fresh orange juice
¼ cup mild honey
⅛ teaspoon almond extract (optional)
¼ cup almonds, ground in a blender, spice mill, or food processor
1 tablespoon grated orange peel
3 seedless navel oranges, peeled, white membranes removed, and thinly sliced
½ cup Grand Marnier
Additional orange slices and mint sprigs for garnish

Warm the Grand Marnier in a saucepan over a low flame. Either light the liqueur while it is in the pan and pour it, flaming, over the crêpes, or pour the warm liqueur over the crêpes and light. If you wish, continue spooning the blue-flaming liqueur over the crêpes until the flame goes out. Garnish with orange slices and mint sprigs. Serve hot.

Serves 6

Bavarian Crème au Café

This has been an immensely successful dessert at my house. The mint extract makes it especially delightful. It's so light that guests don't feel "weighted down," even after having seconds.

There are several steps involved here, and I recommend that you make it the day before you wish to serve it. (It will keep for several days, yet can be made as little as five hours before serving.) It has a melt-in-your-mouth consistency that makes it a good complement to any kind of meal, light to heavy, though naturally you wouldn't want to serve it after an egg-oriented meal. It's a protein-rich dessert as well.

It will help to have the necessary equipment ready.

FOR THE CUSTARD:
A heavy-bottomed saucepan for heating the egg yolks and milk
A whisk
A small bowl or pan for dissolving the gelatin in the coffee
A small saucepan for heating the 1½ cups milk
A wooden spoon
A candy thermometer
A rubber spatula
A strainer set over a 3-quart bowl

FOR THE EGG WHITES:
A large bowl
A clean, dry egg beater or balloon whisk
A spatula

5 eggs plus 3 egg yolks, at room temperature
⅔ cup mild honey, or 1 cup sugar
2 tablespoons (2 envelopes) unflavored gelatin
½ cup strong coffee
1½ cups low-fat milk
½ teaspoon peppermint extract
¼ cup Kahlúa
1 teaspoon vanilla extract
2 teaspoons brandy
¼ teaspoon cream of tartar
⅛ teaspoon salt, preferably sea salt
1 cup heavy cream, chilled

FOR THE WHIPPED CREAM:

A clean, dry egg beater or whisk, chilled

A 1-quart bowl, chilled

A 2-quart decorative mold or soufflé dish, or 6 to 8 ramekins

Making the custard:

Separate the eggs, placing the whites in the large bowl for the egg whites and the yolks, plus the 3 extra, in the large saucepan (keep the whites you didn't use in a covered jar in the refrigerator). Gradually whip the honey or sugar into the yolks and beat with a whisk until the mixture is frothy.

Dissolve the gelatin in the coffee in a small bowl or pan, stirring well to make sure all the crystals are dissolved. Set aside in a pan of water on the stove.

In another saucepan, heat the milk over medium heat until you see the surface begin to tremble; do not allow it to boil. Now drizzle the milk slowly into the egg yolks, beating all the while with a whisk.

Place this mixture over a low to medium flame (if you're not working with a heavy-bottomed saucepan, the flame should be low) and heat through, stirring with a wooden spoon all the while, until the custard begins to thicken. (Under no circumstances let this mixture boil, as that will curdle the egg yolks. If the eggs do begin to curdle, remove the pan from the heat immediately and stir vigorously or blend in a blender, then return to the heat.) As the temperature reaches 168 degrees, the mixture will begin to thicken and steam. Stir until the mixture is creamy and coats your spoon evenly, then remove from the heat and stir for 1 minute to cool.

Heat the coffee-gelatin mixture through over a pan of water to dissolve again, then add it to the custard, carefully scraping every last bit out of the bowl or pan with a rubber spatula. Strain the mixture into the 3-quart bowl, then stir in the peppermint extract, 2 tablespoons of the Kahlúa, the vanilla, and the brandy, and set aside.

continued

Beating the egg whites:

Start to beat the egg whites with the clean, dry beater or whisk. As they begin to foam, add the cream of tartar and the salt. Beat until the egg whites form stiff, shining peaks, then stir ¼ into the custard and gently fold in the rest. Set aside.

Beating the cream:

Leaving ½ cup of the cream in the refrigerator to chill further, beat the remainder in the chilled 1-quart bowl, circulating the beater or whisk to incorporate as much air as possible. (If your bowl and beater are not chilled, place the bowl in ice water.) Beat the cream until doubled in volume and until it adheres softly to a spoon when lifted, but not until it is stiff.

Stir the Bavarian cream mixture so it begins to set evenly. If you don't do this, the gelatin will settle at the bottom. Allow it to cool for about 5 minutes, stirring every minute or so, then gently fold in the whipped cream.

Pour the Bavarian cream into the mold of your choice or into individual ramekins. (If you are using a soufflé dish, you may have to prepare a collar [see page 111], although you need only do this if you have more cream than the soufflé dish will hold.) Cover well and chill for 4 to 5 hours, or overnight. Keep chilled until you are ready to serve.

Just before serving time, whip the remaining cream and flavor it with the remaining 2 tablespoons of Kahlúa. Serve the Bavarian cream in the soufflé dish or ramekins, or unmolded on a serving plate. (To unmold, dip in very hot water for a few seconds and reverse onto a chilled serving plate; refrigerate again to set.) Top with the Kahlúa-flavored whipped cream.

Serves 6 to 8

Apricot Soufflé

This soufflé, made with egg whites only, is intense and ethereal at the same time. Dessert soufflés, like main-dish soufflés, may be assembled up to two hours in advance and held, covered.

Put the apricots in a bowl and pour on the boiling water. Soak for 2 hours. Drain, reserving the soaking water.

Preheat the oven to 400 degrees. Butter a 2-quart soufflé dish. Sprinkle in the sugar and tilt the dish to distribute the sugar evenly over the surface.

Purée the apricots in a food processor, along with their soaking liquid and the honey. Stir in the amaretto. Blend until smooth.

Beat the 8 egg whites, adding a little salt and the cream of tartar after they begin to foam, until they form stiff (but not dry), shiny peaks. Stir ¼ of the egg whites into the apricot mixture, then fold in the remainder. Spoon the mixture into the prepared soufflé dish and bake for 30 minutes, until puffed and the top is browned.

Serve immediately. The soufflé should be runny in the middle.

Serves 6

1 pound dried apricots

2 cups boiling water, or enough to cover the apricots

Unsalted butter for the soufflé dish

1 tablespoon sugar

2 tablespoons mild honey, or to taste

3 tablespoons amaretto

8 egg whites

Pinch of salt

Pinch of cream of tartar

Gingerbread Soufflé

Unsalted butter for the soufflé
   dish
1 tablespoon sugar
¾ cup low-fat milk
2 tablespoons unsalted butter
1 teaspoon freshly grated gingerroot, or ½ teaspoon ground
   ginger
1 teaspoon ground cinnamon
2 tablespoons unbleached white
   flour
1 tablespoon mild honey
Salt, preferably sea salt
1 tablespoon dry sherry
¼ cup ginger marmalade
3 tablespoons molasses
4 egg yolks, at room temperature
6 egg whites, at room temperature
¼ teaspoon cream of tartar
Plain nonfat yogurt, whipped
   cream, or vanilla ice cream

Imagine the sweet spiciness of gingerbread in a downy soufflé. A little of the sauce settles at the bottom, becoming cakey, and the top becomes crusty as the soufflé bakes. So, to capture all the gingerbread goodness, scoop all the way to the bottom of the dish as you serve.

This impressive dessert also makes a delicious puddinglike leftover.

Preheat the oven to 400 degrees; butter a 2-quart soufflé dish. Sprinkle in the sugar and tilt the soufflé dish to distribute the sugar evenly over the surface.

Bring the milk to a simmer in a saucepan. Melt the butter in another heavy-bottomed saucepan over medium-low heat and sauté the ginger for 1 minute, until it is just beginning to color. Stir in the cinnamon and add the flour. Stir together to make a roux and cook, stirring with a wooden spoon, for 1 minute. Do not allow the mixture to brown. Remove from the heat and whisk in the hot milk, all at once. Whisk over low heat until the mixture has thickened, and continue to cook, stirring constantly, for another 2 or 3 minutes. Remove from the heat and stir in the honey, salt, sherry, ginger marmalade, and molasses. Beat in the egg yolks, 1 at a time. (The soufflé mixture can be refrigerated at this point, tightly covered.)

Beat the 6 egg whites until they form stiff, shiny peaks, adding the cream of tartar and a pinch of salt when they begin to foam. Stir ¼ of the beaten egg whites into the sauce, then fold in the remaining egg whites. Pour into the prepared soufflé dish and bake for 25 to 30 minutes, until puffed and the top is browned.

Serve immediately, topped with yogurt, whipped cream, or vanilla ice cream.

Serves 6

Soufflé Grand Marnier

This is not as rich as the classic soufflé Grand Marnier, but it's just as impressive and delicious.

Preheat the oven to 400 degrees; butter a 2-quart soufflé dish. Sprinkle in the sugar and tilt the soufflé dish to distribute the sugar evenly over the surface.

Heat the milk in a saucepan to a bare simmer. In a separate heavy saucepan, melt the butter and stir in the flour. Cook, stirring with a wooden spoon or a whisk, for 1 minute (do not allow the mixture to brown), and remove from the heat. Whisk in the hot milk all at once, then return the saucepan to the heat. Cook over medium-low heat, stirring constantly with a whisk, for a few minutes after the mixture thickens. Remove from the heat and whisk in the honey, marmalade, Grand Marnier, and orange zest. Whisk in the egg yolks, 1 at a time. Return to the heat and stir for 1 minute over low heat, being careful not to allow the mixture to boil; then remove from the heat and allow to cool.

Beat the 6 egg whites until they begin to foam, then add the salt and cream of tartar. Continue to beat until the egg whites are stiff and form shiny peaks.

Stir a small amount of the egg whites into the soufflé mixture and fold in the rest. Pour into the prepared soufflé dish. Bake for 30 minutes, until the soufflé is puffed and brown, and serve, garnishing each plate with sliced oranges.

Serves 6

Unsalted butter for the soufflé dish

1 tablespoon sugar

¾ cup low-fat milk

2 tablespoons unsalted butter

2 tablespoons unbleached white flour

2 tablespoons mild honey

3 heaped tablespoons orange marmalade

¼ cup Grand Marnier

Finely chopped zest of 1 orange

4 eggs, separated, plus 2 egg whites, at room temperature

⅛ teaspoon salt, preferably sea salt

¼ teaspoon cream of tartar

2 oranges, peeled, white membranes removed, and thinly sliced

Light Cheesecake

2 cups plain nonfat yogurt, home-
    made (page 202) or
    commercial
Butter for the pan
½ cup granola without raisins
1 pound nonfat cottage cheese
4 eggs
½ cup sugar
1 teaspoon vanilla extract
3 tablespoons fresh lemon juice
Finely chopped zest of 1 lemon
    (about 1 teaspoon)
¼ teaspoon salt, preferably sea salt
2 tablespoons unbleached white
    flour

Maybe "light cheesecake" is an oxymoron. But it is possible to make something like a cheesecake that is not the intense, ultrarich cream cheese cake that we know and love. This does have that intense, concentrated, wonderful cheesecake quality.

The day before you wish to bake, line a strainer with cheesecloth, place it over a bowl, and place the yogurt in the strainer. Let sit overnight in the refrigerator. By morning the yogurt will be very thick and creamy.

Preheat the oven to 350 degrees.

Butter an 8-inch springform pan or an 8- or 10-inch cake pan generously. Blend the granola in a food processor so that it has a uniform, mealy texture, and spread it over the pan, turning and tilting the pan so that the mixture coats all of the sides and the bottom in a thin layer. Shake the pan to layer what doesn't adhere to it evenly over the bottom. Refrigerate.

Blend together the cottage cheese and yogurt in the clean bowl of a food processor fitted with the steel blade until smooth. Add the eggs, sugar, vanilla, lemon juice, lemon zest, salt, and flour. Taste and add more sugar, lemon juice, or vanilla if you desire. Pour into the prepared pan and bake in the preheated oven for 1 hour, or until the top begins to brown. When the top just begins to brown, turn off the oven; leave the door closed and let the cheesecake sit in the oven for another hour.

Remove from the oven and refrigerate for several hours before cutting.

Serves 8 to 10

Couscous with Fruit

Couscous is superb with fruit; it makes an excellent breakfast as well as a dessert. Leftovers can be heated through in a double boiler and served with yogurt.

Place the couscous in a bowl and toss with the salt. Combine the water and apple juice and pour 1¼ cup of the mixture over the couscous. Let sit for 10 minutes, until the liquid is absorbed and the couscous is fluffy. (Stir after 5 minutes with a wooden spoon, or rub the couscous between your fingers so that it doesn't lump.)

Melt the butter in a heavy-bottomed saucepan or in the bottom part of a couscoussière over medium-low heat and sprinkle in the cinnamon, ½ teaspoon of the nutmeg, and ½ teaspoon of the allspice. Add the apples, nuts, dried apricots, and currants and sauté for 5 minutes. Stir in the pear and the remaining water and apple juice. Bring to a simmer.

Place the couscous in a colander, sieve, or the top part of the couscoussière and set it over the fruit mixture. Wrap a kitchen towel or cheesecloth around the space between the sides of the colander and the pot so that the steam will come up only through the colander. Now cover the couscous with a towel or with the lid of the pot. Simmer 10 minutes, until the fruit is tender and fragrant and the couscous fluffy.

Transfer the couscous to a wide serving dish and pour on the fruit. Toss together gently, sprinkle on the remaining ¼ teaspoon nutmeg and ¼ teaspoon allspice, and serve, with yogurt on the side.

Serves 6

1 cup couscous

¼ teaspoon salt, preferably sea salt

½ cup water

2 cups apple juice

1 tablespoon butter

1 teaspoon ground cinnamon

¾ teaspoon freshly grated nutmeg

¾ teaspoon ground allspice

2 apples, peeled (if waxed), cored, and chopped

3 tablespoons pine nuts or slivered almonds

⅓ cup chopped dried apricots

3 tablespoons currants

1 large, ripe pear, cored and chopped

1½ cups plain nonfat yogurt for serving

Indian Pudding

1 quart low-fat or skim milk,
    scalded

6 tablespoons yellow cornmeal,
    preferably stone-ground

⅓ cup molasses

2 to 3 tablespoons mild honey

3 eggs, beaten

¾ teaspoon salt, preferably sea salt

1 teaspoon ground ginger

½ teaspoon freshly grated nutmeg

1 tablespoon unsalted butter

½ cup raisins

Plain nonfat yogurt

Indian pudding is an old American recipe. Cornmeal was referred to by the Pilgrims as "Indian"; hence the name. Recipes for it appear in cookbooks as far back as the seventeenth century, and often call for the addition of "a little Indian." This is a spicy dessert, high in protein; it makes a good leftover. Most versions are sweeter than this one.

Preheat the oven to 325 degrees; butter a 2-quart casserole, soufflé dish, or dutch oven.

Bring the milk to the boiling point in a 2- or 3-quart heavy-bottomed saucepan. Pour in the cornmeal in a slow stream, stirring all the while with a whisk or wooden spoon. Bring to a gentle boil and cook over low heat, stirring, for about 15 minutes, until the mixture is thick and creamy (it should have the consistency of a runny cream-of-wheat). Add the molasses and honey and cook for another 5 minutes.

Remove from the heat and stir in the beaten eggs, the salt, ginger, nutmeg, butter, and raisins; mix well.

Pour the pudding into the prepared casserole, soufflé dish, or dutch oven and bake for 1 to 1½ hours, until a knife comes out clean and the top is just beginning to brown. Serve with plain nonfat yogurt.

Serves 6 to 8

Dessert Pie Crusts

These crusts are made with some whole-wheat flour, which gives them a rich, nutty flavor. They aren't as easy to roll out as white flour crusts, but I find that the flavor is worth the extra trouble.

PARTIALLY WHOLE-WHEAT DESSERT CRUST

Butter the tart pan or pie pan. Mix together the flours and salt. Cut in the butter, which should be very cold and cut into small pieces. Do this in a food processor, using the pulse action, or with folks, or using your hands. To do this manually, work quickly and pick up handfuls of the flour and butter with both hands and roll them between your thumbs and first two fingers. Keep picking up handfuls until the butter is evenly distributed through the flour and the mixture resembles oatmeal. Then briskly rub the mixture between the palms of your hands until you have a mixture resembling coarse cornmeal.

Mix in the honey. If the dough comes together, gather it into a ball. If it seems dry, add the ice cold water, then gather into a ball. Wrap in plastic and refrigerate for a few hours before rolling out.

Remove the dough from the refrigerator and let soften for 45 minutes before rolling out. Place the dough on a floured surface, or on a lightly floured piece of waxed paper, and flatten it with a rolling pin. Sprinkle the dough with flour. Then place a piece of waxed paper over the top and roll out. When the dough is rolled out sufficiently to fit your tart pan, peel off the top piece of waxed paper, and if you have used waxed paper underneath the dough, reverse the dough into the buttered pan. If you have not used paper beneath the dough, use a spatula to loosen it from the surface and line the pan. Don't worry if the dough breaks. Just

continued

1 scant cup whole-wheat flour or whole-wheat pastry flour
1 scant cup unbleached white flour, plus extra for rolling
¼ teaspoon salt, preferably sea salt
4 ounces (1 stick) cold unsalted butter
2 tablespoons mild honey
1 tablespoon ice cold water, if necessary

press the pieces together with your fingers. If the dough doesn't line the pan easily, cut and patch. Whole-wheat doughs don't ease into pans the way white flour doughs do; patching is always necessary. But the finished crust will be fine.

To get an attractive edge around the top of the pan, gently press the dough up the edge from the bottom, so that you have some extra at the top, then pinch little creases along the edge.

The crust can be refrigerated or frozen at this point.

Makes one 12- to 14-inch crust

1 scant cup whole-wheat pastry flour

½ cup unbleached white flour

½ cup finely ground almonds

¼ teaspoon salt, preferably sea salt

4 ounces (1 stick) cold unsalted butter

2 tablespoons mild honey

¼ teaspoon almond extract (optional)

1 tablespoon ice cold water, if necessary

SWEET ALMOND PIE CRUST

This nutty, fragrant crust is great for fruit tarts and pumpkin pie. The almonds add oil to the mixture, so the tablespoon of water probably won't be necessary.

Mix together the flours, ground almonds, and salt. Cut in the butter, as in the preceding recipe. Mix in the honey and almond extract. If the dough comes together, gather it up into a ball. If it's dry, add the water, a teaspoon at a time, then gather in a ball, wrap in plastic, and refrigerate for several hours. Follow the preceding directions for rolling out.

Makes one 12- to 14-inch crust

Apple, Peach, or Pear Pie or Tart

I have a weakness for any fruit tart or pie. Each season brings new possibilities. The same combination of honey and spices works well for apples, peaches, and pears.

Preheat the oven to 350 degrees.

Roll out ⅔ of the pie crust dough to fit a 9- or 10-inch pie pan, saving the remaining dough for a lattice or regular top crust. Or roll out the whole amount and fit a 12- or 14-inch pie pan. Brush with the beaten egg. Pierce the crust in several spots with a fork or the sharp tip of a knife, and pre-bake in the preheated oven for 5 minutes, then remove the pan from the oven and raise the oven heat to 450 degrees.

Combine the sliced fruit with all the other ingredients. Place in the pie shell (or tart shell), and for a double crust, cover with a lattice or regular top crust, pricking the top crust to allow steam to escape. Beat the pinch of cinnamon for a double crust into the remaining egg. Brush the lattice or top crust with the mixture.

Bake at 450 degrees for 10 minutes, then turn down the heat and bake at 350 degrees for another 30 minutes. Serve warm or cooled.

Makes one 12- or 14-inch tart or one
9- or 10-inch double-crust pie

1 recipe Partially Whole-Wheat Dessert Crust (page 253) or Sweet Almond Pie crust (page 254)
1 egg, beaten
5 cups peeled, sliced apples, peaches, or pears
¼ cup mild honey
Pinch of salt, preferably sea salt
1 tablespoon cornstarch or arrow-root, dissolved in a little water
½ teaspoon ground cinnamon, plus a pinch for a double crust
½ teaspoon freshly ground nut-meg
¼ teaspoon ground allspice
1 teaspoon vanilla extract
1 tablespoon fresh lemon juice
1 tablespoon brandy or calvados (apple brandy)

Berry or Cherry Pie

1 recipe Partially Whole-Wheat
   Dessert Crust or Sweet
   Almond Pie crust (pages
   253–254)

1 egg, beaten

3 tablespoons water or fresh
   orange juice

2 tablespoons fresh lemon juice

2 tablespoons crème de cassis or
   other fruity liqueur (use kirsch
   for cherry tarts)

2 tablespoons cornstarch

4 cups berries or pitted cherries,
   washed, stemmed, and picked
   over

⅓ cup mild honey or sugar

*What a luxurious way to show off the dark, concentrated
essence of fresh-picked berries.*

Preheat the oven to 350 degrees.

Roll out ⅔ of the pie pastry and fit it into a 9- or 10-
inch pie pan, saving the other ⅓ for a lattice topping, or roll
out the whole amount and fit in a 12- or 14-inch tart pan.
Brush with the beaten egg. Pierce the dough in several
places with a fork or the tip of a sharp knife and prebake
the shell for 5 minutes, then remove the pan and raise the
oven heat to 450 degrees.

Combine the orange and lemon juice and the crème de
cassis or liqueur. Dissolve the cornstarch in this mixture.
Combine with the berries or cherries and honey or sugar
and turn into the pie crust. Cover with a lattice topping and
bake at 450 degrees for 10 minutes, then turn the heat
down to 350 degrees and bake for another 30 minutes. If
the crust begins to brown too much, cover loosely with foil.

Makes one 12- or 14-inch tart, or one
9- or 10-inch double-crust pie

Pecan Pie

When I was growing up in Connecticut, pecan pie was a rare treat. Then I had the luxury of living in Texas, where pecan trees grew in my back yard and spilled their pecans all through the fall. That's where I developed my lasting fondness for pecan pies. This one is not sickly sweet like some, but it's plenty rich all the same.

Preheat the oven to 350 degrees.

Roll out your crust to fit a 12- or 14-inch pie pan. Pierce the dough in several places with a fork or the tip of a sharp knife and prebake the shell for 5 minutes. Remove the pan and raise the oven heat to 375 degrees.

Cream the butter with the honey; beat in the eggs. Add the vanilla, rum, nutmeg, and salt. Fold in the pecans. Pour the mixture into the pie shell.

Bake at 375 degrees for 35 to 40 minutes, until a knife comes out clean when inserted in the center.

Makes one 12- or 14-inch pie

1 recipe Partially Whole-Wheat
   Dessert Crust (page 253)
4 tablespoons (½ stick) unsalted
   butter
½ cup mild honey
3 eggs
1 teaspoon vanilla extract
1 tablespoon rum
¼ teaspoon freshly grated nutmeg
½ teaspoon salt, preferably sea salt
2 cups broken pecans

Pumpkin Pie

1 recipe Sweet Almond Pie crust
    (page 254)

3 eggs

2 cups cooked, puréed pumpkin,
    canned or fresh (see Note)

½ cup low-fat milk

½ cup mild honey

1 tablespoon molasses

1½ teaspoons vanilla extract

1 to 2 tablespoons rum, to taste

1½ teaspoons ground cinnamon

½ teaspoon ground ginger

¼ teaspoon ground mace

¼ teaspoon ground cloves

¼ teaspoon freshly grated nutmeg

¼ teaspoon salt, preferably sea salt

Whipped cream, plain nonfat
    yogurt, or vanilla ice cream

The addition of molasses makes this a dark and spicy pie.

Preheat the oven to 350 degrees. Beat the eggs and brush the crust with a bit of the beaten egg. Prebake the crust for 7 minutes, remove from the heat, and turn up the oven to 425 degrees.

Beat together the remaining beaten eggs with the pumpkin, milk, honey, molasses, vanilla, rum, spices, and salt. Pour into the pie shell. Bake at 425 degrees for 10 minutes, then reduce the heat to 350 degrees and bake for another 30 to 40 minutes, until set. If the crust begins to burn on the edges, cover loosely with aluminum foil.

Cool completely and serve with whipped cream, plain yogurt, or vanilla ice cream.

Note: To make fresh pumpkin purée, preheat the oven to 425 degrees. Remove the seeds and strings from 2 pounds of pumpkin, cut in wedges, and place on an oiled baking sheet. Cover with foil and bake until thoroughly soft, about 45 minutes. Peel away the skin and purée the pumpkin in a food processor fitted with the steel blade. Measure out 2 cups for the above recipe, and freeze what excess remains.

Makes one 12- or 14-inch pie

Sweet Potato Pie

Substitute cooked, mashed sweet potatoes for the pumpkin and follow the above recipe.

Mince Pie

Some mince pies are too sweet for me; this one is just right. There's really no need for much additional sweetener here, as the dried fruits and the fruit juice contain so much natural sugar already.

Preheat the oven to 350 degrees.

Roll out ⅔ of the pie crust dough and fit it into a 9- or 10-inch pie pan, reserving the rest for a lattice topping, or roll out the entire crust for a 12- or 14-inch pie. Follow the directions on page 253 and prebake the pie shell for 5 minutes, then remove from the oven and turn the heat up to 375 degrees.

Cover the currants and raisins with sherry and soak while preparing the other ingredients, or for 15 minutes. Pour off the sherry.

In a large saucepan, combine the apples, currants, raisins, prunes, apricots, dates, nuts, orange juice and rind, lemon juice and rind, and apple cider. Bring to a simmer, then cover and cook over low heat for 20 minutes. Add the spices and brandy and stir in the honey; simmer another 5 minutes. Stir in the flour and mix well.

Pour the filling into the pie shell and spread it evenly. Roll out the other ⅓ of the crust and make a lattice topping.

Bake at 375 degrees for 40 minutes, then serve, topped with plain yogurt.

*Makes one latticed 9- or 10-inch pie,
or one unlatticed 12- or 14-inch pie*

1 recipe Partially Whole-Wheat Dessert Crust or Sweet Almond Pie crust (pages 253–254)
⅓ cup currants
½ cup raisins
1 cup dry sherry
2 tart apples, peeled and chopped
⅓ cup chopped pitted prunes
⅓ cup chopped dried apricots
¼ cup chopped pitted dates
½ cup broken pecans or walnuts
Juice and grated rind of ½ orange
Juice and grated rind of ½ lemon
¼ cup apple cider
½ teaspoon ground cinnamon
½ teaspoon ground cloves
¼ teaspoon freshly grated nutmeg
1 tablespoon brandy
¼ cup mild honey
3 tablespoons unbleached white flour
½ to ¾ cup plain nonfat yogurt, homemade (see page 202) or commercial

Buckwheat Cake

½ cup unbleached white flour

1 tablespoon baking powder

½ teaspoon baking soda

½ teaspoon salt

1 cup coarse buckwheat meal

⅓ cup raw brown (turbinado) sugar

2 eggs

2 tablespoons mild honey

1 teaspoon vanilla extract

1 cup plain nonfat yogurt

½ cup low-fat or skim milk

3 tablespoons unsalted butter

⅓ cup raspberry preserves

I first ate a cake made from coarse buckwheat flour when I was skiing in the Dolomites, in Northern Italy. Coarse buckwheat flour has a rich, earthy/nutty flavor, and the cake has a texture not unlike cornbread. This will keep for several days in the refrigerator, wrapped tightly in plastic wrap.

Preheat the oven to 400 degrees. Cut a piece of waxed paper to fit the bottom of a 10-inch cake pan (or a heavy-bottomed enameled gratin, in which case you won't need the waxed paper). Don't put the waxed paper in the pan yet.

Sift together the flour, baking powder, baking soda, and salt. Combine with the buckwheat meal and sugar in a bowl. Mix together well.

Beat together the eggs and honey. Beat in the vanilla, yogurt, and milk.

Place the butter in the cake pan or gratin and place in the preheated oven. When the butter has melted (be careful that it doesn't brown), remove the pan from the heat.

Quickly blend together the liquid mixture with the flour mixture. Don't overbeat. Add the melted butter and stir together well.

Brush the butter that remains in the pan over its bottom and sides. Place the waxed paper in the bottom of the pan, then turn it over to make sure it is well coated with butter.

Pour the batter into the baking pan and place in the hot oven. Bake 35 to 40 minutes, until firm and brown, and a tester comes out clean. Remove from the heat.

Allow the cake to cool in the pan for 15 minutes or more, then remove from the pan and cool on a rack.

When the cake is completely cool, cut it laterally into two equal layers using a long serrated knife. Spread the cut side of the bottom half with an even layer of raspberry preserves. Replace the top half. Wrap in plastic and foil, and refrigerate for a day. Cut in wedges or squares and serve.

Serves 16

Strawberry and Cassis Sherbet

This sherbet is a frozen meringue flavored with strawberries and cassis. The reason I have added cassis is that nowadays it's hard to find ripe, full-bodied strawberries. The cassis gives the sherbet a delightful lift.

If you've never made a meringue before, you will be amazed by the chemical transformation that occurs. I couldn't believe it, the first time I made one, as I beat in the hot syrup and watched the fluffy egg whites become satiny and smooth. The change is nothing short of miraculous, and for me it was especially exciting to see that I could do this easily with a honey syrup.

Be sure to make your syrup in a large saucepan, more than double the volume of your honey and water. It will bubble up furiously; I have carelessly clogged up many a burner with the overflow. Also, keep the heat moderate or your syrup will caramelize.

3 cups fresh or frozen strawberries, washed and stemmed
3 to 4 tablespoons fresh lemon juice
½ cup crème de cassis
3 egg whites, at room temperature
Scant ¼ teaspoon cream of tartar
Pinch of salt, preferably sea salt
⅓ cup water
⅔ cup mild honey, or ¾ cup sugar
Fresh mint, fresh sliced strawberries, and lime slices for garnish

Purée the strawberries in a blender and stir in the lemon juice and the cassis. Set aside.

Put the egg whites into a clean, dry 3-quart bowl or in the bowl of an electric mixer. Begin to beat the egg whites slowly. When they start to foam, add the cream of tartar and the salt and beat into stiff, shinning peaks. Set aside (or if you have a free-standing mixer, turn it down to low speed), and prepare the syrup as follows:

Bring the water and honey or sugar to a boil in a large heavy-bottomed saucepan over medium heat. Tilt the pan to combine the ingredients evenly and to obtain a clear liquid. Boil rapidly but over moderate heat to the "soft ball" stage on a candy thermometer (238 degrees). To test without a thermometer, drop a small amount into ice water. It should form a ball that will flatten out when you lift it with your fingers.

Now, beating the whites at moderate speed, dribble the hot syrup into the egg whites. Continue beating at high

continued

speed for 5 minutes or so: You will see the egg white mixture go through a miraculous metamorphosis and become a satiny meringue. Continue beating until the egg whites are cool and form stiff, satiny peaks when a bit is lifted with a spoon. Gradually beat the strawberry-cassis purée into the meringue.

Freeze in a sorbetière according to the instructions, or turn into a shallow pan or ice trays and freeze for about 2 hours, until mushy and almost set (let soften if frozen solid). Scrape into a food processor fitted with the steel blade and pulse the mixture (or beat at high speed with an electric mixer) to break up the ice crystals. Turn back into the pan or trays and repeat the process again in an hour. (This second blending may be omitted, but your sherbet may still have ice crystals as a result.) Now turn into a pretty serving bowl, a mold, or individual cups, and cover. Freeze for at least 2 hours for individual portions, 4 hours for bowls or molds.

Allow the sherbet to soften slightly in the refrigerator before serving; individual servings will take 10 minutes to soften, and a large bowl will take 20 minutes. If you wish to unmold the sherbet, quickly dip it into warm water and reverse onto a chilled platter. Cover and return to the freezer for 30 minutes to set the "dribbles," then refrigerate for 20 to 30 minutes before serving.

Serve garnished with mint, fresh sliced strawberries, and slices of lime.

Serves 8 to 10

Homemade Applesauce

Applesauce is very easy to make. This one is tart and spicy. Serve it for dessert with yogurt, or for breakfast.

In a large saucepan, combine the apple slices, water, and lemon juice. Bring to a boil, then reduce the heat, cover, and simmer for about 30 minutes, stirring occasionally, or until the apples begin to fall apart.

Add the spices and honey to taste, then stir and continue cooking for 15 to 30 minutes, stirring occasionally, depending on how mushy you want your applesauce to be. Press with the back of a wooden spoon or a potato masher, leaving some large chunks.

Serve hot or chilled.

Makes about 3 cups

8 large tart apples, such as Gravenstein, Granny Smith, or McIntosh, peeled and sliced
1 cup water
1½ tablespoons fresh lemon juice
1 teaspoon ground cinnamon
½ teaspoon ground cloves
½ teaspoon freshly grated nutmeg
½ teaspoon ground allspice
¼ teaspoon ground mace
2 to 4 tablespoons mild honey, to taste

Cranberry–Pear Tart

This gorgeous tart makes a marvelous Thanksgiving dessert.

Preheat the oven to 350 degrees. Prebake the crust for 7 minutes. Remove from the heat and set aside. Turn up the heat to 400 degrees.

Combine the orange juice, cornstarch, and all but 2 tablespoons of the honey in a large saucepan and whisk together until the cornstarch is dissolved. Add half the cranberries and bring to a boil, stirring. Remove from the heat and stir in the remaining cranberries and the orange zest.

Toss the pears with the lemon juice and the remaining 2 tablespoons of honey. Arrange them in an overlapping ring around the outside edge of the tart shell. Pour the cranberry mixture into the middle. Bake for 25 to 30 minutes. Mean-
continued

One 12-inch dessert crust (either of the crusts on pages 253–254)
¾ cup fresh orange juice
2 tablespoons cornstarch
½ cup mild honey
One 10-ounce bag of fresh cranberries
2 tablespoons finely chopped orange zest
3 large Comice pears, peeled, cored, and thinly sliced
2 tablespoons fresh lemon juice
2 tablespoons apricot jam

while, melt the jam in a saucepan with any honey and lemon left over from the pears. Remove the tart from the oven and brush the pears with the melted jam. Cool before serving.

Serves 8

Index

Tomatoes (cont'd)
  in Spicy Tofu Salad, 222–23
  in Stuffed Eggplant, 134–35
  in Tabouli, 220
  in Thick Cabbage Soup, 84
  in Tortilla Soup, 60–61
  uncooked, pasta with basil and, 184
  in Vegetable Paella, 142
Torte, deep-dish vegetable, 108–9
Tortillas, 97
  Black Bean Enchiladas, 97–99
  Extraordinary Chalupas, 100–101
  soup, 60–61
Turbinado sugar, xxii
Turkish Cucumber Soup, 92
Turnips, xxx
  in Noodle-Bean Soup, 82
  stir-fried with tofu, 144–45

Utensils, xxv–xxvi

Vegesal, xxiii
Vegetable Paella, 142
Vegetable Platter with Dips, 40–42
Vegetable salt, xxiii
Vegetable Shish Kebab, 143
Vegetable stock, 49
Vegetables, xxxiv
  cheese soufflé with, 111
  couscous with, 154–55

marinated, à la Grecque, 38–39
marinated, vinaigrette, 35
as omelet fillings, 123
stir-fried with tofu, 144–45
See also names of individual vegetables
Vegetarian food, xiii, xiv–xv
  entertaining, xli-xlvi
  and meaty holidays, xlvii
Vichyssoise, 76
Vinaigrettes, 197, 205
  low-fat yogurt, 206
  marinated vegetables with, 35

Walnut oil, xx
  dressing, 207
Walnuts, in Spicy Tofu Salad, 222–23
Water chestnuts, and snow peas, Chinese-
  style, 166
Watercress and Mushroom Salad, 226
Wheat berries, xxxv
  cream of, soup, 67
  in Curry Salad, 150
Wheat germ, xvii
Whipped cream, xl
whole-wheat crusts, 102–3, 253–54
Whole-Wheat-Sesame Pita Bread, 12
Wild rice. *See* Rice, wild
Wine:
  marsala, peaches with, 240
  port:

grapefruit with, 241
melon with, 239
red:
  Fettuccine with Wild Mushrooms, 181
  pears poached in, 236
  raspberries in, 240
sherry, in Black Bean Soup, 85
sweet, Mediterranean Fruit Compote,
  237
white:
  bananas poached in, 235
  sauce, 199
Winter Squash Gratin, 171
Won Tons with Spinach and Tofu Filling in
  Ginger-Garlic Broth, 146–47

Yeast breads, basic technique, 3–7
Yeasted Olive Oil Pastry, 104
Yogurt, xvi–xvii, 47, 197, 202
  in Bulgarian Cucumber Soup, 91
  in Couscous with Fruit, 251
  in Dill Soup, 77
  in Extraordinary Chalupas, 100–101
  in Light Cheesecake, 250
  low-fat, vinaigrette, 206
  raitas, 172
  in Turkish Cucumber Soup, 92
  See also Dressings

Zucchini. *See* Squash, zucchini